Gary R. Elkins, PhD, ABPP, ABPH, is a professor of psychology and neuroscience at Baylor University, where he is the director of the Mind–Body Medicine Research Laboratory. He is internationally recognized for his work in clinical and experimental hypnosis, psychotherapy, and behavioral medicine. Dr. Elkins is the author of the *Handbook of Medical and Psychological Hypnosis: Foundations, Applications, and Professional Issues*, which was named the 2017 Best Book in Hypnosis by the Society for Clinical and Experimental Hypnosis. He is also the author of the groundbreaking book *Hypnotic Relaxation Therapy: Principles and Applications.* Dr. Elkins is the editor-in-chief of the *International Journal of Clinical and Experimental Hypnosis*, associate editor of *BCM Complementary and Alternative Medicine*, and consulting editor of *Psychology of Consciousness: Theory, Research, and Practice.* Dr. Elkins has board certification from the American Board of Professional Psychology (ABPP) and from the American Board of Psychological Hypnosis (ABPH). He is a past president of the American Society of Clinical Hypnosis, the Society of Psychological Hypnosis, the ABPH, and the Society for Clinical and Experimental Hypnosis. With more than 40 years of experience in hypnosis and more than 100 publications, he conducts an ongoing program of research in clinical and mindful hypnotherapy. Dr. Elkins teaches workshops nationally and internationally and maintains a private practice with a specialization in hypnotherapy and clinical health psychology.

Nicholas Olendzki, PsyD, is a psychotherapist specializing in mindfulness, integrative psychotherapy, and hypnotherapy interventions. He completed his doctoral degree in clinical psychology in the Department of Psychology and Neuroscience at Baylor University, where he was a Presidential Scholar. Dr. Olendzki is certified in mindfulness and psychotherapy through the Institute of Meditation and Psychotherapy and received additional training through the Center for Mindfulness at University of Massachusetts Medical School. He is a contributing author to *Handbook of Medical and Psychological Hypnosis: Foundations, Applications, and Professional Issues.* Dr. Olendzki has made contributions as a coinvestigator on mindfulness studies, exploring the impact of mindfulness on physiological conditions at the Center for Mindfulness at University of Massachusetts Medical School and mindful hypnotherapy at the Mind–Body Medicine Research Laboratory at Baylor University. He is currently engaged in clinical practice at the University of Massachusetts, Dartmouth.

MINDFUL HYPNOTHERAPY
The Basics for Clinical Practice

Gary R. Elkins, PhD, ABPP, ABPH
Nicholas Olendzki, PsyD

SPRINGER PUBLISHING COMPANY

Springer Publishing Company, LLC
11 West 42nd Street
New York, NY 10036
www.springerpub.com

Acquisitions Editor: Sheri W. Sussman
Compositor: S4Carlisle Publishing Services

ISBN: 978-0-8261-2773-0
ebook ISBN: 978-0-8261-2774-7

***A supplementary audio recording is available for download at* http://connect.springerpub.com/content/book/978-0-8261-2774-7; access via clicking on the SHOW SUPPLEMENTARY tab.**
Audio Recording ISBN: 978-0-8261-9352-0

Printed by LSI

Library of Congress Cataloging-in-Publication Data

Names: Elkins, Gary Ray, 1952- author.
Title: Mindful hypnotherapy : the basics for clinical practice / Gary Elkins, PhD, ABPP, ABPH, Nicholas Olendzki, PsyD.
Description: New York : Springer Publishing Company, [2019] | Includes bibliographical references and index.
Identifiers: LCCN 2018026712| ISBN 9780826127730 | ISBN 9780826127747 (e-book)
Subjects: LCSH: Hypnotism--Therapeutic use. | Mindfulness.
Classification: LCC RC495 .E385 2019 | DDC 615.8/512--dc23 LC record available at https://lccn.loc.gov/2018026712

Printed in the United States of America.

To my wife, Guillerma, for her support and daily example of loving kindness.

GRE

To my family, with all of my love.

NO

Also by Gary R. Elkins, PhD, ABPP, ABPH

Handbook of Medical and Psychological Hypnosis: Foundations, Applications, and Professional Issues

Relief from Hot Flashes: The Natural, Drug-Free Program to Reduce Hot Flashes, Improve Sleep, and Ease Stress

Hypnotic Relaxation Therapy: Principles and Applications

CONTENTS

PREFACE

This book is a comprehensive guide to the basics of mindful hypnotherapy (MH), incorporating everything you need to understand the approach, apply it to clients in your clinical practice, and use it for your own personal edification and growth. MH is a treatment that combines the qualities from two highly effective and well-established treatment approaches: mindfulness and hypnotherapy. These approaches have separately been shown to be effective in the treatment of a wide array of disorders, ranging from elevated stress or adjustment problems to more debilitating conditions such as major depressive disorder, posttraumatic stress disorder (PTSD), substance use disorders, chronic pain, anxiety disorders, and more.

Readers opening this book for the first time may be curious about how hypnosis and mindfulness may be integrated. While mindfulness and hypnosis are different in many respects, they can be understood in a complementary manner. To begin with, the contemporary definition of *hypnosis* is "a state of consciousness involving focused attention and reduced peripheral awareness characterized by an enhanced capacity for response to suggestion" (Elkins, Barabasz, Council, & Spiegel, 2015), while *mindfulness* is commonly defined as "paying attention in a particular way, on purpose, in the present moment, and nonjudgmentally" (Kabat-Zinn, 1994). At their very broadest level, mindfulness and hypnosis are both special ways of paying attention to one's experiences.

The two practices have very different cultural origins, and their fundamental aims have historically been thought of as incompatible. For example, mindfulness is a psychological state characterized by paying attention to present-moment experiences as they occur, with an attitude of openness, curiosity, and compassion. A mindful state of mind entails setting aside the constant and usually automatic instinct to emotionally embrace certain experiences and emotionally resist others; instead, the individual chooses to adopt a stance of equanimity toward his or her experiences. This attitude of equanimity and openness to experiences is often described as "nonjudgmentalness" or a "nonjudgmental awareness." The conscious cultivation of a mindful state in an effort to attain physical and psychological benefits likely originated in the ancient religion of Buddhism, where it is believed to be one of the important factors leading to enlightenment (a state of being characterized by a permanent cessation of psychological suffering). At its core, mindfulness aims to reduce suffering by changing one's *relationship* with experiences, not by changing the experiences themselves. For example, if a person feels chronic back pain, he or she may feel less distress by adopting an open and curious attitude toward the pain and *more* distress if he or she mentally and emotionally "fights" against the pain.

In contrast, the historical origin of hypnosis is found in the evolution of psychiatry and Western medicine, which traditionally focus on changing *experiences,* rather than attitudes toward experiences. The techniques of inducing a hypnotic state and therapeutic suggestion may be traced to the work of Franz Anton Mesmer in the mid-1700s in Europe (Austria and France). The term "hypnosis" was originally introduced in the early 1800s by a Scottish physician by the name of James Braid. At that time, hypnosis was thought to be a special kind of sleep. In fact, the word "hypnosis" is derived from the Greek word "hypnos," which means sleep. However, it has been shown that the hypnotic state and sleep have little in common in regard to brain activity or subjective experience. It is noteworthy that Dr. Braid eventually concluded that hypnosis involved a focus of attention and response to suggestions and was not in any way reflective of sleep. Hypnosis is now widely understood as a state of consciousness involving focused attention and characterized by an enhanced capacity for response to suggestion and most commonly occurs along with deep relaxation (Elkins, 2014). Rather than serving as a stand-alone treatment, hypnotherapy involves integrating hypnosis into existing treatment modalities (Elkins, 2017).

In the latter part of the 20th century, countercultural trends in the West led to a greater awareness of meditation and mindfulness. Eventually, the development of a secular mindfulness-based intervention for pain in the early 1980s by John Kabat-Zinn sparked a popular revolution in clinical practice, which brought these practices into the limelight as potential treatments. Treatments involving mindfulness became collectively known as the "third wave" of cognitive therapy (discussed further in Chapter 2), and mindfulness became the treatment modality of choice for many clinicians. It is this comingling of cultures in medicine that set the stage for the development of MH.

Development of Mindful Hypnotherapy

MH was codeveloped at Baylor University by Dr. Nicholas Olendzki and Dr. Gary R. Elkins. The intervention was born out of a significant gap in the empirical literature on mindfulness and hypnotherapy. For decades, the two approaches have been recognized as occupying a similar domain within mind–body interventions but have thus far operated in parallel rather than in tandem. Within the empirical literature, most studies are limited to a simple comparison between mindfulness and hypnotherapy, and only in recent years have a small handful of researchers begun to speculate on what a combined approach might look like. While there has been a growing interest within the fields of mindfulness and hypnotherapy in combining the strengths of these two interventions into a single therapy, at the time that Dr. Olendzki and Dr. Elkins began developing MH, there had been no empirical literature evaluating the actual merits of this approach and no manualized or systematic guide for an integrated intervention.

The specific formulation of MH developed naturally out of discussions between the two authors. Dr. Elkins's considerable expertise in hypnotherapy and Dr. Olendzki's knowledge in the field of mindfulness led to free-ranging discussions regarding the origin of the two fields, mutual overlap in applications and phenomenological experiences of the two fields, and concrete differences between mindfulness and hypnosis. Early incarnations of MH with individual clients met with very positive results and helped to shape and standardize the intervention.

Mindful Hypnotherapy in Comparison to Other Mindfulness-Based Interventions

MH is not intended to be an accurate and unwavering vehicle for Buddhist teachings (sometimes referred to as the *Dharme* or *Dhamma*) or an unaltered representation of secular mindfulness as it is taught in Mindfulness-Based Stress Reduction (MBSR), Acceptance and Commitment Therapy, Dialectical Behavioral Therapy, and other clinical interventions. These are all excellent practices that can be extremely helpful in reducing the suffering of those who practice them. Rather, MH draws liberally from each of these traditions, adapts and expands upon the source material as needed, and delivers this novel intervention according to hypnotic principles (Elkins, 2014).

One way to think about MH is as follows. Consider the metaphor of a tree. Trees are typically tall and strong, they are plentiful in certain parts of the world, they provide shade, and they have many other interesting qualities. The strength and plenitude of trees have historically made wood a common construction material, but which kind of wood is best? The answer would certainly depend upon what you're trying to build. The wood of some trees is lightweight but weaker, while other trees bear stout and heavy wood. Observing this, one might decide to use the lightweight wood of a balsa tree for model planes and surfboards, and heavy woods like oak for houses or furniture. Both types of wood are useful under certain circumstances and less useful under others. Whichever wood you choose to use retains some of the qualities of the tree it comes from (e.g., lightness/heaviness, wood hue). In both cases, whatever is made from the wood is going to be *terrible* at photosynthesis. You've taken what used to be a spectacular tree and made it unsuitable for many of the things that a tree can do. However, by harvesting wood from a balsa tree or an oak tree, you can fashion a final product that is suitable for a different purpose yet retains *some* of the qualities that a tree has.

Similarly, MH, MBSR, and other mindfulness-based psychological interventions can be an avenue for self-transformation and psychological wellness, retaining many of the beneficial qualities inherent in their Buddhist roots. However, in making mindfulness into a secular intervention, it has been shaped and changed, and mindfulness itself is only one aspect of a rich and nuanced religious tradition. In adapting these practices to a secular psychological intervention, much is lost, but a good deal is gained as well (just like transforming an oak tree into a chair makes it better in some ways and worse in others). Just like an oak tree will be suitable for some purposes and a balsa tree will be suitable for others, different mindfulness interventions will be suitable for different clients, and some clients will not be appropriate candidates for any type of mindfulness intervention. MH offers a novel intervention that is influenced by a variety of modalities and theoretical orientations, and the final product is a seamless integration of mindfulness and hypnotherapy.

This Book

This book is intended to be an additional tool in the therapist's toolbox—a new approach that delivers a mindfulness-based intervention within a hypnotic context. The book is divided into three sections. The first section (*Foundations*) provides the conceptual basis for MH, research, discussion of hypnotic abilities, and basics for formulating hypnotic inductions and suggestions. The second section (*Mindful Hypnotherapy by Session*) provides a treatment manual for MH over eight sessions. It includes transcripts, hypnotic inductions, and guidance for individualization and tracking progress using the Mindful Self-Hypnosis Daily Practice

Log. The third section (*Conclusion*) provides an overview of training and personal growth toward becoming a mindful hypnotherapist.

This MH approach is long overdue. Over the course of the past 40 years, the fields of hypnotherapy and mindfulness have been compared and contrasted phenomenologically, physiologically, and neurologically. Most recently, there has been a resurgence of interest in going beyond a simple comparison, venturing into the realm of combining mindfulness and hypnotherapy into a single, seamless intervention. The MH intervention presented here is both the culmination of the work that preceded it and the vanguard of a new frontier of mind–body psychotherapy interventions.

A sample audio recording is provided at https://bcove.video/3VrKQo0 and gives an example of the pacing of hypnotic suggestions.

REFERENCES

Elkins, G. R. (2014). *Hypnotic relaxation therapy: Principles and applications.* New York, NY: Springer Publishing.

Elkins, G. R. (2017). *Handbook of medical and psychological hypnosis: Foundations, applications, and professional issues.* New York, NY: Springer Publishing.

Elkins, G. R., Barabasz, A. F., Council, J. R., & Spiegel, D. (2015). Advancing research and practice: The revised APA division 30 definition of hypnosis. *American Journal of Clinical Hypnosis, 57,* 378–385. doi:10.1080/00029157.2015.1011465

Kabat-Zinn, J. (1994). Wherever you go, there you are: Mindfulness meditation in everyday life. New York, NY: Hyperion.

ACKNOWLEDGMENTS

The original conceptualization for this book began in 2010, when Dr. Olendzki was applying for the doctoral program in clinical psychology at Baylor University. At that time, Dr. Elkins, director of the Mind–Body Medicine Research Laboratory (MBMRL), was conducting a series of studies on the clinical applications of hypnotic relaxation therapy and beginning to explore the integration of hypnosis and mindfulness. Dr. Olendzki, as an applicant to Dr. Elkins at Baylor, already had an extensive background in mindfulness practice and Buddhist philosophy. Dr. Olendzki had further served as the clinical research coordinator for a large study of mindfulness at the Center for Mindfulness in Medicine, Health Care, and Society at the University of Massachusetts Medical School. It was a perfect match, and the collaboration between Dr. Elkins and Dr. Olendzki to develop mindfulness-based hypnotherapy began!

We want to thank Dr. James Carmody at the University of Massachusetts Medical School for his training and prior mentorship of Dr. Olendzki in mindfulness and the introduction to the scientific method in expanding the understanding of mindfulness-based interventions. In a similar manner, we wish to acknowledge the support and facilities provided by the Department of Psychology and Neuroscience at Baylor University for hypnosis research and the development of MH and our ongoing research. In particular, we wish to thank Dr. Charles Weaver, chair of the Department of Psychology and Neuroscience at Baylor, for his strong support and encouragement.

Additionally, we would like to thank Carolyn Ahearn, Vicki Patterson, Emily Pendleton, and Lauren Simicich for their review and suggestions for edits to the book chapters and references. Also, thanks to the members (colleagues and students) of the MBMRL at Baylor University who were there during the development of this book and provided feedback on the MH approach and suggestions and comments on the transcripts and clinical methods described in this book.

Finally, we want to thank our clients and the individuals who volunteered for clinical studies of the MH program. The feedback from our clients and study participants proved invaluable in the refinement of MH, and this process continues to this day!

To the clinicians who read this book, we express our thanks for your consideration in learning about hypnosis and its integration with mindfulness. If you are an experienced clinician, we hope you will find some ideas that you can use in your practice. If you are new to hypnotherapy or mindfulness, please consider this a basic text that can introduce you to therapeutic approaches that are increasingly recognized as effective and important. Your openness to new concepts and ideas is acknowledged and will be appreciated by your clients and patients!

Gary R. Elkins, PhD, ABPP, ABPH, Baylor University, Waco, Texas
Nicholas Olendzki, PsyD, University of Massachusetts–Dartmouth

SECTION I

FOUNDATIONS

CHAPTER 1

CONCEPTUAL BASIS FOR MINDFUL HYPNOTHERAPY

Until you are willing to be confused about what you already know, what you know will never grow bigger, better, or more useful.

—*Milton H. Erickson (1980)*

Introduction

Mindfulness is a contemplative practice involving focused attention, attentiveness to the present moment, and nonjudgmental awareness. It is a way of experiencing the world that can facilitate powerful life changes and open the door to greater well-being. Clinical interventions that use mindfulness offer a unique perspective that can help people improve clients' lives. Hypnosis is defined as "a state of consciousness involving focused attention and reduced peripheral awareness characterized by an enhanced capacity for response to suggestion" (Elkins, Barabasz, Council, & Spiegel, 2015). Hypnotherapy presents an intriguing synchronicity with some aspects of mindfulness, in that it also is a practice that involves focused attention, experiencing the world differently, and improving clients' lives. However, these two practices differ in many respects, such as the use of hypnotic suggestions during hypnotherapy to empower patients to achieve treatment goals.

Mindful hypnotherapy (MH) is an intervention that intentionally uses hypnosis (hypnotic induction and suggestion) to integrate mindfulness for personal or therapeutic benefit. In MH, we utilize hypnosis as a powerful delivery vehicle for mindfulness. Hypnosis is a medium that enables mindfulness to be absorbed and integrated more easily, efficiently, and effectively. This can be expressed alternately as follows: Imagine that the scientists of the future created a wonder drug that could reduce all suffering by 50%. Now, imagine that the medicine came in only one pill form and that the pill was the size of a golf ball. What would happen next? There would be great interest in smaller pills or alternative ways of accessing the "medicine." This metaphor highlights a core truth that lies at the heart of MH: It's not just a medicine or treatment that is important, but how that medicine is delivered.

Hypnotherapy: A Medium for Mindful Change

Clinicians who are trained only in mindfulness may have preconceived notions about hypnosis. Likewise, individuals who are trained only in hypnosis may have self-limiting ideas about mindfulness. For example, given the history of hypnosis, some might think of it as it has sometimes been portrayed in "hypnotist shows," as a form of entertainment or mind control. Hypnotherapy is neither entertainment nor a method of "mind control." Hypnosis and hypnotherapy involve a focus of attention and receptivity to suggestions and are directed toward empowering clients to achieve their personal goals. They are respectful of clients and used in a flexible manner by therapists with sufficient training and experience. During a hypnotic state, an individual is uniquely receptive to exploring experiences with an open mind and with avid curiosity. By clearly explaining mindfulness and guiding a client's experiences directly in a hypnotic state, we can pave the way for the client having similar experiences with mindfulness in the future. This helps to expedite a client's orientation toward greater mindfulness and helps the client explore the beneficial effects of mindfulness on his or her own during daily life.

Clinicians who are familiar with hypnosis but lack a background of training in mindfulness may have misconceptions about it being unscientific, strange, and inextricable from its religious roots (these issues are further addressed in Chapters 2 and 3 of this book). Mindfulness may be misunderstood as being "the same as hypnosis" or as just a relaxation or stress management technique. It is not. Mindfulness and hypnosis can, however, be combined for a synergistic effect.

One of the challenges to effectively integrating mindfulness into treatment is conveying the subtle, yet radical wisdom that mindfulness entails.[1] This is important because a lack of understanding of nonjudgmental awareness, for example, can dilute the impact of mindfulness practice and delay its clinical utility. When a client misperceives a mindfulness concept, the distortion often occurs when the client comes face to face with unfamiliar concepts or when even the clinician does not have sufficient training and experience with mindfulness practice. For

[1] In this case, the word "*radical*" is being used in the sense of transforming the fundamental nature of something and something that flies in the face of the ordinary way of thinking.

example, consider the following description of *mindfulness* that a client will sometimes provide, even several sessions into a mindfulness-based treatment:

> I have been doing this mindfulness thing for a couple of weeks now and I think I'm finally getting the hang of it! Yesterday I was feeling really angry at my mother-in-law, but I hate being angry and I know that blowing up at her is only going to make things worse. So: I just put those feelings in a box, put a smile on my face, took a deep breath, and went on with my life. It was very *Zen*.

The client's approach to this situation may have been the best option available to the client given the circumstances. Regardless of its effectiveness or ineffectiveness, it demonstrates the use of coping skills that are almost diametrically opposed to mindfulness. In this case, the client has misconstrued equanimity as nonengagement, has confused nonjudgmental awareness with trying to control feeling, and has assumed that if something is unpleasant it must be escaped (in this case, by compartmentalizing the experience and pretending that everything is fine).

Hypnosis shares similarities to mindfulness in that it involves guiding clients to achieve a focus of attention. However, it is different from mindfulness in its theoretical foundations and in the very intentional use of suggestions to guide experience and achieve a range of specific goals. Hypnotherapy interventions typically are directed toward *change* or alteration in thoughts, feelings, physiology, or behavior. An example of a client using self-hypnosis is illustrated in the following comment by the client using hypnosis for pain control.

> The other day, I was at the doctor's having a biopsy, and it was really painful and unpleasant. I was able to be use the self-hypnosis that you taught me, and I just went to another place in my mind. I tuned out the pain and just focused on a relaxing memory. Before I knew it, the procedure was over, and I went on with my day.

In this case, the client is using *hypnosis* to relax and cope with a painful procedure. This can be effective and there are benefits to using self-hypnosis in this way. However, it is not an illustration of the power of nonjudgmental awareness, acceptance, daily practice, or the deeper wisdom of mindfulness. The benefits of mindfulness go beyond simply finding a technique or method for coping with a stressful or painful situation or event. The power of mindfulness can be life changing and extends to all forms of suffering—emotional, physical, interpersonal, existential, and spiritual. Consider the following comment from an individual who had begun mindfulness practice on a daily basis:

> Since learning mindfulness, my experience of every aspect of my life has changed. I have a sense of stillness and I'm able to "be with what is" no matter what is happening, and I am less stressed. The time I take to meditate gives me perspective on the events of the day. Things just do not overwhelm me as they did in the past .... I feel that I am more present in the moment ... less worried ... less stressed ... living in the *now*.

This chapter began with a quote from Dr. Milton Erickson, one of the most important figures in contemporary psychotherapy and hypnosis: "Until you are willing to be confused about what you already know, what you know will never grow bigger, better, or more useful." There is great potential for the integration of hypnosis and mindfulness (Yapko, 2011); however, to achieve this, clinicians and individuals must be *open and flexible* in their understanding of both concepts. To be confused is to be open to learning, and learning creates new understanding and potential for growth and thereby potentially *grows bigger, better, and more useful*. Acceptance and change are not incompatible. It is mind-expanding to go beyond existing schemas and create new ones.

Empirical Basis for Integration

Although there is a need for more research at the intersection of mindfulness and hypnosis, the scholarly articles that do exist on the subject suggest that there is a reasonable basis for integration. In several early examples of hypnosis and meditation research, peer-reviewed articles compared the phenomenological and physiological correlates of mindfulness and hypnosis (Forte, Brown, & Dysart, 1987; Sabourin, Cutcomb, Crawford, & Pribram, 1990; Walrath & Hamilton, 1975). Findings indicate that although the physiological response to mindfulness meditation is fairly similar to that to hypnosis (Walrath & Hamilton, 1975), the phenomenological experience of the two states is distinct (Brown, Forte, Rich, & Epstein, 1982). For example, Brown et al. (1982) studied 122 subjects divided into four groups. The self-hypnosis group practiced 1 hour daily for 2 weeks, a mindfulness meditation group went on a 2-week intensive retreat, and a second mindfulness meditation group went on a 2-day intensive retreat. The study also included a *waking dreaming* condition that was part of an ongoing therapy program. Following the interventions, the participants completed a self-administered Profile of

Trance, Imaging, and Meditation Experience (TIME) questionnaire, and results indicated that subjects in the hypnosis condition experienced a change in attention with a special focus on the role of suggestion. In contrast, individuals in the meditation arms reported a greater awareness of their stream of experiences as they occurred, a subjective slowing of time, and an altered sense of self (feeling as though mental and physical events are an impersonal process). In addition, the more experienced meditators experienced a sense of weightlessness.

In a special issue on mindfulness and hypnosis, several authors contributed articles to the *Journal of Mind–Body Regulation* with different theoretical perspectives on the overlap between these two interventions. In one article, Lynn, Malaktaris, Maxwell, Mellinger, and van der Kloet (2012) argue that hypnosis and mindfulness inhabit a common domain involving suggestion. After comparing and contrasting mindfulness and hypnotic approaches to suggestion, the authors discuss some of the clinical implications for their conclusions. For instance, mindfulness and hypnosis could theoretically be used interchangeably according to variable client characteristics, or hypnosis could be used to *enhance* the effectiveness of a mindfulness intervention. The authors go on to highlight the fact that hypnosis and meditation have barely been explored from an empirical standpoint and suggest that controlled empirical trials studying the overlap of hypnosis and mindfulness are "vitally important" (Lynn et al., 2012, p. 21). In the same issue, Grant (2012) offers a cautionary commentary highlighting some of the methodological difficulties of meaningfully comparing hypnosis to mindfulness. He rightfully calls attention to the fact that meditation and even mindfulness can include a diverse array of interventions, and he also points out that several benefits of mindfulness are attained only by long-term practice, whereas secular clinical interventions often focus on the effects of short-term practice. While none of his arguments are prohibitive for empirically investigating the possibility that hypnosis and mindfulness inhabit a common domain, they do emphasize the importance of clear definitions of the constructs under investigation and careful methodology when investigating those constructs.

Harrer (2009) adds to the diverse theoretical perspectives on mindfulness and hypnosis by presenting the two as having a complementary and synergistic relationship. According to this view, each intervention presents unique expressions of the same central constructs. Harrer presents eight constructs with analogues in hypnosis and mindfulness for the reader's consideration, such as the fact that hypnosis is often characterized by attentional *absorption*, whereas mindfulness is usually described in terms of an *open awareness*. Rather than viewing these two poles of attention as diametrically opposed, Harrer suggests that there is a spectrum of clinically useful experiences between the two and that using only hypnosis *or* mindfulness is unnecessarily restrictive. A logical consequence of Harrer's line of reasoning is that it may be possible to integrate mindfulness and hypnosis into a personalized intervention that has the potential to be superior to either intervention alone. Along similar lines, Lynn, Surya Das, Hallquist, and Williams (2006) suggest that

> hypnosis and mindfulness-based approaches can be used in tandem to create adaptive response sets and to deautomatize maladaptive response sets ... mindfulness can serve as a template for generating an array of suggestions that provides cognitive strategies to contend with problems in living and to ameliorate stress and negative affect more generally. (p. 143)

Consistent with this sentiment, Lynn, Barnes, Deming, and Accardi (2010) published a sample hypnotic mindfulness induction for use in Mindfulness-Based Cognitive Therapy (MBCT) courses. In this same article, these authors identify the combination of mindfulness and hypnosis as "a natural marriage with excellent prospects." More recently, Facco (2017) provided a conceptualization of some common features of hypnosis and meditation, such as "induction based on focused attention; capability to reach an intentional control of both biologic–somatic activities and conscious–unconscious processes; and activation/deactivation of several brain areas and circuits" such as the default modality brain network (Facco, 2017, p. 169). Furthermore, Yapko (2011) has provided a theoretical argument for the integrated use of mindfulness and hypnosis and addresses similarities and differences.

Mentally substituting familiar coping strategies and concepts for the novel, mindful ones is common in the beginning phases of mindfulness treatment. This is because it is deeply counterintuitive for most people to pay attention to that which is unpleasant, let alone to do so with an attitude of openness rather than aversion. Our experience is that many clients do eventually learn what mindfulness is and how to integrate a mindful perspective into their lives. For some, this is accomplished by the end of their treatment with a mindfulness-based intervention. For others, it requires participating in several mindfulness treatments or courses before they begin to shift their thinking in a meaningful way and let go of their instinctual reactivity.

The structure of MH involves the integration of mindfulness and hypnotherapy methods to accentuate the benefits of both. To achieve optimal integration, it is often useful to have a plan for how skills and understanding will be introduced over the course of treatment. This structured or semistructured approach can be adapted as needed based on client needs and situational factors. The majority of this book focuses on providing an introduction to basic MH concepts and their practical application in MH sessions. A brief overview of MH's typical structure is provided in the following section.

Structure of Mindful Hypnotherapy

MH uses a step-by-step process to build the client's understanding of mindfulness. This "scaffold" approach begins with the most familiar concepts and gradually introduces ones that are less familiar. Unfolding the concept of mindfulness step by step and week by week means that by the time a client is introduced to a new concept or topic, the client has already become familiar with a similar skill that can be used to understand the new concept. In addition, each new facet of mindfulness adds a richness of context to the other facets. A client learning how to notice the present moment in session 1 will often experience immediate relief and benefit but will have a richer idea of the implications of present-moment awareness by the end of the eight sessions. In order, the sessions of MH focus on:

- Being in the present moment (Chapter 8)
- Paying attention to physical experiences nonjudgmentally (Chapter 9)
- Paying attention to thoughts and emotions nonjudgmentally (Chapter 10)
- Teaching self-hypnosis (Chapter 11)
- Teaching self-compassion (Chapter 12)
- Raising awareness of one's values and sense of meaning (Chapter 13)
- Integrating sessions (Chapter 14)
- Transitioning to long-term practice (Chapter 15)

In practical terms, this scaffolding process begins with the idea of "being in the present moment" in session 1. Although most of us get caught up in focusing on the future or the past, the idea that living in the present might be beneficial for healing is not a foreign one. When clients are asked to "slow down," to just breathe for a moment, and to notice what it's like to be *here, now*, they usually report that this is a calming and pleasant experience; what's more, few clients are surprised by this experience. Therefore, its familiarity and normalcy can be a good starting point to individuals who are new to mindfulness and hypnosis.

Even at the beginning of session 2, many clients will be mentally primed for the content that follows if they have been doing their homework. This is because paying attention to the present moment (session 1) will necessarily involve some degree of awareness about what is seen, heard, felt, and otherwise experienced through the senses in the present moment. As clients have *been present* throughout the week, they may have noticed the feeling of rain on their skin, the interesting pattern on their living room rug, or the annoying hum of the air conditioning in their apartment. The conceptual *stretch* in this session comes from inviting a client to pay attention to such things with curiosity, rather than trying to push unpleasant experiences away and attempting to cling to pleasant experiences.

Once a client has had practice with nonjudgmental awareness of the physical senses, this skill can be transferred to being nonjudgmentally aware of thoughts and emotions in session 3. MH is presented in this order because many clients find nonjudgmental awareness of thoughts and emotions to be more difficult than nonjudgmental awareness of physical sensations. Thoughts and emotions often feel more visceral, primal, and personal than the mere sensations of the body. However, after becoming more practiced with nonjudgmental awareness of body, a client may find that this experience can be used as a scaffold to understanding mindfulness of thoughts and emotions.

Session 4 gives the client a break from new mindfulness concepts and shifts the clinical focus to teaching self-hypnosis. Self-hypnosis enables clients to begin personalizing their hypnosis experiences by modifying their home practice to suit their preferences.

In session 5, clients are invited to consider the importance of compassion for themselves and others. Although these concepts are not unfamiliar per se, they can be difficult to practice. Many clients carry around a harsh *inner critic* or a lack of awareness about what they truly *need* rather than what they crave in the moment. For example, some clients worry that if they show love toward themselves, it will mean they're self-centered. Others worry that if they *let up* on themselves, they will never accomplish anything. Still other clients find themselves procrastinating or engaging in other harmful behavior, even though this is not in their best interests. By session 5, however, most clients will have developed the mental flexibility to engage with compassion and self-compassion in a meaningful way. Furthermore, the foundational work on mindful awareness will allow clients to discern which acts of self-compassion will be of true benefit and strengthen their will to act on this knowledge.

Session 6 capitalizes on a client's growing and holistic understanding of what mindfulness entails and further leverages this understanding to explore valued actions. Once a client is relating to his or her experiences with equanimity rather than reactivity, it opens up a freedom of choice that may not have existed before. A person who is unable to tolerate unpleasant experiences *must* act to change or escape those experiences. A person who cannot tolerate letting go of a pleasant experience *must* act to hold on to or reclaim that experience. However, an individual who can maintain a baseline sense of well-being that is independent of pleasant or unpleasant experiences has the freedom to act in a way that is consistent with one's own sense of meaning and in accordance with one's values.

Finally, sessions 7 and 8 are used to explore the unified impact of the previous sessions, to clear up misunderstandings or questions, and to transition to long-term maintenance of these behaviors. Mindfulness is a practice that has a relatively simple premise, but the long-term potential of mindfulness can be explored for a lifetime. MH is designed to be a time-limited intervention that helps clients benefit from the strengths of both mindfulness and hypnosis. The intervention is based on fostering autonomy and grants clients the tools to make the practice their own long after the intervention has concluded. It is our firm belief that MH has the potential to empower clients to overcome a wide variety of obstacles in life and that it can be a potent contribution to the fields of clinical hypnotherapy and mindfulness alike.

■ CLINICIAN NOTE

Standardization

The session structure for MH outlined in this book is meant to describe a template for uniting mindfulness and hypnotherapy. This particular structure and content has met with excellent success in the authors' experience, and it is well received by clients. It is our hope that presenting our standardized format will help clinicians implement MH more easily and will facilitate rigorous empirical testing. Readers with a good grasp of mindfulness and hypnotherapy may apply the integration in a flexible manner to achieve goals and results.

Summary

In summary, hypnosis and mindfulness can be integrated and used in tandem for therapeutic benefit and to create adaptive response sets. The conceptual basis for MH is that hypnosis can serve as a delivery method for mindfulness-based suggestions and experiences. Further, mindful hypnotic inductions involve focused attention and provide a framework for accessing conscious and unconscious processes and mindful hypnotic suggestions. MH uses a step-by-step process over eight or more sessions to introduce experiences of present-moment awareness, nonjudgmental awareness, learning self-hypnosis, compassion, awareness of values, integration, and transition to long-term practice of mindful self-hypnosis. Within this structure, sessions can be personalized to maximize MH benefits. Learning MH involves flexibility and openness to new understandings of both mindfulness and hypnosis.

REFERENCES

Brown, D., Forte, M., Rich, P., & Epstein, G. (1982). Phenomenological differences among self hypnosis, mindfulness meditation, and imaging. *Imagination, Cognition and Personality, 2*, 291–309. doi:10.2190/jwc1-axly-6r0l-g2nk

Elkins, G. R., Barabasz, A. F., Council, J. R., & Spiegel, D. (2015). Advancing research and practice: The revised APA division 30 definition of hypnosis. *American Journal of Clinical Hypnosis, 57*, 378–385. doi:10.1080/00029157.2015.1011465

Erickson, M. H., & Rossi, S. I. (1980). *The collected works of Milton H. Erickson.* New York, NY: Irvington.

Facco, E. (2017). Meditation and hypnosis: Two sides of the same coin? *International Journal of Clinical and Experimental Hypnosis, 62*(2), 169–188. doi:10.1080/00207144.2017.1276361

Forte, M., Brown, D., & Dysart, M. (1987). Differences in experience among mindfulness meditators. *Imagination, Cognition and Personality, 7*, 47–60. doi:10.2190/53EL-UTVW-DN4T-F60D

Grant, J. A. (2012). Towards a more meaningful comparison of meditation and hypnosis. *Journal of Mind–Body Regulation, 2*, 71–74. Retrieved from https://journalhosting.ucalgary.ca/index.php/mbr/article/view/16008/12660

Harrer, M. E. (2009). Mindfulness and the mindful therapist: Possible contributions to hypnosis. *Contemporary Hypnosis, 26*, 234–244. doi:10.1002/ch.388

Lynn, S. J., Barnes, S., Deming, A., & Accardi, M. (2010). Hypnosis, rumination, and depression: Catalyzing attention and mindfulness-based treatments.

International Journal of Clinical and Experimental Hypnosis, 58, 202–221. doi:10.1080/00207140903523244

Lynn, S. J., Malaktaris, A., Maxwell, R., Mellinger, D. I., & van der Kloet, D. (2012). Do hypnosis and mindfulness practices inhabit a common domain? Implications for research, clinical practice, and forensic science. *Journal of Mind–Body Regulation, 2*, 12–26. Retrieved from https://journalhosting.ucalgary.ca/index.php/mbr/article/download/16000/12655

Lynn, S. J., Surya Das, L., Hallquist, M. N., & Williams, J. C. (2006). Mindfulness, acceptance, and hypnosis: Cognitive and clinical perspectives. *International Journal of Clinical and Experimental Hypnosis, 54*, 143–166. doi:10.1080/00207140500528240

Sabourin, M. E., Cutcomb, S. D., Crawford, H. J., & Pribram, K. (1990). EEG correlates of hypnotic susceptibility and hypnotic trance: Spectral analysis and coherence. *International Journal of Psychophysiology, 10*, 125–142. doi:10.1016/0167-8760(90)90027-b

Walrath, L. C., & Hamilton, D. W. (1975). Autonomic correlates of meditation and hypnosis. *American Journal of Clinical Hypnosis, 17*, 190–197. doi:10.1080/00029157.1975.10403739

Yapko, M. D. (2011). *Mindfulness and hypnosis: The power of suggestion to transform experience*. New York, NY: W. W. Norton.

CHAPTER 2

MINDFULNESS AND HYPNOSIS: RESEARCH CONTEXT

Research is to see what everybody else has seen, and to think what nobody else has thought.

—Albert Szent-Györgyi (1957)

Introduction

For more than 2,000 years, mindfulness was taught alongside a broader set of Buddhist beliefs (see Chapter 3), and was constrained almost exclusively to the Asiatic countries, where Buddhism was more common. In the West, meditation and mindfulness were relatively obscure practices throughout the 19th century and the first half of the 20th century. During this time, mindfulness was primarily practiced by displaced Buddhist monks and to some extent by lay Buddhist immigrants. When these practices became more prevalent during the countercultural spiritual explorations of the late 1950s and 1960s, Buddhism drew increasing attention from academics (Olendzki, 2014).

As a direct result of mindfulness and meditation becoming more prevalent in the West in the second half of the 20th century, these practices became a matter of empirical scrutiny, and researchers began to wonder what impact they had on physiology and mental health. By the mid-1970s, a significant number of such studies had begun to accumulate, and Smith (1975) reported that "at least 100 scholarly books and journals have argued that meditation [a practice related to mindfulness] does have psychotherapeutic potential."

It is important to note that these studies were mainly observational in nature. Mindfulness and meditation were embedded within their religious and cultural roots, and as such they were rarely used by psychologists as interventions in a secular therapy context. Therefore, even those studies that found a link between these practices and health benefits usually used participants who were already engaged in regular meditation. To give a contemporary parallel, prayer would generally not be recommended as an intervention to an atheist in a clinical context, despite findings that prayer may have beneficial effects on those who engage in the practice (Andrade & Radhakrishnan, 2009; Levine, Aviv, Yoo, Ewing, & Au, 2009; Sternthal, Williams, Musick, & Buck, 2012). Similarly, therapists in the 1960s and 1970s may have felt that the ritualistic and religious trappings of these practices made them less accessible to individuals whose religious beliefs differed from meditation's culture of origin, or the therapists themselves may have felt discomfort with teaching them. Whatever the cause, the so-called third wave of cognitive behavioral interventions, which are characterized by integrating mindfulness into *clinical* interventions, did not begin in earnest until the advent of Mindfulness-Based Stress Reduction (MBSR) in the early 1980s.

Mindfulness-Based Stress Reduction and Related Programs

Although a full review of mindfulness research is beyond the scope of this chapter, a brief overview of MBSR and the more prominent mindfulness interventions that followed is helpful to understanding the influences that shaped mindful hypnotherapy (MH). MBSR began as a 10-week group mindfulness intervention that had a significant positive impact on chronic pain tolerance and mood (Kabat-Zinn, 1982). Like later iterations of MBSR, the intervention included a body-scan meditation, mindfulness of breathing, and hatha yoga. The 10-week intervention was reduced to 8 weeks early on in MBSR's development, and subsequent research provided ever-growing support for MBSR as an effective treatment for chronic pain and anxiety reduction (Arch et al., 2013; Baer, Carmody, & Hunsinger, 2012; Cavanagh et al., 2013). With time, MBSR's reach and influence grew into an international phenomenon. The success of MBSR inspired similar programs such as Mindfulness-Based Cognitive Therapy (MBCT) and Mindfulness-Based Relapse Prevention (Bowen et al., 2009; Witkiewitz, Marlatt, & Walker, 2005), which modified the standard course material of MBSR to be more germane to depression relapse and drug addiction, respectively.

As MBSR gained greater popularity, other mindfulness-based and mindfulness-influenced therapies that diverged from the standard eight-week intervention were being developed. The earliest of these was Dialectical Behavioral Therapy (DBT; Linehan, 1987). DBT was developed as an intervention that uses a team of therapists to provide group therapy and individual therapy to help clients with parasuicidal behaviors. The success of DBT in treating these behaviors in borderline patients was a remarkable accomplishment and helped DBT to gain rapid recognition and early adoption in the psychotherapy community. Similar to MBSR's establishment and gradual expansion, the success of DBT for a specific population with a specific problem (borderline personality disorder) was a kind of *proof of concept*. Over time, this inspired researchers to study DBT for a wide variety of conditions and populations. Consequently, DBT gained empirical support for treating other chronic psychological issues, such as eating disorders (Chen, Matthews, Allen, Kuo, & Linehan, 2008; Safer, Telch, & Agras, 2001; Telch, Agras, & Linehan, 2001) and substance-use disorders (Axelrod, Perepletchikova, Holtzman, & Sinha, 2011; Linehan et al., 1999).

During the same time period when MBSR was gaining popularity and DBT was just starting to grow, Acceptance and Commitment Therapy (ACT) was developing (Hayes, 1987; Hayes & Wilson, 1993); it coalesced into a complete and distinct therapy by 1994 (Hayes & Wilson, 1994). One of the ways that ACT distinguished itself from MBSR or DBT was by being the first mindfulness-based treatment that was delivered on an individual basis, with no group component integrated into the intervention. ACT is based on Relational Frame Theory (RFT) and uses mindfulness principles to address a wide range of issues, including depression and anxiety (Hayes & Twohig, 2008), psychosis (Bach & Hayes, 2002; Gaudiano & Herbert, 2006), chronic pain (Dahl, Wilson, & Nilsson, 2004; Vowles & McCracken, 2008), and substance use (Gifford et al., 2004; Hayes et al., 2004; Luoma, Kohlenberg, Hayes, & Fletcher, 2012).

Clinical Research on Mindfulness Interventions

Among the conditions for which mindfulness has been studied, stress and anxiety are perhaps the most promising avenues of research. Although there have been a limited number of large randomized controlled trials (RCTs) of mindfulness interventions, the evidence from several meta-analyses shows a consensus that mindfulness can be efficacious in the treatment of stress and anxiety disorders (Grossman, Niemann, Schmidt, & Walach, 2004; Hofmann, Sawyer, Witt, & Oh, 2010; Piet, Würtzen, & Zachariae, 2012; Powers, Zum Vorde Sive Vording, & Emmelkamp, 2009). For example, a meta-analysis by Powers et al. (2009), which included active-treatment RCTs, found that ACT performed equally to established anxiety treatments, such as behavioral and cognitive-behavioral therapy (CBT; Powers et al., 2009). Furthermore, the literature suggests that these gains tend to be well maintained at long-term follow-up (Carlson, Speca,

Faris, & Patel, 2007; Grossman, Tiefenthaler-Gilmer, Raysz, & Kesper, 2007; Miller, Fletcher, & Kabat-Zinn, 1995).

Evidence also suggests that mindfulness can be of benefit in the treatment of mental health conditions such as depression (Kenny & Williams, 2007; Strauss, Cavanagh, Oliver, & Pettman, 2014), eating disorders (Daubenmier et al., 2011; Kristeller, Wolever, & Sheets, 2013), addictions (Bowen et al., 2006, Bowen et al., 2009; Vidrine et al., 2009), and posttraumatic stress disorder (PTSD; Kearney, McDermott, Malte, Martinez, & Simpson, 2013; Omidi et al., 2013). Further, MBSR and related mindfulness programs have been shown to be of benefit in the treatment of chronic pain (Carson et al., 2005; Kabat-Zinn, 1982; Kabat-Zinn, Lipworth, & Burney, 1985; Kabat-Zinn, Lipworth, Burney, & Sellers, 1986; Wong et al., 2011), fibromyalgia (Astin et al., 2003; Kaplan, Goldenberg, & Galvin-Nadeau, 1993; Sephton et al., 2007), cancer symptoms (Piet et al., 2012), irritable bowel syndrome (Aucoin, Lalonde-Parsi, & Cooley, 2014; Gaylord et al., 2011; Zernicke et al., 2013), and arthritis (Fogarty, Booth, Gamble, Dalbeth, & Consedine, 2015; Zautra et al., 2008). Clearly, mindfulness interventions have a broad applicability, and the list of conditions for which mindfulness may be efficacious is ever expanding.

Clinical Research on Hypnosis Interventions

There is also an expanding body of clinical research on hypnosis interventions to treat a wide range of medical and psychological concerns (Elkins, 2017). Clinical and experimental studies provide support for hypnotherapy in the treatment of irritable bowel syndrome (Galovski & Blanchard, 1998; Palsson, Turner, & Whitehead, 2006; Prior, Colgan, & Whorwell, 1990), hot flashes (Elkins et al., 2008; Elkins, Fisher, Johnson, Carpenter, & Keith, 2013), sleep disturbances (Cordi, Hirsiger, Merillat, & Rasch, 2015; Cordi, Schlard, & Rasch, 2014; Elkins et al., 2013), some dermatological problems (Spanos, Stenstrom, & Johnson, 1988; Spanos, Williams, & Gwynn, 1990), smoking cessation (Elkins et al., 2006; Green & Lynn, 2000), weight loss (Kirsch, 1996; Kirsch, Montgomery, & Sapirstein, 1995), and treatment of chronic depressive syndromes and PTSD (Bryant, Creamer, O'Donnell, Silove, & McFarlane, 2008; Gruzelier, 2006; Spiegel, Hunt, & Dondershine, 1988). Other areas of application of hypnotherapy include tension and migraine headaches (Olness, MacDonald, & Uden, 1987), pain associated with labor and delivery (Brown & Hammond, 2007), and medical procedures (Elkins et al., 2006; Enqvist, Björklund, Engman, & Jakobsson, 1997; Lang et al., 2000; Montgomery, David, Winkel, Silverstein & Bovbjerg, 2002; Patterson & Ptacek, 1997).

Several empirical studies have been conducted on the use of hypnotherapy for pain management (Brown & Hammond, 2007; Hawkins,

2001; Jensen, 2011; Jensen, Barber, Romano, Hanley, et al., 2009; Jensen, Barber, Romano, Molton, et al., 2009; Jensen et al., 2011; Montgomery, DuHamel, & Redd, 2000; Patterson & Jenson, 2003). Outcomes for hypnosis interventions have included decreased pain and use of pain medications, as well as reduced suffering from pain (Elkins, Jensen, & Patterson, 2007; Elkins, Johnson, & Fisher, 2012; Jensen, 2011). Studies have generally been positive in regard to hypnotherapy in the treatment of pain conditions such as chronic low-back pain (Jensen, Barber, Romano, Hanley, et al., 2009; Jensen, Barber, Romano, Molton, et al., 2009; McCauley, Thelen, Frank, Willard, & Callen, 1983; Spinhoven & Linssen, 1989), fibromyalgia (Castel, Perez, Sala, Padrol, & Rull, 2007; Haanen et al., 1991), osteoarthritis (Gay, Philippot, & Luminet, 2002), pain-related disability (Jensen, Abresch, Carter, & McDonald, 2005: Jensen, et al., 2011), and cancer-related pain (Elkins, Cheung, Marcus, Palamara, & Rajab, 2004; Neron & Stephenson, 2007; Spiegel & Bloom, 1983).

Many hypnotic inductions involve relaxation, decreased rumination, and inward focus of attention (Elkins, 2014), which may be experienced as anxiety reducing and may be of benefit in stress reduction. While research is limited, Flammer (2006) conducted a meta-analysis of 18 RCTs focused on generalized anxiety and phobias. The findings indicated that there was a large effect size for hypnotherapy in reducing anxiety when compared to the wait-list control. In addition, hypnosis practice may have a beneficial effect on reducing stress and its effects on immunity (Keicolt-Glaser, Marucha, Atkinson, & Glaser, 2001).

Research on Integrating Hypnosis Interventions With Standard or Cognitive-Behavioral Therapy Interventions

In addition to the studies that have found clinical hypnosis to be effective as a primary treatment, there is evidence to suggest that hypnosis may enhance treatment gains when it is integrated or combined with cognitive-behavioral or other standard therapies. For example, Kirsch et al. (1995) reviewed 18 studies and found that clients receiving cognitive-behavioral hypnotherapy showed greater improvement than at least 70% of clients receiving nonhypnotic treatment. Although there is a need for further research on the impact of integrating hypnosis into the standard treatment for anxiety disorders specifically (Golden, 2012), some initial evidence indicates that integrating hypnosis into standard therapy can produce greater therapeutic gains than therapy without hypnosis. For example, one study of public-speaking anxiety investigated the efficacy of a hypnotic delivery of cognitive-behavioral treatment versus a nonhypnotic delivery of the same intervention (Schoenberger, Kirsch, Gearan, Montgomery, & Pastyrnak, 997).

In the study, participants were randomized into two groups. CBT was administered to both groups, with the only difference being that in the CBT plus hypnosis group, suggestions for entering a hypnotic trance were given before relaxation instructions, while in the nonhypnosis group, instructions for relaxation were given without suggestions for trance. In a pre–post comparison of anxiety symptoms in a public-speaking scenario, participants showed a significantly greater reduction in anxiety symptoms in the CBT plus hypnosis condition than in the nonhypnosis CBT condition. This significant increase in effectiveness corresponds to a larger effect in the hypnosis condition, and the client's pre-intervention expectation of hypnosis efficacy was found to moderate treatment gains.

■ CLINICIAN NOTE

Hypnosis Intervention Research

Research has examined hypnotherapy as the primary intervention for some disorders and the integration or addition of hypnotherapy to cognitive-behavioral or other established therapies. Research suggests that hypnotherapy may have a significant additive effect and may *boost* the impact when integrated with other methods or interventions.

In another comparison of CBT and cognitive therapy with hypnosis, Alladin and Alibhai (2007) found that the hypnosis condition significantly reduced anxiety and depression when compared to CBT without hypnosis in a sample of 84 depressed patients. In this study, CBT, based on the work by Beck, Rush, Shaw, and Emery (1979), was compared to cognitive therapy with hypnotic suggestions for ego strengthening, expansion of awareness, positive mood induction, and posthypnotic suggestions for diminishing depression and motivation. A repeated-measures analysis of variance (ANOVA) showed that both conditions significantly improved, but the hypnosis condition improved 16% more on measures of anxiety than the nonhypnosis condition and improved 5% more on measures of depression.

In a third study of the additive effects of hypnosis to standard therapy, Bryant, Moulds, Guthrie, and Nixon (2005) recruited 87 civilian trauma survivors who met the diagnostic criteria for acute stress disorder and randomized them into three groups for six sessions of treatment. The CBT group was given a standard progression of psychoeducation, imaginal exposure, cognitive restructuring, and in vivo exposure. The CBT plus hypnosis condition received an identical treatment, but also had a hypnotic induction prior to imaginal exposure, which included suggestions for engaging fully and deeply in the exercise. The third group had supportive counseling (SC) only, including problem-solving skills, education about trauma in general, and an explicit avoidance of cognitive restructuring or hypnosis. Postintervention analysis revealed that both CBT and CBT plus hypnosis had significantly greater reductions in PTSD symptoms compared to SC, and the rate at which clients reexperienced symptoms of PTSD was significantly lower in the CBT plus hypnosis group as compared to the CBT group. Contrary to the authors' hypothesis, CBT plus hypnosis did not result in significant clinical gains over CBT beyond the finding regarding reexperiencing. However, the authors noted in retrospect that limiting the hypnosis intervention to reexperiencing and not using hypnosis in cognitive restructuring, in vivo exposure, and anxiety management was a limiting factor that may explain the lack of findings in these domains.

Context for Integrating Mindfulness and Hypnosis

Despite the variable quality of empirical mindfulness research, studies have generally established that mindfulness can help ameliorate the suffering in people's lives and improve their quality of life. However, treatments like MBSR or MBCT group sessions are typically 2 to 2.5 hours long (including one all-day mindfulness retreat) and require an hour of homework per day, 6 days a week over the course of 8 weeks. In contrast to MBSR, ACT for stress and anxiety does not typically necessitate an all-day retreat and each session is delivered individually within the standard therapy hour. However, like many contemporary interventions, ACT is often delivered over the course of 12 or more sessions. While this investment of time is certainly worthwhile for both individual and group mindfulness interventions, it would be a great advantage if clients could achieve a comparable depth of understanding and clinical improvement in a briefer span of time using fewer sessions. With MH, at least some of these ideals and experiences of these other interventions can be imparted in a compressed amount of time using hypnotherapy to let the experiences and perspectives *sink in* more deeply and efficiently.

Another potential benefit of integrating mindfulness and hypnotherapy is that there may be synergistic effect among these interventions. For example, mindfulness delivered within the context of hypnosis may elicit greater treatment participation from individuals with an interest in hypnotherapy and may lead to greater symptom reduction. Despite widespread use of mindfulness-influenced and mindfulness-based treatments, they have not consistently been found to be superior to standard CBT in well-controlled empirical studies of stress and anxiety. While some studies have found mindfulness and CBT to be approximately equivalent (Forman, Herbert, Moitra, Yeomans, & Geller, 2007; Khoury et al., 2013;

Manicavasgar, Parker, & Perich, 2011; Öst, 2008), other studies have found slight advantages to CBT. For example, in an RCT comparing MBSR to cognitive-behavioral group therapy (CBGT) for social anxiety disorder, participants improved in both groups, but measures of social anxiety were lower in those clients who had received CBGT (Koszycki, Benger, Shlik, & Bradwejn, 2007). Despite the lack of evidence that mindfulness is *superior* to alternative interventions, it remains a popular approach for clients and treatment providers alike. If mindfulness can be presented in a format that improves upon treatment outcomes or achieves them in a briefer span of time, this would be a valuable contribution to medicine.

Mindfulness interventions typically focus on nonjudgmental *awareness* of experiences, whereas hypnosis interventions typically focus on using a hypnotic state to directly *change* those experiences. However, it is not incompatible for an intervention to focus on *both* nonjudgmental awareness and change. MH seeks to foster nonjudgmental acceptance of whatever experiences naturally unfold while simultaneously integrating hypnotic suggestions for symptom change. As symptoms and experiences change through MH, clients are encouraged to maintain an open-minded curiosity throughout the process. In light of existing research in mindfulness, hypnotherapy, and the author's own clinical experiences, MH may be of particular benefit for the treatment of anxiety, stress, chronic pain, depression, sleep disturbances, irritable bowel syndrome, and behavioral issues. The basics of MH are provided in this book, which provides the guidelines and "treatment manual" needed for further research.

Summary

In recent years there has been an emerging body of empirical research supporting both mindfulness and hypnosis interventions. In some cases, mindfulness and hypnosis have been shown to be of benefit for similar problems (i.e., stress, anxiety, pain, depression, irritable bowel syndrome). In other research, hypnosis has been found to offer some advantages of brevity and effect on symptoms (i.e., acute and procedural pain, hot flashes, dermatological symptoms, sleep quality, habits). However, the mechanisms by which these interventions achieve benefits may be similar in some regards (i.e., relaxation, focus of attention, awareness) and different in other aspects (i.e., hypnotizability, hypnotic state, expectancy, goal-directed suggestions). Also, studies provide substantive evidence that when hypnotherapy is integrated into standard cognitive-behavioral treatment, therapeutic gains tend to be superior to CBT alone. On the basis of this general trend, it is theorized that not only are third-wave cognitive therapies compatible with hypnosis, but treatment gains may even be *enhanced* by a hypnotic delivery and reinforcement of content. MH builds upon this existing body of research to provide an added tool that can be individualized and affect both acceptance and change as outcome goals.

REFERENCES

Alladin, A., & Alibhai, A. (2007). Cognitive hypnotherapy for depression: An empirical investigation. *International Journal of Clinical and Experimental Hypnosis, 55*, 147–166. doi:10.1080/00207140601177897

Andrade, C., & Radhakrishnan, R. (2009). Prayer and healing: A medical and scientific perspective on randomized controlled trials. *Indian Journal of Psychiatry, 51*(4), 247–253. doi:10.4103/0019-5545.58288

Arch, J. J., Ayers, C. R., Baker, A., Almklov, E., Dean, D. J., & Craske, M. G. (2013). Randomized clinical trial of adapted mindfulness-based stress reduction versus group cognitive behavioral therapy for heterogeneous anxiety disorders. *Behaviour Research and Therapy, 51*, 185–196. doi:10.1016/j.brat.2013.01.003

Astin, J. A., Berman, B. M., Bausell, B., Lee, W. L., Hochberg, M., & Forys, K. L. (2003). The efficacy of mindfulness meditation plus Qigong movement therapy in the treatment of fibromyalgia: A randomized controlled trial. *Journal of Rheumatology, 30*(10), 2257–2262.

Aucoin, M., Lalonde-Parsi, M. J., & Cooley, K. (2014). Mindfulness-based therapies in the treatment of functional gastrointestinal disorders: A meta-analysis. *Evidence-Based Complementary and Alternative Medicine, 2014*, 140724. doi:10.1155/2014/140724

Axelrod, S. R., Perepletchikova, F., Holtzman, K., & Sinha, R. (2011). Emotion regulation and substance use frequency in women with substance dependence and borderline personality disorder receiving dialectical behavior therapy. *American Journal of Drug and Alcohol Abuse, 37*, 37–42. doi:10.3109/00952990.2010.535582

Bach, P., & Hayes, S. C. (2002). The use of acceptance and commitment therapy to prevent the rehospitalization of psychotic patients: A randomized controlled trial. *Journal of Consulting and Clinical Psychology, 70*, 1129–1139. doi:10.1037//0022-006x.70.5.1129

Baer, R. A., Carmody, J., & Hunsinger, M. (2012). Weekly change in mindfulness and perceived stress in a mindfulness-based stress reduction program. *Journal of Clinical Psychology, 68*, 755–765. doi:10.1002/jclp.21865

Beck, A., Rush, A., Shaw, B., & Emery, G. (1979). *Cognitive therapy of depression*. New York, NY: Guilford.

Bowen, S., Chawla, N., Collins, S. E., Witkiewitz, K., Hsu, S., Grow, J., … Marlatt, A. (2009). Mindfulness-based relapse prevention for substance use disorders: A pilot efficacy trial. *Substance Abuse, 30*, 295–305. doi:10.1080/08897070903250084

Bowen, S., Witkiewitz, K., Dillworth, T. M., Chawla, N., Simpson, T. L., Ostafin, B. D., … Marlatt, G. A. (2006). Mindfulness meditation and substance use in an incarcerated population. *Psychology of Addictive Behaviors, 20*(3), 343–347. doi:10.1037/0893-164X.20.3.343

Brown, D. C., & Hammond, C. D. (2007). Evidence-based clinical hypnosis in obstetrics, labor, and delivery and preterm labor. *International Journal of Clinical and Experimental Hypnosis, 55*(3), 355–371. doi:10.1080/00207140701338654

Bryant, R. A., Creamer, M., O'Donnell, M., Silove, D., & McFarlane, A. C., (2008). A multisite study of initial respiration rate and heart rate as predictors of post-traumatic stress disorder. *Journal of Clinical Psychiatry, 69*(11), 1694–1701. doi:10.4088/jcp.v69n1104

Bryant, R. A., Moulds, M. L., Guthrie, R. M., & Nixon, R. D. (2005). The additive benefit of hypnosis and cognitive-behavioral therapy in treating acute stress disorder. *Journal of Consulting and Clinical Psychology, 73*, 334–340. doi:10.1037/0022-006X.73.2.334

Carlson, L. E., Speca, M., Faris, P., & Patel, K. D. (2007). One year pre–post intervention follow-up of psychological, immune, endocrine and blood pressure outcomes of Mindfulness-Based Stress Reduction (MBSR) in breast and prostate cancer outpatients. *Brain, Behavior, and Immunity, 21*, 1038–1049. doi:10.1016/j.bbi.2007.04.002

Carson, J. W., Keefe, F. J., Lynch, T. R., Carson, K. M., Goli, V., Fras, A. M., & Thorp, S. R. (2005). Loving-kindness meditation for chronic low back pain: Results from a pilot trial. *Journal of Holistic Nursing, 23*(3), 287–304. doi:10.1177/0898010105277651

Castel, A., Pérez, M., Sala, J., Padrol, A., & Rull, M. (2007). Effect of hypnotic suggestion on fibromyalgic pain: Comparison between hypnosis and relaxation. *European Journal of Pain, 11*(4), 463–468. doi:10.1016/j.ejpain.2006.06.006

Cavanagh, K., Strauss, C., Cicconi, F., Griffiths, N., Wyper, A., & Jones, F. (2013). A randomised controlled trial of a brief online mindfulness-based intervention. *Behaviour Research and Therapy, 51*, 573–578. doi:10.1016/j.brat.2013.06.003

Chen, E. Y., Matthews, L., Allen, C., Kuo, J. R., & Linehan, M. M. (2008). Dialectical behavior therapy for clients with binge-eating disorder or bulimia nervosa and borderline personality disorder. *International Journal of Eating Disorders, 41*, 505–512. doi:10.1002/eat.20522

Cordi, M. J., Hirsiger, S., Mérillat, S., & Rasch, B. (2015). Improving sleep and cognition by hypnotic suggestion in the elderly. *Neuropsychologia, 69*, 176–182. doi:10.1016/j.neuropsychologia.2015.02.001

Cordi, M. J., Schlarb, A. A., & Rasch, B. (2014). Deepening sleep by hypnotic suggestion. *Sleep, 37*(6), 1143–1152. doi:10.5665/sleep.3778

Dahl, J., Wilson, K. G., & Nilsson, A. (2004). Acceptance and commitment therapy and the treatment of persons at risk for long-term disability resulting from stress and pain symptoms: A preliminary randomized trial. *Behavior Therapy, 35*, 785–801. doi:10.1016/S0005-7894(04)80020-0

Daubenmier, J., Kristeller, J., Hecht, F. M., Maninger, N., Kuwata, M., Jhaveri, K., ... Epel, E. (2011). Mindfulness intervention for stress eating to reduce cortisol and abdominal fat among overweight and obese women: An exploratory randomized controlled study. *Journal of Obesity, 2011*, 651936, 13. doi:10.1155/2011/651936

Elkins, G. R. (2014). *Hypnotic relaxation therapy: Principles and applications.* New York, NY: Springer Publishing.

Elkins, G. R. (2017). *Handbook of medical and psychological hypnosis: Foundations, applications, and professional issues.* New York, NY: Springer Publishing.

Elkins, G. R., Cheung, A., Marcus, J., Palamara, L., & Rajab, H. (2004). Hypnosis to reduce pain in cancer survivors with advanced disease: A prospective study. *Journal of Cancer Integrative Medicine, 2*(4), 167–172.

Elkins, G. R., Fisher, W. I., Johnson, A. K., Carpenter, J. S., & Keith, T. Z. (2013). Clinical hypnosis in the treatment of post-menopausal hot flashes: A randomized controlled trial. *Menopause, 20*, 291–298. doi:10.1097/GME.0b013e31826ce3ed

Elkins, G. R., Jensen, M. P., & Patterson, D. R. (2007). Hypnotherapy for the management of chronic pain. *International Journal of Clinical and Experimental Hypnosis, 55*(3), 275–287. doi:10.1080/00207140701338621

Elkins, G. R., Johnson, A., & Fisher, W. (2012). Cognitive hypnotherapy for pain management. *American Journal of Clinical Hypnosis, 54*(4), 294–310. doi:10.1080/00029157.2011.654284

Elkins, G. R., Marcus, J., Stearns, V., Perfect, M., Rajab, M. H., Ruud, C., ... Keith, T. (2008). Randomized trial of a hypnosis intervention for treatment of hot flashes among breast cancer survivors. *Journal of Clinical Oncology, 26*(31), 5022–5026. doi:10.1200/JCO.2008.16.6389

Elkins, G. R., White, J., Patel, P., Marcus, J., Perfect, M. M., & Montgomery, G. H. (2006). Hypnosis to manage anxiety and pain associated with colonoscopy for colorectal cancer screening: Case studies and possible benefits. *International Journal of Clinical and Experimental Hypnosis, 54*(4), 416–431. doi:10.1080/00207140600856780

Enqvist, B., Björklund, C., Engman, M., & Jakobsson, J. (1997). Preoperative hypnosis reduces postoperative vomiting after surgery of the breasts: A prospective, randomized, and blinded study. *Acta Anaesthesiologica Scandinavica, 41*(8), 1028–1032. doi:10.1111/j.1399-6576.1997.tb04831.x

Flammer, E. (2006). Die wirksamkeit von hypnotherapie bei angstörungen [The effectiveness of hypnotherapy in anxiety disorders]. *Hypnose-ZHH, 1*(2), 173–198.

Fogarty, F. A., Booth, R. J., Gamble, G. D., Dalbeth, N., & Consedine, N. S. (2015). The effect of Mindfulness-Based Stress Reduction on disease activity in people with rheumatoid arthritis: A randomised controlled trial. *Annals of the Rheumatic Diseases, 74*(2), 472–474. doi:10.1136/annrheumdis-2014-205946

Forman, E. M., Herbert, J. D., Moitra, E., Yeomans, P. D., & Geller, P. A. (2007). A randomized controlled effectiveness trial of Acceptance and Commitment Therapy and cognitive therapy for anxiety and depression. *Behavior Modification, 31*, 772–799. doi:10.1177/0145445507302202

Galovski, T. E., & Blanchard, E. B. (1998). Treatment of irritable bowel syndrome with hypnotherapy. *Applied Psychophysiological Biofeedback, 23*(4), 219–232. doi:10.1023/A:1022209631047

Gaudiano, B. A., & Herbert, J. D. (2006). Acute treatment of inpatients with psychotic symptoms using Acceptance and Commitment Therapy: Pilot results. *Behaviour Research and Therapy, 44*, 415–437. doi:10.1016/j.brat.2005.02.007

Gay, M. C., Philippot, P., & Luminet, O. (2002). Differential effectiveness of psychological interventions for reducing osteoarthritis pain: A comparison of Erickson [correction of Erickson] hypnosis and Jacobson relaxation. *European Journal of Pain, 6*(1), 1–16. doi:10.1053/eujp.2001.0263

Gaylord, S. A., Palsson, O. S., Garland, E. L., Faurot, K. R., Coble, R. S., Mann, J. D., . . . Whitehead, W. E. (2011). Mindfulness training reduces the severity of irritable bowel syndrome in women: Results of a randomized controlled trial. *American Journal of Gastroenterology, 106*(9), 1678–1688. doi:10.1038/ajg.2011.184

Gifford, E. V., Kohlenberg, B. S., Hayes, S. C., Antonuccio, D. O., Piasecki, M. M., Rasmussen-Hall, M. L., & Palm, K. M. (2004). Acceptance-based treatment for smoking cessation. *Behavior Therapy, 35*, 689–705. doi:10.1016/s0005-7894(04)80015-7

Golden, W. L. (2012). Cognitive hypnotherapy for anxiety disorders. *American Journal of Clinical Hypnosis, 54*, 263–274. doi:10.1080/00029157.2011.650333

Green, J. P. & Lynn, S. J. (2000). Hypnosis and suggestion-based approaches to smoking cessation: An examination of the evidence. *International Journal of Clinical and Experimental Hypnosis, 48*, 195–224. doi:10.1080/00207140008410048

Grossman, P., Niemann, L., Schmidt, S., & Walach, H. (2004). Mindfulness-Based Stress Reduction and health benefits: A meta-analysis. *Journal of Psychosomatic Research, 57*, 35–43. doi:10.1016/S0022-3999(03)00573-7

Grossman, P., Tiefenthaler-Gilmer, U., Raysz, A., & Kesper, U. (2007). Mindfulness training as an intervention for fibromyalgia: Evidence of postintervention and 3-year follow-up benefits in well-being. *Psychotherapy and Psychosomatics, 76*, 226–233. doi:10.1159/000101501

Gruzelier, J. H. (2006). Frontal functions, connectivity and neural efficiency underpinning hypnosis and hypnotic susceptibility. *Contemporary Hypnosis, 23*(1), 15–32. doi:10.1002/ch.35

Haanen, H. C., Hoenderdos, H. T., van Romunde, L. K., Hop, W. C., Mallee, C., Terwiel, J. P., & Hekster, G. B. (1991). Controlled trial of hypnotherapy in the treatment of refractory fibromyalgia. *Journal of Rheumatology, 18*(1), 72–75. PMID: 2023202

Hawkins, R. M. F. (2001). A systematic meta-review of hypnosis as an empirically supported treatment for pain. *Pain Reviews, 8*(2), 47–73. doi:10.1191/0968130201pr175ra

Hayes, S. C. (1987). A contextual approach to therapeutic change. In N. S. Jacobson (Ed.), *Psychotherapists in clinical practice: Cognitive and behavioral perspectives* (pp. 327–387). New York, NY: Guilford.

Hayes, S. C., & Twohig, M. (2008). *ACT verbatim for depression and anxiety: Annotated transcripts for learning acceptance and commitment therapy.* Oakland, CA: New Harbinger Publications.

Hayes, S. C., & Wilson, K. G. (1993). Some applied implications of a contemporary behavior-analytic account of verbal events. *Behavior Analyst, 16*, 283–301. doi:10.1007/bf03392637

Hayes, S. C., & Wilson, K. G. (1994). Acceptance and Commitment Therapy: Altering the verbal support for experiential avoidance. *Behavior Analyst, 17*, 289–303. doi:10.1007/bf03392677

Hayes, S. C., Wilson, K. G., Gifford, E. V., Bissett, R., Piasecki, M., Batten, S. V.,...Gregg, J. (2004). A preliminary trial of twelve-step facilitation and acceptance and commitment therapy with polysubstance-abusing methadone-maintained opiate addicts. *Behavior Therapy, 35*, 667–688. doi:10.1016/S0005-7894(04)80014-5

Hofmann, S. G., Sawyer, A. T., Witt, A. A., & Oh, D. (2010). The effect of mindfulness-based therapy on anxiety and depression: A meta-analytic review. *Journal of Consulting and Clinical Psychology, 78*, 169–183. doi 10.1037/a0018555

Jensen, M. P. (2011). *Hypnosis for chronic pain management: Therapist guide.* Oxford, UK: Oxford University Press.

Jensen, M. P., Abresch, R. T., Carter, G. T., & McDonald, C. M. (2005). Chronic pain in persons with neuromuscular disease. *Archives of Physical Medicine and Rehabilitation, 86*(6), 1155–1163. doi:10.1016/j.apmr.2004.11.028

Jensen, M. P., Barber, J., Romano, J. M., Hanley, M. A., Raichle, K. A., Molton, I. R., ... Patterson, D. R. (2009). Effects of self-hypnosis training and EMG biofeedback relaxation training on chronic pain in persons with spinal-cord injury. *International Journal of Clinical and Experimental Hypnosis, 57*(3), 239–268. doi:10.1080/00207140902881007

Jensen, M. P., Barber, J., Romano, J. M., Molton, I. R., Raichle, K. A., Osborne, T. L., ... Patterson, D. R. (2009). A comparison of self-hypnosis versus progressive muscle relaxation in patients with multiple sclerosis and chronic pain. *International Journal of Clinical and Experimental Hypnosis, 57*(2), 198–221. doi:10.1080/00207140802665476

Jensen, M. P., Ehde, D. M., Gertz, K. J., Stoelb, B. L., Dillworth, T. M., Hirsh, A. T., ... Kraft, G. H. (2011). Effects of self-hypnosis training and cognitive restructuring on daily pain intensity and catastrophizing in individuals with multiple sclerosis and chronic pain. *International Journal of Clinical and Experimental Hypnosis, 59*(1), 45–63. doi:10.1080/00207144.2011.522892

Kabat-Zinn, J. (1982). An outpatient program in behavioral medicine for chronic pain patients based on the practice of mindfulness meditation: Theoretical considerations and preliminary results. *General Hospital Psychiatry, 4*, 33–47. doi:10.1016/0163-8343(82)90026-3

Kabat-Zinn, J., Lipworth, L., & Burney, R. (1985). The clinical use of mindfulness meditation for the self-regulation of chronic pain. *Journal of Behavioral Medicine, 8*(2), 163–190. doi:10.1007/bf00845519

Kabat-Zinn, J., Lipworth, L., Burney, R., & Sellers, W. (1986). Four-year follow-up of a meditation-based program for the self-regulation of chronic pain: Treatment outcomes and compliance. *Clinical Journal of Pain, 2*(3), 159–774. doi:10.1097/00002508-198602030-00004

Kaplan, K. H., Goldenberg, D. L., & Galvin-Nadeau, M. (1993). The impact of a meditation-based stress reduction program on fibromyalgia. *General Hospital Psychiatry, 15*(5), 284–289. doi:10.1016/0163-8343(93)90020-O

Kearney, D. J., McDermott, K., Malte, C., Martinez, M., & Simpson, T. L. (2013). Effects of participation in a mindfulness program for veterans with posttraumatic stress disorder: A randomized controlled pilot study. *Journal of Clinical Psychology, 69*(1), 14–27. doi:10.1002/jclp.21911

Kenny, M. A., & Williams, J. M. G. (2007). Treatment-resistant depressed patients show a good response to Mindfulness-Based Cognitive Therapy. *Behaviour Research and Therapy, 45*(3), 617–625. doi:10.1016/j.brat.2006.04.008

Khoury, B., Lecomte, T., Fortin, G., Masse, M., Therien, P., Bouchard, V., ... Hofmann, S. G. (2013). Mindfulness-based therapy: A comprehensive meta-analysis. *Clinical Psychology Review, 33*, 763–771. doi:10.1016/j.cpr.2013.05.005

Kiecolt-Glaser, J. K., Marucha, P. T., Atkinson, C., & Glaser, R. (2001). Hypnosis as a modulator of cellular immune dysregulation during acute stress. *Journal of Consulting and Clinical Psychology, 69*(4), 674–682. doi:10.1037//0022-006x.69.4.674

Kirsch, I. (1996). Hypnotic enhancement of cognitive-behavioral weight loss treatments: Another meta-reanalysis. *Journal of Consulting and Clinical Psychology, 64*(3), 517–519. PMID: 8698945

Kirsch, I., Montgomery, G., & Sapirstein, G. (1995). Hypnosis as an adjunct to cognitive-behavioral psychotherapy: A meta-analysis. *Journal of Consulting and Clinical Psychology, 63*, 214–220. doi:10.1037//0022-006x.63.2.214

Koszycki, D., Benger, M., Shlik, J., & Bradwejn, J. (2007). Randomized trial of a meditation-based stress reduction program and cognitive behavior therapy in generalized social anxiety disorder. *Behaviour Research and Therapy, 45*, 2518–2526. doi:10.1016/j.brat.2007.04.011

Kristeller, J., Wolever, R. Q., & Sheets, V. (2014). Mindfulness-based eating awareness training (MB-EAT) for binge eating: A randomized clinical trial. *Mindfulness*, *5*(3), 282–297. doi:10.1007/s12671-012-0179-1

Lang, E. V., Benotsch, E. G., Fick, L. J., Lutgendorf, S., Berbaum, M. L., Berbaum, K. S., ... Spiegel, D. (2000). Adjunctive non-pharmacological analgesia for invasive medical procedures: A randomised trial. *Lancet*, *355*(9214), 1486–1490. doi:10.1016/S0140-6736(00)02162-0

Levine, E. G., Aviv, C., Yoo, G., Ewing, C., & Au, A. (2009). The benefits of prayer on mood and well-being of breast cancer survivors. *Supportive Care in Cancer*, *17*(3), 295–306. doi:10.1007/s00520-008-0482-5

Linehan, M. M. (1987). Dialectical behavioral therapy: A cognitive behavioral approach to parasuicide. *Journal of Personality Disorders*, *1*, 328–333. doi:10.1521/pedi.1987.1.4.328

Linehan, M. M., Schmidt, H., Dimeff, L. A., Craft, J. C., Kanter, J., & Comtois, K. A. (1999). Dialectical behavior therapy for patients with borderline personality disorder and drug-dependence. *American Journal on Addictions*, *8*, 279–292. doi:10.1080/105504999305686

Luoma, J. B., Kohlenberg, B. S., Hayes, S. C., & Fletcher, L. (2012). Slow and steady wins the race: A randomized clinical trial of Acceptance and Commitment Therapy targeting shame in substance use disorders. *Journal of Consulting and Clinical Psychology*, *80*, 43–53. doi:10.1037/a0026070

Manicavasgar, V., Parker, G., & Perich, T. (2011). Mindfulness-Based Cognitive Therapy vs. cognitive behaviour therapy as a treatment for non-melancholic depression. *Journal of Affective Disorders*, *130*, 138–144. doi:10.1016/j.jad.2010.09.027

McCauley, J. D., Thelen, M. H., Frank, R. G., Willard, R. R., & Callen, K. E. (1983). Hypnosis compared to relaxation in the outpatient management of chronic low back pain. *Archives of Physical Medicine and Rehabilitation*, *64*(11), 548–552. doi:10.1080/00029157.1995.10403175

Miller, J. J., Fletcher, K., & Kabat-Zinn, J. (1995). Three-year follow-up and clinical implications of a mindfulness meditation-based stress reduction intervention in the treatment of anxiety disorders. *General Hospital Psychiatry*, *17*, 192–200. doi:10.1016/0163-8343(95)00025-M

Montgomery, A. H., DuHamel, K. N., & Redd, W. H. (2000). A meta-analysis of hypnotically induced analgesia: How effective is hypnosis? *International Journal of Clinical Hypnosis*, *48*(2), 138–153. doi:10.1080/00207140008410045

Montgomery, G. H., David, D., Winkel, G., Silverstein, J. H., & Bovbierg, D. H. (2002). The effectiveness of adjunctive hypnosis with surgical patients: A meta-analysis. *Anesthesia and Analgesia*, *94*(6), 1639–1645. doi:10.1213/00000539-200206000-00052

Neron, S., & Stephenson, R. (2007). Effectiveness of hypnotherapy with cancer patients' trajectory: Emesis, acute pain, and analgesia and anxiolysis in procedures. *International Journal of Clinical and Experimental Hypnosis, 55*(3), 336–354. doi:10.1080/00207140701338647

Olendzki, A. (2014). From early Buddhist traditions to Western psychological science. In A. Le, C. T. Ngnoumen, & E. J. Langer (Eds), *The Wiley Blackwell handbook of mindfulness* (pp. 531–562). West Sussex, UK: John Wiley & Sons.

Olness, K., MacDonald, J. T., & Uden, D. L. (1987). Comparison of self-hypnosis and propranolol in the treatment of juvenile classic migraine. *Pediatrics, 79*(4), 593–597.

Omidi, A., Mohammadi, A., Zargar, F., & Akbari, H. (2013). Efficacy of Mindfulness-Based Stress Reduction on mood states of veterans with post-traumatic stress disorder. *Archives of Trauma Research, 1*(4), 151–154. doi:10.5812/atr.8226

Öst, L.-G. (2008). Efficacy of the third wave of behavioral therapies: A systematic review and meta-analysis. *Behaviour Research and Therapy, 46*, 296–321. doi:10.1016/j.brat.2007.12.005

Palsson, O. S., Turner, M. J., & Whitehead, W. E. (2006). Hypnosis home treatment for irritable bowel syndrome: A pilot study. *International Journal of Clinical and Experimental Hypnosis, 54*(1), 85–99. doi:10.1080/00207140500328666

Patterson, D. R., & Jenson, M. P. (2003). Hypnosis and clinical pain. *Psychological Bulletin, 129*(4), 495–521. doi:10.1037/0033-2909.129.4.495

Patterson, D. R., & Ptacek, J. T. (1997). Baseline pain as a moderator of hypnotic analgesia for burn injury treatment. *Journal of Consulting and Clinical Psychology, 65*, 60–67. doi:10.1037//0022-006X.65.1.60

Piet, J., Würtzen, H., & Zachariae, R. (2012). The effect of mindfulness-based therapy on symptoms of anxiety and depression in adult cancer patients and survivors: A systematic review and meta-analysis. *Journal of Consulting and Clinical Psychology, 80*, 1007–1020. doi:10.1037/a0028329

Powers, M. B., Zum Vorde Sive Vording, M. B., & Emmelkamp, P. M. (2009). Acceptance and Commitment Therapy: A meta-analytic review. *Psychotherapy and Psychosomatics, 78*(2), 73–80. doi:10.1159/000190790

Prior, A., Colgan, S. M., & Whorwell, P. J. (1990). Changes in rectal sensitivity after hypnotherapy in patients with irritable bowel syndromes. *Gut: An International Journal of Gastroenterology and Hepatology, 31*(8), 896–898. doi:10.1136/gut.31.8.896

Safer, D. L., Telch, C. F., & Agras, W. S. (2001). Dialectical Behavior Therapy for bulimia nervosa. *American Journal of Psychiatry, 158*, 632–634. doi:10.1176/appi.ajp.158.4.632

Schoenberger, N. E., Kirsch, I., Gearan, P., Montgomery, G., & Pastyrnak, S. L. (1997). Hypnotic enhancement of a cognitive behavioral treatment for public speaking anxiety. *Behavior Therapy, 28*, 127–140. doi:10.1016/S0005-7894(97)80038-X

Sephton, S. E., Salmon, P., Weissbecker, I., Ulmer, C., Floyd, A., Hoover, K., & Studts, J. L. (2007). Mindfulness meditation alleviates depressive symptoms in women with fibromyalgia: Results of a randomized clinical trial. *Arthritis Care and Research, 57*(1), 77–85. doi:10.1002/art.22478

Smith, J. C. (1975). Meditation as psychotherapy: A review of the literature. *Psychological Bulletin, 82*, 558–564. doi:10.1037/h0076888

Spanos, N. P., Stenstrom, R. J., & Johnson, J. C. (1998). Hypnosis, placebo, and suggestion in the treatment of warts. *Psychosomatic Medicine, 45*, 333–339.

Spanos, N. P., Williams, V., & Gwynne, M. L. (1990). Effects of hypnotic, placebo, and salicylic acid treatments on wart regression. *Psychosomatic Medicine, 52*(1), 109–114. doi:10.1097/00006842-199001000-00009

Spiegel, D., & Bloom, J. R. (1983). Group therapy and hypnosis reduce metastatic breast carcinoma pain. *Psychosomatic Medicine, 45*, 333–339. doi:10.1097/00006842-198308000-00007

Spiegel, D., Hunt, T., & Dondershine, H. E. (1988). Dissociation and hypnotizability in posttraumatic stress disorder. *American Journal of Psychiatry, 145*(3), 301–305. doi:10.1176/ajp.145.3.301

Spinhoven, P., & Linssen, A. C. (1989). Group therapy and hypnosis reduce metastatic breast carcinoma pain. *Psychosomatic Medicine, 45*, 333–339. doi:10.1097/00006842-198308000-00007

Sternthal, M. J., Williams, D. R., Musick, M. A., & Buck, A. C. (2012). Religious practices, beliefs, and mental health: Variations across ethnicity. *Ethnicity and Health, 17*(1–2), 171–185. doi:10.1080/13557858.2012.655264

Strauss, C., Cavanagh, K., Oliver, A., & Pettman, D. (2014). Mindfulness-based interventions for people diagnosed with a current episode of an anxiety or depressive disorder: A meta-analysis of randomised controlled trials. *PLoS One, 9*(4), e96110. doi:10.1371/journal.pone.0096110

Szent-Györgyi, A. (1957). *Bioenergetics*. Cambridge, MA: Academic Press.

Telch, C. F., Agras, W. S., & Linehan, M. M. (2001). Dialectical Behavior Therapy for binge eating disorder. *Journal of Consulting and Clinical Psychology, 69*, 1061–1065. doi:10.1037/0022-006X.69.6.1061

Vidrine, J. I., Businelle, M. S., Cinciripini, P., Li, Y., Marcus, M. T., Waters, A. J., ... Wetter, D. W. (2009). Associations of mindfulness with nicotine dependence, withdrawal, and agency. *Substance Abuse, 30*(4), 318–327. doi:10.1080/08897070903252973

Vowles, K. E., & McCracken, L. M. (2008). Acceptance and values-based action in chronic pain: A study of treatment effectiveness and process. *Journal of Consulting and Clinical Psychology, 76*, 397–407. doi:10.1037/0022-006X.76.3.397

Witkiewitz, K., Marlatt, G. A., & Walker, D. (2005). Mindfulness-based relapse prevention for alcohol and substance use disorders. *Journal of Cognitive Psychotherapy, 19*, 211–228. doi:10.1891/jcop.2005.19.3.211

Wong, S. Y. S., Chan, F. W. K., Wong, R. L. P., Chu, M. C., Kitty Lam, Y. Y., Mercer, S. W., & Ma, S. H. (2011). Comparing the effectiveness of

Mindfulness-Based Stress Reduction and multidisciplinary intervention programs for chronic pain: A randomized comparative trial. *Clinical Journal of Pain, 27*(8), 724–734. doi:10.1097/AJP.0b013e3182183c6e

Zautra, A. J., Davis, M. C., Reich, J. W., Nicassario, P., Tennen, H., Finan, P., . . . Irwin, M. R. (2008). Comparison of cognitive behavioral and mindfulness meditation interventions on adaptation to rheumatoid arthritis for patients with and without history of recurrent depression. *Journal of Consulting and Clinical Psychology, 76*(3), 408–421. doi:10.1037/0022-006X.76.3.408

Zernicke, K. A., Campbell, T. S., Blustein, P. K., Fung, T. S., Johnson, J. A., Bacon, S. L., & Carlson, L. E. (2013). Mindfulness-Based Stress Reduction for the treatment of irritable bowel syndrome symptoms: A randomized wait-list controlled trial. *International Journal of Behavioral Medicine, 20*(3), 385–396. doi:10.1007/s12529-012-9241-6

CHAPTER 3

BUDDHIST CONCEPTS AND MINDFULNESS

To enjoy good health, to bring true happiness to one's family, to bring peace to all, one must first discipline and control one's own mind. If a man can control his mind he can find the way to Enlightenment, and all wisdom and virtue will naturally come to him.

—The Teachings of Buddha, *Bukkyo Dendo Kyokai (2008)*

Introduction

Mindful hypnotherapy (MH) is a secular intervention that draws upon Buddhist concepts and philosophy to formulate hypnotic suggestions and interventions. As such, MH is suitable for therapists and clients with a wide array of faiths and beliefs, as well as those who are atheist or agnostic. In this chapter, a few Buddhist concepts and stories are presented to give readers a basic, contextual understanding of where our secular MH intervention originated. A full review of Buddhist source material is, of course, beyond our scope, and the brief snapshot provided in this chapter simply recognizes the rich traditions from which it is drawn. Here we present a select set of Buddhist teachings that inform some of the core concepts of MH in the hopes that it will prompt further independent exploration. Just like the mindfulness interventions that came before MH, the material in this chapter is a *version* of the origins of mindfulness that is filtered through our own experiences and cognitive filter. A common refrain throughout Buddhism and secular mindfulness interventions alike is to experience things for yourself and base your understanding on what you directly observe to be true. In this spirit, we encourage individuals who are new to mindfulness to use this chapter as a beginning and, for those new to hypnotherapy, this book as an introduction: something to foster interest and point you toward your own path to discovery by investigating the source materials for yourself.

A significant portion of early Buddhist thought is remarkably pragmatic, methodical, and worldly in its approach to understanding suffering. The predominant focus of its teachings is on the subject of reducing suffering through psychological transformation. Over the long span of time that mindfulness has been in existence as an oral tradition, many useful rhetorical devices have been developed to help people understand these concepts and integrate them into their lives. Jon Kabat-Zinn and other pioneers of mindfulness in medicine drew upon an in-depth knowledge of Buddhism to forge their own trademark interventions.

Origins of Mindfulness

The origins of mindfulness can be found some 2,500 years ago in the introspective and contemplative approaches in India during the time of Siddhartha Gautama (who became better known by his honorific/descriptive title—*the Buddha*—once he began teaching). According to oral history and legend, Siddhartha Gautama was born as a prince. It has been said that during his youth and young adulthood he was protected from the outside world and lived a life of luxury and pleasure. He eventually traveled outside the walls of the place, where he encountered the realities of human suffering—fear, death, illness, pain, and all manner of other sufferings. Siddhartha found himself deeply affected by the awareness of such suffering in the world and set upon a spiritual path toward wisdom and enlightenment. He spent years following severe ascetic disciplines and learning to engage in deeply meditative practices that involved stillness, focus of attention, and careful observation of the internal flow of experiences. Having experienced both extreme indulgence (in his young adulthood) and extreme asceticism, Siddhartha came to embrace a *middle path* between the two. Shortly thereafter, he sat quietly beneath a Bodhi tree, in a state of deep meditation while he contemplated the nature of suffering. According to Buddhist tradition, this was the final step on his own journey to enlightenment and the beginning of his decision to teach others what he had learned.[1] The middle path that the Buddha employed does not involve the self-punishment of the ancient ascetics, but rather embraces a philosophy of self-care without overindulgence. Buddhists believe that this balanced approach helps support self-awareness, compassion,

[1] Although *enlightenment* is a complex and multifaceted concept beyond the scope of this chapter, it involves a kind of insight into the nature of experiences. In Buddhism, this *awakening* to this new understanding of subjective experiences is said to have a large impact on the psychological experience of suffering.

and the willingness to experience *what is* without judgment, and leads to personal transformation and true relief from suffering.

Within Buddhist teachings, mindfulness is one element of the *eightfold path* to enlightenment (Tirch, Siberstein, & Kolts, 2016), a group of eight psychological and behavioral changes that help to reduce the experience of suffering. As the term *mindfulness* has been translated into different languages and adapted in different cultural contexts, definitions of mindfulness in a secular Western context have included a present-centered attention and awareness of experiences (Brown & Ryan, 2017); paying attention in a particular way, on purpose, in the present moment, and nonjudgmentally (Kabat-Zinn, 1994); as well as other definitions (Bishop et al., 2004). Alongside mindfulness, concentration is another important aspect of Buddhist practice. Concentration is generally cultivated through meditation practice, which aims for an altered state of consciousness and serenity that may resemble a hypnotic state (Holroyd, 2003). Mindfulness can be considered similar to the hypnotic state insofar as both involve concentration, focus of attention, and nonjudgmental observation of one's own physical, emotional, and mental processes. Mindfulness practice leads to greater a psychological insight and enables other important, beneficial changes to occur. To understand modern, secular mindfulness practice, it is often helpful to have a fundamental understanding of the Buddhist philosophy. The *four noble truths* are a succinct set of Buddhist beliefs that help explain the psychological foundation and theoretical assumptions behind modern mindfulness practice.

The *Four Noble Truths*

At their heart, Buddhism, medicine, and psychotherapy originate from common concerns: the fact that there is suffering in the world and a desire to alleviate it. Even individuals living a sheltered and privileged existence will be susceptible to myriad forms of physical and emotional suffering. These *givens* of existence, such as physical illness, emotional turmoil, and death, are inevitable. Nevertheless, the history of medicine and psychotherapy are shaped by our attempts to understand and combat *specific* kinds of human suffering and lessen the impact of the pain we cannot avoid.

Researchers in the medical and social sciences have focused on understanding the etiology of suffering more fully, so that we can use this understanding to create more effective interventions. For example, in psychotherapy we might be interested in the kinds of thoughts, behaviors, or experiences that lead to anxiety disorders. When careful research reveals more about the etiology of these disorders, we use our knowledge to craft particular treatments that use this knowledge to treat anxiety, depression, and other mental health concerns. In medicine, an understanding of physical pain and its physiological underpinnings, for example, has led to the development of powerful medicines to counteract pain and address physical dysfunction. At their best, both medicine and psychotherapy can offer a lasting cure to some of the conditions that are under their purview.

The medical/psychological approach to alleviating suffering is methodical. In short, we might distill this scientific approach to the problem of suffering into four steps: (a) recognizing the presence of a problem; (b) investigating and understanding the root causes of the problem; (c) evaluating whether this understanding can be used to address the problem; and (d) articulating the solution to the problem so that this solution can be put into practice. Interestingly enough, some of the core beliefs of Buddhism follow a similar structure when discussing the problem of suffering. Buddhist texts call these four steps the *four noble truths,*[2] and they are a concise summary of some of the ideas that gave rise to secular mindfulness interventions. Loosely interpreted, these four noble truths of Buddhism are:

1. Suffering and dissatisfaction exist.
2. Suffering has an origin/cause, and that cause is *craving* (in both positive and negative forms):
   - Attachment (and not *having* the things that you are attached to)
   - Aversion (to things we *don't* want, but noticing that these things are present anyway)
3. It is possible for suffering to cease through addressing its origin/cause.
4. There is a path that specifies how to address these origins/causes and effectively address the problem of suffering:
   - Right view, right thought, right speech, right action, right livelihood, right effort, right mindfulness, and right concentration[3]

---

[2]The terminology we adopt in this chapter as a shorthand means of referring to the ideas themselves, rather than as a sign of devotion or faith.

[3]In this list, "*right*" is the terminology used in Buddhist texts to indicate that these changes will help individuals reduce the suffering in their lives and the lives of others. Although some of the principles of change in this list are clinically useful considerations, there is an inherent value-judgment built into these terms as they are traditionally phrased. This is one example of why some adaptation is needed to make mindfulness palatable for a broader population. The terms "*right view*" and so on are used throughout this chapter as a matter of clarity as we refer to traditional Buddhist beliefs, not as an assertion that there is only one *right way* to effect beneficial changes.

The First Noble Truth: The Recognition of Suffering

For the modern scientist-clinician, the first noble truth will probably seem logical and can be assimilated seamlessly into a secular worldview. Our bodies are fragile. We bend, break, and bleed. We are subject not only to illness, disease, and death, but also to everyday discomforts like hunger and tiredness. From a psychological perspective, we are similarly battered by the vicissitudes of everyday living. Clients and clinicians alike will experience sadness, loss, frustration, and many other forms of discontent over the course of their lives. Our clients who have mental health concerns bear an even greater burden of mental and emotional suffering. For these individuals suffering from PTSD, anxiety, depression, and other conditions, returning even to the baseline level of universal human suffering would be a welcome change.

Clinical interventions (including mindful hypnotherapy) usually begin with an acknowledgment that there is some manifestation of suffering or harm in excess of what Freud described as *common unhappiness*. When therapy begins, one of our first tasks is generally to identify what form of suffering brought the client to seek services. Is the client depressed? Anxious? Has the client lost a loved one, or is he or she suffering from a substance-use disorder? Acknowledging that there is some form of suffering is the first step in helping the client overcome it and thrive.

As an important side note, Buddhism and psychotherapy both tend to focus on alleviating suffering. However, neither makes any claim that suffering is the only "true" human experience. We also feel joy, relief, love, and happiness. Like suffering, however, the pleasant feelings in life are temporary. Experiences of suffering and pleasure alike will eventually change into other experiences—a process that sometimes takes mere moments and other times takes decades. For example, the experience of stubbing a toe is painful, but the pain usually fades within a minute or two. The pride that a person might feel for their son or daughter may last a lifetime, but over the course of that lifetime, the parent's experience pride may shift to joy, worry, or other things depending on the immediate circumstances and what the person is paying attention to. The impermanence of all experiences is a focus for many Buddhist teachings.

The Second Noble Truth: The Origin of Suffering

The second observation (or noble truth) is that there is a root cause to the suffering we all experience, and the root cause is a kind of deep need or *craving* for things to *be* other than they *are*. This craving for things to be different can be further subdivided into *attachment* and *aversion*, though the essential principle is the same for both. For an example of attachment, consider a person who loves fatty, salty, or sugary foods (an experience many of us can relate to). If we are very attached to the idea of eating our favorite indulgence, we may feel a sense of privation whenever we resist this compulsion. The desire looms larger and larger, and we suffer in proportion to how attached we are to the idea of giving in. Finally, the desire/attachment may become so intolerable that we eat the thing we've been craving. This is generally harmless if it happens occasionally but can lead to serious health consequences if it happens frequently. In contrast, consider what it would be like to let go of *some* of that attachment. If we fully enjoyed the experience of eating our favorite food while it lasted but *let go* of the experience once it's gone, we may not feel the same degree of suffering as we would if we were still longing and craving for the experience after it's gone.

The same principle explains why aversion can cause suffering. If a person suffers from panic attacks, those panic attacks can easily become amplified or attenuated depending on how the person responds to the symptoms. A client with panic disorder may notice discomfort in the chest and become afraid that it is a sign of an impending panic attack. If so, the client's aversion to the possibility of having a panic attack will cause more fear, amplifying the symptoms and enhancing the suffering. In contrast, if the individual accepts the possibility of having a panic attack and regards the unpleasant symptoms with equanimity, the client may be expected to suffer less.

An individual who mentally and emotionally *fights* experiences or tries to pretend that the experiences don't exist will generally suffer more than someone who notices and accepts that the experiences are taking place. This radical acceptance, however, does not preclude the possibility of change. If a person accidentally touches a hot stove, the individual can both acknowledge that it hurts and remove the hand from the stove, so it doesn't keep burning. This dialectic between acceptance and change is a guiding philosophy for MH, which uses mindful awareness and insight to guide therapy toward the most meaningful and wise changes that clients can make in their lives.

The second noble truth is helpful for understanding where most clinical interventions begin to diverge from mindfulness interventions such as MH. Mindfulness interventions are different from standard approaches because they spring from a unique interpretation of *why* we suffer, which in turn gives rise to a unique approach to how to solve the problem (discussed later in this chapter). If people initiate therapy because of discomfort in their lives, most non-mindfulness interventions focus on how to reduce the source of discomfort so that the presence of the unpleasant experience does not cause further suffering. The approach is very intuitive for patients and clinicians alike, and it can be a very successful way to ameliorate distress. An example of this approach would be the use of analgesics for pain. If a person has a headache and has access to painkillers, that individual will often take the painkiller, reduce the pain, and be free from the distress that the headache would have caused. This approach has its limits, however. In some cases, the pain cannot be adequately addressed with the existing medications or treatments. In other cases, the pain *can* be addressed, but doing so would cause further harm. The persistence of the opioid crisis over time is an unfortunate illustration of this point. Severe pain can be treated with powerful narcotics, but doing so may not fully alleviate the pain. Adequate treatment risks the patient becoming addicted to the medication.

The Third Noble Truth: The Relief From Suffering

The third postulate in this logical chain of propositions is that suffering can diminish when attachment and aversion diminish. This conceptualization of suffering and its cause can seem very counterintuitive because most of us are accustomed to the idea of changing our environment to suit our preferences rather than changing our preferences to suit our environment. Our most intuitive conceptualization is that we suffer because our desires are unfulfilled, so the reciprocal idea (that we suffer because we have desires) strikes many people as odd. Nevertheless, mindfulness interventions use this unique interpretation of the origin of suffering to help people overcome their presenting concerns.

Specifically, mindfulness interventions are predicated on the idea that suffering can be reduced by attenuating the strength of our attachment and aversion. This is the root philosophy behind the "nonjudgmental awareness" that is such a staple of mindfulness. Nonjudgmental awareness involves an attitude of curiosity, openness, and emotional acknowledgment of the experiences that are taking place in the present moment. When nonjudgmental awareness is present, attachment and aversion diminish. When strong judgment is present, strong attachment and aversion are likely to be present as well.

If we accept this logical framework of (a) suffering, (b) its origin, and (c) its cessation as reasonable, the implications for treatment are far reaching. One of the most exciting implications is that we may be able to reduce mental and emotional suffering even without changing our external circumstances. An excellent example is chronic pain, which is a problem with physical, mental, and emotional components to it. The first Mindfulness-Based Stress Reduction (MBSR) group was composed mostly of chronic pain patients who were referred by their physicians. These chronic pain patients had reached the limit of what could be safely prescribed but were still experiencing a considerable degree of suffering. Likewise, the mental and emotional resources that the patients were employing to ignore the pain, change it, or *fight back* against it did not seem to bring adequate relief. The existing medical paradigm had reached its limits. During the course of MBSR, these patients nevertheless learned to reduce their suffering by cultivating a nonjudgmental awareness of their pain. By attenuating the strength of their emotional aversion to the pain, their suffering decreased even if the physical pain itself was still present.

The Fourth Noble Truth: The Middle Path

The fourth noble truth focuses on *how* to let go of the attachment and aversion that causes suffering. The Buddhist perspective is that this is best attained by instituting a comprehensive set of life changes that are broken down into eight general categories. Three of these changes involve moral actions and perspectives, three involve mental changes and mental development (including the development of greater mindfulness), and two involve developing a greater insight into the nature of experience. Since some of the changes suggested by the fourth noble truth could come across as excessively prescriptive and religiously inspired, secular mindfulness interventions typically focus only on a select portion of the eightfold path that is advocated by Buddhism. These changes tend to make mindfulness interventions acceptable to a wider audience. The fourth noble truth is also where secular mindfulness interventions diverge most widely from the source material they draw from. For the sake of reference, the eight changes (or eightfold path) advocated by Buddhism are shown in the following list, though only a select few have much influence on MH or other mindfulness interventions:

1. Right view—having an understanding of Buddhist beliefs such as the four noble truths, impermanence, and impersonal nature of experience
2. Right thought—cultivating thoughts that are free from ill will or harm
3. Right speech—avoiding lying, slander, mean-spirited speech, and frivolous speech
4. Right action—avoiding killing, stealing, and sexual misconduct such as cheating
5. Right livelihood—avoiding professions that involve lying, cheating, killing, and other offenses
6. Right effort—using will and mental energy to foster healthy states of mind and overcome unhealthy states of mind

7. Right mindfulness—perceiving things clearly for what they are, without mental elaboration (seeing thoughts as just thoughts, emotions as just emotions, and so on)
8. Right concentration—using meditation to focus the mind

Buddhist Concepts and Secularism

Secular mindfulness interventions do not draw explicitly from the previous list, but their influence can be seen most strongly with the inclusion of mindfulness as a central theme of treatment. Influences from other items on the list are generally more subtle. In cases such as mindful self-compassion (MSC) and MH, the interventions include an emphasis on generally increasing compassionate thoughts, feelings, and actions. Nearly all mindfulness interventions also make use of meditation as a means to focus the mind and generally enhance well-being. The meditation employed in mindfulness interventions does not generally focus on getting to the *deeper* states of meditation, however.[4] Other aspects of the fourth noble truth are rarely incorporated into mindfulness interventions, such as right speech or right livelihood.

Despite the fact that mindfulness interventions would be an *incomplete* solution to the problem of suffering from a Buddhist perspective, empirical evidence supports their efficacy from a psychotherapeutic perspective. Since the advent of MBSR and other mindfulness interventions in the

CLINICIAN NOTE

Meditation and Hypnosis

Practices involving attentional focus, suggestions for calmness, and letting go of judgmental thoughts can be found in many religious practices—Buddhist, Christian, Jewish, Muslim, and Hindu. Depending on the tradition, these practices may be considered to be forms of prayer or may be called *meditation* or *centering*. Like these, mindful hypnosis involves suggestions to focus attention, experiencing calmness, awareness of self, and letting go of conscious effort.

---

[4]The experiential states of meditation described in Buddhism have some similarities to what some people experience in deep states of hypnosis (see Holroyd, 2003). Future research may give more understanding of the similarities that are meaningful as well as the differences.

1980s, there has been an explosion of research and clinical interest in this approach, and mindfulness has been successful in treating a broad array of physical and psychological concerns (see Chapter 2). Increasing mindfulness seems to result in a greater sense of well-being that is accomplished by changing a person's *relationship* with his or her experiences rather than changing the experience itself. MH continues this secular tradition of mindfulness interventions, with the aim of making it easier for clients to gain a deep understanding of the intervention's core concepts.

On a practical level, MH draws from this rich tradition by attempting to attenuate the suffering caused by attachment and aversion. In keeping with the hypnotic principle of positive language (see Chapter 5), the intervention generally tries to accomplish this by increasing individuals' nonjudgmental awareness of their experiences. MH also aims to foster self-kindness and invites clients to align their actions with their emerging, mindful perspective. So many mental health problems come from the inability to tolerate unpleasant mental and emotional states, and aversion drives people to a variety of maladaptive and unhealthy behaviors. When individuals are curious, open, and interested in the moment-to-moment changes in their experiences, this shift tends to decrease the intensity of their emotional *need* to experience something different[5] and leaves them with greater freedom to choose their course of action. Likewise, the mental and attitudinal changes facilitated by MH tend to increase individuals' ability to notice important things that may have escaped their attention before. As clients become more aware of the things (and perspectives) that cause them distress and harm, they gain a greater capacity to improve their lives and help themselves to thrive.

Buddhist Concepts Through Metaphors and Storytelling

As previously stated, Buddhism and medicine (including psychotherapy) achieve reduced suffering by different means. Generally speaking, modern medicine tries to achieve greater comfort for patients by changing the experiences that a person has. If a patient suffers from pressure ulcers, the typical (and appropriate) response is to heal the ulcer itself and prevent future ulcers by regularly repositioning a bedbound patient. If an individual has social anxiety disorder, successful treatment usually involves reducing a person's fear and dread in social situations. This traditional approach can be so intuitive, appealing, and effective that it can blind clients and clinicians to the fact that suffering can *also* be decreased by

[5]*Preferences* for physical and mental comfort will remain intact, of course.

changing a person's relationship with his or her experiences. One of the first tasks in a mindfulness intervention is to open a client's eyes to the possibility of reducing suffering through altering the person's relationship with experiences. Once clients see and experience the utility of this approach for themselves, it tends to be a turning point in treatment.

The tendency to focus on changing one's circumstances (an "external" approach to reducing suffering) instead of changing one's attitude toward one's own experiences (the "internal" approach to reducing suffering) has been the prevailing attitude throughout human history. For clinicians who have some exposure to the source material that inspired secular mindfulness interventions, there are a variety of metaphors and teaching stories that could help facilitate a client's understanding of this internal approach to reduced suffering.[6] Although some of these stories and metaphors are written in an archaic style, others require little or no modification to be comprehensible, useful, and palatable to a non-Buddhist client. A review of these stories could fill several volumes, and modern mindfulness teachers continue to generate additional stories and metaphors to connect to their students. Therefore, we will present two examples here to demonstrate the general principle and refer interested readers to other sources (e.g., the resources discussed in Chapter 16 and Appendix C). For an example of an ancient metaphor, there is a simile of *the second arrow* that is common in Buddhist circles, but only sometimes finds its way into clinical practice. In its archaic form, the metaphor states that

> when the uninstructed worldling is being contacted by a painful feeling, he sorrows, grieves, and laments; he weeps beating his breast and becomes distraught. He feels two feelings—a bodily one and a mental one. Suppose that they were to strike a man with a dart, and then they would strike him immediately afterwards with a second dart, so that the man would feel a feeling caused by two darts. So too, when the uninstructed worldling is being contacted by a painful feeling . . . he feels two feelings—a bodily one and a mental one.

The passage goes on to explain that if individuals are able to notice their pain without resistance, they would feel the physical pain but would not compound the suffering by their emotional and mental reaction to it, as though they were shot with only one arrow rather than two. The

---

[6]The use of metaphors and stories is merely a rhetorical feature of Buddhism, not an integral aspect of its core tenets. Nevertheless, they are discussed in this chapter due to their potential utility for use during mindful hypnotherapy.

essence of the message is easy to grasp in story form, and a creative clinician can adapt the story as needed to suit a client's individual circumstances and temperament. For example, for a client with small children, this might be told as a lighthearted story about the pain of stepping on a Lego block in the middle of the night, and the frustration and surprise that makes that pain worse, as though the person had stepped on a second Lego block and doubled the pain. For a client with an anxiety disorder, the essence of this Buddhist simile may be woven into a larger discussion about how the fear *of* panic attacks makes panic attacks twice as intense, so that if the client were somehow able to accept the intense fear and distress of panic at face value without fighting it, the client's distress might be cut in half. Another question that is worth consideration is "to what extent are my clients stabbing *themselves* with the second arrow," either intentionally or unintentionally. Some clients feel some degree of attachment to their suffering because it is familiar. If mental anguish and ruminative thoughts have become preferable to the fear of the unknown, metaphors such as this one could be useful in the process of exploring these issues.

Another, more modern example of a "teaching story" is described by Ajahn Brahm in his book *Who Ordered This Truckload of Dung?* (2005). The titular story describes returning home one day to find that there is a truckload of dung that has been dumped on your front lawn. No one saw who had done it, so now you're stuck with a problem that you didn't create. How would you get that dung off your lawn? You could try stuffing handfuls of dung into your pockets, down your shirt, and into your pants, but you might find that people don't react well to you. Eventually, you may even find yourself with a few less friends! Thankfully, there's another solution, and that's to get to work shoveling the dung into a wheelbarrow and carting it off. You could put some in your garden and other parts of it at the base of trees. Some days you might make more progress than others, but eventually you may find that the dung is gone, your flowers are thriving, and the trees are bearing delicious fruit.

In this story, the truckload of dung represents the trauma, depression, and other concerns that are so burdensome to our clients. The weight of these past events or negative self-talk may feel like carrying this problem around in their pockets all day. Although the prospect of facing these difficult thoughts and feelings may be daunting at first, with bravery and patience we can learn to turn toward these experiences rather than turning away from them. The process can be extraordinarily difficult at times, but the end result is often worthwhile. We may even discover something invaluable about ourselves in the process.

There are many similes and teaching stories woven throughout the Pali Cannon (a core collection of Buddhist teachings), though a more accessible source may be the multitude of stories and metaphors that can be found in meditation halls and retreat centers around the world. Storytelling is a common way of teaching important truths succinctly and memorably, and, therefore, it is a common feature of *Dharma talks* that explain Buddhist doctrine or mindfulness. These Dharma talks can give mindful hypnotherapists new ideas on how to explain mindfulness well to their clients and can introduce metaphors, similes, and imagery that may be useful during hypnosis. More information on the use of metaphors and imagery in hypnosis can be found in Chapters 4 and 5.

As discussed in the Preface, we present a version of mindfulness that can be useful for self-transformation and healing by drawing from a variety of sources. We believe that psychological interventions are made stronger when there is a solid foundational philosophy upon which to build. Knowing the context for *why* they are doing what they are doing and why it works helps therapists build a sense of mastery. Understanding the foundation upon which an intervention is built also enables a therapist to improvise and adapt with greater confidence. In developing MH, we drew upon our own experiences with therapeutic mindfulness interventions, secular mindfulness practice, and even the Buddhist philosophy from which these practices arose.

Summary

Mindfulness interventions were originally inspired by Buddhist philosophy and practice. Mindfulness interventions such as MH have been secularized, however; they have been removed from their religious context and divested of the cultural trappings that may have made them inaccessible to clients seeking a relief from their suffering. We believe that having some knowledge of the *source material* for mindfulness is a worthwhile investment because from a utilitarian perspective it allows practitioners to understand mindfulness more deeply and adapt this rich source material for their own use. Mindfulness is only one of the eight things that Buddhist doctrine recommends to reduce and eliminate suffering. Nevertheless, secular mindfulness interventions have proved effective in helping clients reduce their distress by changing their relationship with their experiences. Hypnotherapy can be a powerful tool for facilitating experiential learning for mindfulness concepts, but it is incumbent upon the hypnotherapist to wield this tool with sufficient knowledge and wisdom. While the knowledge of Buddhism and nonclinical mindfulness practice is not a prerequisite for becoming a mindful hypnotherapist, knowing more about the intervention's origins can provide an undeniable advantage. In general, the knowledge of mindfulness's *source material* can provide clinicians with new ideas on how to teach their clients and can provide new ideas for metaphors and imagery for use during hypnotherapy. There are a number of resources (see Appendix B) related to the subjects of Buddhism, mindfulness, and hypnotherapy, to which we refer readers of this book.

REFERENCES

Bishop, S., Lau, M., Shapiro, S., Carlson, L., Anderson, N., Carmody, J., … Devins, G. (2004). Mindfulness: A proposed operational definition. *Clinical Psychology: Science and Practice*, *11*(3), 230–241. doi:10.1093/clipsy/bph077

Brahm, A. (2005). *Who ordered this truckload of dung?: Inspiring stories for welcoming life's difficulties*. Sommerville, MA: Wisdom Publications.

Brown, K., & Ryan, R. (2017). *Mindfulness: The roots of mindfulness: History, philosophy, and definitions*. New York, NY: Routledge.

Bukkyo Dendo Kyokai [Society for the Promotion of Buddhism]. (2008). *The teachings of Buddha*. Tokyo, Japan: Kosaido Printing.

Holroyd, J. (2003). The science of meditation and the state of hypnosis. *American Journal of Clinical Hypnosis*, *46*(2), 109–128. doi:10.1080/00029157.2003.10403582

Kabat-Zinn, J. (1994). *Wherever you go, there you are: Mindfulness meditation in everyday life*. New York, NY: Hyperion.

Tirch, D., Silberstein, L., & Kolts, R. (2016). *Buddhist psychology and cognitive-behavioral therapy: A clinician's guide*. New York, NY: Guilford Press.

CHAPTER 4

HYPNOTIC INDUCTION TECHNIQUES AND MINDFULNESS

I fell into a trance
My head began to buzz
And when I woke back up
I wasn't who I was
My pain was gone, my heart was light
I soon began to see
That all my life the things that hurt
Were not a part of me
I flow into a trance
A peaceful heart to see
And now when I awake
I know the real me

—*Eric K. Willmarth, PhD (personal communication)*

Introduction

Hypnotic induction techniques are methods that are used to achieve *a state of consciousness involving focused attention and reduced peripheral awareness* (Elkins, Barabasz, Council, & Spiegel, 2015). This distinctive state of consciousness is the essence of hypnosis and the aim of hypnotic inductions. Given that a *hypnotic state* and a *mindful state* both involve an altered state of consciousness characterized by focused attention, there are likely to be neurological and physiological similarities between the two. However, the two states of mind begin to diverge insofar as the hypnotic state "is characterized by an enhanced capacity for response to suggestion" (Elkins et al., 2015).

Achieving a hypnotic state has positive benefits, as it involves absorption and focused attention and may (or may not) involve relaxation. Furthermore, within a hypnotic state the individual may be more receptive to positive ideas (Kroger, 2008) and may be able to experience suggested alterations in physiology, sensations, emotions, thoughts, or behaviors (Elkins et al., 2015). These changes can be of great clinical utility, since they enable the client and clinician to collaborate in making direct changes to symptoms and experiences in the service of overcoming their presenting concerns. Hypnotic inductions are simply procedures that are designed to induce hypnosis. They involve a focus of attention and generally include suggestions to deepen the hypnotic state. This chapter presents an overview of the structure and processes of hypnotic inductions. Clinicians planning to integrate mindful hypnotherapy (MH) into their practice should familiarize themselves with the information discussed here, since hypnotic inductions are a fundamental skill that is used throughout the intervention.

Hypnosis and Mindfulness as a State of Consciousness

The hypnotic state and mindfulness both involve highly focused attention, decreased critical judgment, and increased absorption (Tellegen & Atkinson, 1974). Responses in the hypnotic state are partly or fully experienced as involuntary or effortless. This is sometimes considered to be reflective of an adaptive dissociation (Elkins, 2014) in which external reality fades and the individual is more aware of the own internal reality of thoughts, feelings, sensations, behaviors, and subjectively experienced phenomena. The hypnotic state is further characterized by nonjudgmental responsiveness to suggestions and imagery (Spiegel & Spiegel, 2004), as is mindfulness.

FOCUSED ATTENTION AND HYPNOSIS

Hypnotic inductions can vary a great deal and utilize individual skills and preferences. However, all hypnotic inductions begin with or early on include suggestions for focusing attention. Individuals learn to intently focus their attention during hypnosis such that other things fade into the background. The focus of attention can be on an object or something outside the individual or on an internal image or sensation. Similarly, the traditional mindfulness practice uses a variety of different objects of focus. Mindful awareness of sound and of the breath are commonly used. Other traditional approaches include walking meditation (focusing on the sensations in the soles of the feet) and body scan meditation such as used in Mindfulness-Based Stress Reduction. MH borrows from both mindfulness and hypnotherapy traditions, using a variety of different experiences as a focus for attention, including those just mentioned.

These include a proprioceptive awareness of the breath, the sound of a *singing bowl*, and a visual point on the wall for the client to focus upon.

CLINICIAN NOTE

Hypnotic State

There are likely many similarities between the hypnotic state of consciousness and a mindful state. Both may involve focused attention, internal awareness, decreased attachment, or an attitude of nonjudgmental awareness as well as increased self-regulation.

HYPNOTIC RELAXATION

Hypnotic inductions typically include suggestions for relaxation because the relaxation response (Benson, 1975) is so therapeutically useful. Suggestions for a deep hypnotic state and relaxation (Elkins, 2014) are of great benefit in reducing stress, managing pain, and treating a wide range of medical and psychological problems (Elkins, 2017). Hypnotic relaxation is physical, mental, and emotional. Suggestions for hypnotic relaxation may include awareness of *letting go* of tension and increased physical relaxation. As this occurs, suggestions for feeling calm and peaceful may be given by a hypnotherapist or self-suggested by the clients themselves. Mental images of a calm and peaceful place (such as a beach, lake, or other peaceful image) can also aid in mental relaxation. Despite the pervasiveness of these images and suggestions in hypnotherapy, hypnosis should not be confused with relaxation. Just like mindfulness, a hypnotic state and response to hypnotic suggestion can occur while an individual is not relaxed. In the case of hypnosis, this is referred to as *active-alert hypnosis* (Banyai & Hilgard, 1976). Examples of active-alert hypnosis are the *hypnotic state* that can be achieved by long-distance runners, athletes, and musicians and when one is deep in thought.

Hypnosis as a Natural Phenomenon

The popular perception of hypnosis perpetuated by television, movies, and stage shows is that hypnosis is a bizarre or even paranormal phenomenon that can be produced only by a hypnotist. In contrast, the truth is that hypnotic state is a natural ability that everyone is capable of to some extent. This capacity for focused attention, absorption, mental imagery, relaxation, hypnotic state, and access to unconscious resources is healthy and adaptive. The hypnotic state can occur following a formal hypnotic induction, but it can also occur naturally while a person is watching an interesting movie, reading a book, or involved in another absorbing activity. A hypnotherapist is well versed in the potential benefits of a hypnotic state and is trained to help clients bring about this state of mind intentionally. In a clinical setting, therapists and clients collaborate toward using a hypnotic state to empower the clients to achieve their goals. Since hypnotherapy is such a collaborative process, a strong therapeutic alliance based on trust and good communication is essential. Some aspects of the therapeutic alliance as it relates to MH in the clinical setting are discussed in the following section.

Therapeutic Alliance in Mindful Hypnotherapy

THE HYPNOTHERAPEUTIC RELATIONSHIP

The hypnotherapeutic relationship is one of trust and caring. These characteristics are of paramount importance in MH and should be fully established prior to a hypnotic induction. The nature of a hypnotic induction is one in which the client is psychologically vulnerable since critical judgment is largely suspended so that hypnotic suggestions can be experienced. The process of a hypnotic induction is best achieved when the client is open to the experience of hypnosis and willing to accept the hypnotic suggestions provided by the therapist. This is most likely to be successful within a positive and caring interpersonal relationship between the client and the therapist. Therefore, it is important to not rush to a hypnotic induction until these factors have been addressed.

COLLABORATION

The goal of hypnotherapy is to help and empower the clients to achieve their goals (Elkins, 2014). It is a collaborative relationship and it is important to explore and fully understand clients' personal goals. The therapist should explain the premise of mindful hypnosis, identify any misconceptions about hypnosis or mindfulness, and discuss session and overall goals for therapy. The hypnotic induction should be described and discussed with the client and any questions answered. It is equally important to determine that the planned hypnotic induction is acceptable to the clients and within their preferences. The mindful hypnotherapist and the client work together, collaboratively, toward the session goals and hypnotic induction.

EMPATHY

The hypnotherapeutic relationship also involves empathy. The therapist must have an understanding of problems and issues from the client's perspective and the representation of issues as experienced by the client. Deep empathy requires that the therapist use basic counseling skills that foster understanding, care, and unconditional positive regard to elicit a client's perspective and use reflective listening to assure that the communication has been understood. It is essential that the therapist convey empathy for a client's concerns and experiences.

ATTUNEMENT

The response to hypnotic suggestions is a private, internal experience that the client is most aware of. The mindful hypnotherapist cannot directly know the client's internal experience, and the client may remain silent or talk minimally during a hypnotic induction or mindful practice.[1] Therefore, the mindful hypnotherapist should carefully observe the client and notice the nonverbal indications of response to suggestions. The therapist should pace hypnotic suggestions and induction to best match the client's individual responses and elicit feedback from the client when appropriate. Also, it is very helpful to complete posthypnotic inquiries to elicit information from clients on their internal and very subjective experiences in response to suggestions and the hypnotic induction. This process is analogous to the post-meditation inquiry that is common in mindfulness-based interventions. In both mindfulness and hypnosis, this inquiry helps to foster communication, highlight particular aspects of the client's experiences, and guide future discussions.

Setting and Environment for Hypnotic Induction

ENVIRONMENT

Whether a hypnotic induction is completed in a clinical setting or the client is practicing mindful self-hypnosis at home, the environment should be one that is safe and protective. Sufficient time should be set aside for the hypnotic induction and suggestions to be completed and experienced. Clients should be in a place where they will not be disturbed and where they are safe and protected. Extraneous noise or interruptions should be minimized as possible. It is common for lights to be dimmed, and a particular spot or object is often used as a focus of attention.

POSTURE

The posture for the client should be relaxed. This may involve the client sitting in a recliner, lying down, or sitting in a chair. If a client

---

[1]Note that silence or minimal talking is not a *necessary* feature of mindfulness or hypnosis. Either practice can include a great deal of talking, but they usually do not because talking can be a particularly distracting experience, drawing individuals away from other things they may be trying to attend to during hypnosis/meditation.

is already familiar with mindfulness or associates mindfulness with a seated *cross-legged* position, a hypnotic induction can also be performed in a traditional lotus or half-lotus meditation posture. It is entirely the client's preference, but it should be a position in which the client can *let go*, relax, and be very comfortable. There is no particular posture that is especially preferred beyond the client's preference and the degree to which the client wishes to become physically relaxed. A sitting position without neck support requires some muscle tone to maintain sitting upright. For some clients this may be the ideal position to become absorbed in the experience of mindful hypnosis, while others may find that a reclined position enables them to experience mindful hypnosis more fully.

Preinduction Preparation of the Client

Prior to completing the hypnotic induction, it is important to review the client's progress, answer any questions, and introduce the strategic theme for the session. Preparing the client for hypnosis generally includes reviewing the hypnotic induction and eliciting any information that could inform individualizing the specific imagery or suggestions to match the client's preferences and the session goals. Introducing the strategic theme for the session can be helpful to set cognitive expectancies for the session and posthypnotic experiences. If the client has completed any homework assignments or is using self-hypnosis audio recordings, those should also be reviewed and discussed prior to the hypnotic induction portion of the session.

REVIEWING PROGRESS

Some clients may have some prior experience with mindfulness or some expectancies that may be helpful to discuss prior to hypnotic induction. Also, clients may have some preferences for mental imagery, hypnotic induction techniques that work best for them, or ideas about how to enhance their practice of mindful self-hypnosis. If prior homework assignments have been given, those should be reviewed during the general discussion of progress as well.

PREPARING THE CLIENT

Preparing the client includes reviewing the following things with them: the overall plan for the session, the structure of the session, and the hypnotic induction that is anticipated. It is important to answer any questions and orient the client to the overall experience and expectations for continued progress. This might include some psychoeducational material (Yapko, 2011) about mindfulness or hypnosis. It may be helpful to provide handouts, readings, or other material if appropriate.

INTRODUCING STRATEGIC THEMES FOR MINDFULNESS

Each session has a strategic theme. The strategic theme for the session should be discussed with the client, as this lays the groundwork for understanding the session goals and cognitive expectancies for the session and beyond. It is empowering to the client to have a good understanding of the strategic theme of the session and how it fits within the overall MH sessions and program. The strategic theme for the session should be well defined and can be modified based on the client's progress, preferences, and other factors to best meet the client's goals.

General Structure of Mindful Hypnotic Induction

Several hypnotic induction techniques are discussed in this chapter. Although hypnotic inductions vary in their degree of structure, they generally include some of the components listed in the following subsections. Hypnotic inductions can either follow a transcript or be individually tailored to the client. With experience and practice, more naturalistic hypnotic inductions may be utilized. Although the components are not always in the same order in all inductions, the general structure can be summarized as including the following elements.

FOCUSING OF ATTENTION

There are many ways to instruct clients to focus attention and initiate hypnotic induction. Since this step typically occurs at the very beginning of a hypnotic induction, clients' response to the suggestion to focus attention and begin a hypnotic induction is largely experienced as conscious and voluntary (Elkins, 2014). The same procedure can be used both in the session and during self-hypnosis practice. Examples of hypnotic inductions are provided throughout this book, and the approaches can be quite varied. However, one of the most commonly used hypnotic inductions is the *focus on breathing hypnotic induction.* This involves asking the client to focus on his or her breathing. It is easy to learn and can be integrated into self-hypnosis practice. An example is provided below.

> Place one hand on your stomach and the other on your chest...Just settle back into the comfort of the chair...now allow your eyelids to close...and begin to focus your attention on your breathing...Your breathing is always with you...sometimes more in your awareness and sometimes less aware...consciously...Notice the feelings that go

> along with breathing in and breathing out... Notice the coolness of the air in your nostrils as you breathe in and the feeling of letting go and drifting deeper relaxed as you breathe out...allowing a feeling of deeper relaxation to come to you with every breath...each time you breathe out...thinking the word "relax"...and the body and the mind respond to this word...relax...Taking a deep breath of air...and as you breathe out...normally and naturally...a wave of relaxation can seem to come to you. Your forehead relaxes...your neck and shoulders relax.... And notice that your breathing may have already become a little slower...a little deeper...and as it does, you can drift...into an even deeper state of hypnosis...deeper relaxed...a relaxation that spreads to your back... your shoulders...chest...and stomach...breathing in and out just takes you to a deeper level of relaxation...so that now...even your legs and feet...relax further...calmer...and your breathing...each time you breathe out...takes you into a deeper state of hypnotic relaxation...whether you are aware of your breathing...consciously...or not. (Elkins, 2014)

EYE CLOSURE

Suggestions for eye closure can be paced with the client's preference and responses. With most clients, eye closure can help reduce distractions and increase internal awareness and progress toward a hypnotic state. In cases where a client has undergone significant trauma, eye closure might bring with it a sense of unease and anxiety. If this is the case, the hypnotic induction might be personalized by inviting clients to keep their eyes open for as long as they wish, focused on a neutral stimulus such as the wall or floor. For clients who do not have any compunctions about closing their eyes, suggestions for eye closure could include something like the following:

> As you are ready...the muscles around your eyelids can begin to relax...and as they do, the eyelids begin to feel very heavy...as the eyelids feel heavy... just let them close...as you are ready to enter a deep state of hypnotic relaxation.

RELAXATION

Suggestions for relaxation are directed toward physical, emotional, and mental relaxation. The initial suggestions for relaxation may be most directed toward physical relaxation:

> Now you can take a deep breath of air...hold it...and as you exhale, become more deeply relaxed. Letting all the tension go...and

becoming...soon...more relaxed state...muscles relaxing...and feeling calmer.

Once physical relaxation has been achieved, this can be a good indicator of the client's readiness to let go of the sense of emotional and mental tension. Although deep relaxation can lead to a greater subjective sense of ease and calmness in the hypnotic state, complete relaxation is not necessarily a prerequisite for a successful hypnotic induction. As with other aspects of hypnosis, it is important to be attuned and responsive to the client's verbal and nonverbal indicators when proceeding through the hypnotic induction.

OBSERVING THE IMMEDIATE EXPERIENCE

As the client achieves eye closure and relaxation, suggestions can be given for the client to observe the immediate internal experiences. Suggestions at this stage typically involve clients becoming less aware of their external reality and more aware of the unfolding experiences of their own internal reality. Examples of suggestions could include:

> As you become aware of a greater degree of relaxation, you observe your breathing...the sensations of breathing in...and breathing out...and every breath taking you into a deeper state of hypnotic relaxation...just observing the present moment experiences as they occur.

DEEPENING THE HYPNOTIC STATE

Suggestions for increased physical, emotional, and mental relaxation can serve to deepen the hypnotic state. The feeling of calmness provides a beginning to achieve a deeper and more meaningful awareness and response to suggestions. Deepening suggestions may be indicated by counting or progress toward a goal in imagery. For example:

> Now, as I begin to count the numbers from 10 to 1, each number that I count will serve as a cue to enter a deeper state of hypnotic relaxation...a deeper and deeper state of hypnosis and very deeply relaxed...and able to respond to each suggestion...just as you would like.

GOAL-DIRECTED SUGGESTIONS

MH is goal directed, and goals should be collaboratively agreed upon by the therapist and the client during the preinduction phase of hypnotherapy. For example, if the overall goal for the session is nonjudgmental awareness of thoughts or feelings, then suggestions should be consistent with this goal. An example of such suggestions is:

> As you experience a deeper and deeper state of hypnosis...so deeply relaxed...in this hypnotic state you can notice and observe your thoughts...without judging them...just observing them...the way you could watch and observe...clouds drifting across the sky...just watching and noticing...no need to judge the clouds...they just drift by...no need to judge the thoughts...they just drift by within your awareness.

MENTAL IMAGERY AND SUGGESTION

As in the example provided earlier, hypnotic suggestions are often given as mental images. Mental imagery can be an effective way of conveying a complex idea succinctly. While this can be a useful tool during the course of any clinical encounter, mental imagery becomes especially effective during hypnosis due to the changes in cognitive processing that tend to occur. As the hypnotic state becomes deeper, clients experience a greater degree of dissociation. As this occurs, the mental images are experienced as more than a simple rhetorical device; in subjects with a moderate or high hypnotic ability, they are experienced as an internal reality. Instead of just *imagining* being at the beach, the client *experiences* being at the beach and can feel as though he or she is in another place. For example:

> As you can hear my voice, with one part of your mind...you can be aware that you are here sitting comfortably...and yet with another part of your mind you can find that you are soon near the ocean...at a beautiful beach...hearing the waves as they come in...and go out...experiencing being at a beautiful beach...now.

Suggestions for mental imagery should be detailed and consistent with the client's preference. The suggestions for mental imagery should include details of visual imagery, sounds, feelings, taste, and sensations as appropriate. Suggestions for experiencing mindfulness are provided either through direct suggestion, imagery, or indirect suggestions (additional guidance for formulating hypnotic suggestions and metaphors is provided in Chapter 5 of this book).

INDIVIDUALIZATION AND REPETITION

The wording of specific imagery and suggestions should be individualized to match the client's preferences and goals. For some clients, the imagery of a beach may be preferred, while others may connect more deeply with the image of being in the mountains or a place that was significant to them as a child. Certain hypnotic suggestions can also be repeated and varied to help them sink in more deeply. Examples of suggestions could include:

> As you drift into a deeper hypnotic state, you can experience a light and weightless feeling in your left arm...soon it becomes lighter and lighter...as if there were several balloons attached to the wrist...and soon it drifts up...watch the balloons...and the arm just drifts up.

LETTING GO AND INVOLUNTARINESS

The response to hypnotic suggestions is largely experienced as occurring with little conscious effort or *trying* to respond. Rather, the suggestions are for the client to have an experience of *letting go* and *allowing* the responses to occur rather than *making* them occur. Examples of suggestions could include:

> As you drift into a state of hypnotic relaxation...letting go...more and more ... letting go of any concerns...letting go of any tension...and allowing the experiences to come to you...there is nothing you have to do...and nothing you have to try to do...consciously...just letting go...more and more.

REINFORCEMENT OF RESPONSE

As the mindful hypnotherapist observes positive responses to suggestions, it is important to encourage and provide reinforcement throughout the session. Suggestions for particular responses should be followed by reinforcement once a response occurs. For example:

> As you notice your eyelids are closing...just allow it to occur...[when the client's eyelids begin to close] very good...you are doing very well...and it is possible to go on to a deeper hypnotic state...as you relax deeper...[eyelids fully closed] that's right...very good...you are doing very well.

POSTHYPNOTIC SUGGESTION

Posthypnotic suggestions for therapeutic changes persist after the hypnotic session has been completed. It is often the case that acceptance, awareness, or changes are intended to occur in the future and not just while a client is in a hypnotic or mindful state. Posthypnotic suggestions may be given for (a) continued improvement or (b) for response to a suggestion that will occur at a later time (Elkins, 2014). For example:

> And in the future you will find that you are more calm...less stressed...and less bothered by experiences as they occur...no matter what is going on around you...you will have a feeling of grounded-ness...calmness...and inner awareness of your thoughts and feelings as they occur.

Posthypnotic suggestions may be repeated during a hypnotic induction or occur near the end of the sessions.

ALERTING

Alerting is an important phase of most hypnotic inductions. Suggestions for alerting can be given in a direct way or in a more permissive manner. Suggestions should be given for the hypnotic state itself to end and return to conscious alertness, but posthypnotic suggestions and responses may linger, such as in the case of hypnoanalgesia for pain management. As suggestions for alertness and appropriate normal sensations to return are provided, alerting suggestions should remove any unintended hypnotic effects. Suggestions for alerting should be given in a calm and unhurried voice, and they should allow the client to be in control and fully alert. Direct suggestions for alerting could involve counting. For example,

> As I count the numbers from four to one, you can return to conscious alertness...One...more aware of this room, this time and place...Two...returning to conscious alertness and soon your eyelids can begin to open...Three...eye lids opening...feeling calm...refreshed...and relaxed... And four ...all the way back...alert...refreshed...relaxed.

Permissive suggestions for alerting could involve the client alerting at his or her own time. For example:

> Soon...in your own time...and in your own way...returning to conscious alertness...in a way that feels just right for you...and as you return to alertness...your eye lids can open...so that you are alert, refreshed...and relaxed...and back to full conscious alertness.

Summary

Hypnosis can be understood as a state of consciousness involving focused attention and reduced peripheral awareness, as well as an increased capacity for response to suggestion. This state of consciousness is a natural one that everyone is capable of to some degree, but it can be enhanced through the process of a hypnotic induction. The therapeutic alliance is very important to this process and in MH in general. There are many methods of hypnotic induction that involve focusing attention, suggestions for deepening the hypnotic state, and other suggestions that support achieving particular goals. Hypnotic inductions generally follow a structure from initial focus of attention to deepening the hypnotic state, utilization of mental imagery and suggestion, posthypnotic suggestions, and alerting.

REFERENCES

Banyai, E. I., & Hilgard, E. R. (1976). A comparison of active-alert hypnotic induction with traditional relaxation induction. *Journal of Abnormal Psychology, 85*(2), 218–224. doi:10.1037//0021-843x.85.2.218

Benson, J. K. (1975). *The relaxation response*. New York, NY: William Morrow.

Elkins, G. R. (2014). *Hypnotic relaxation therapy: Principles and applications*. New York, NY: Springer Publishing.

Elkins, G. R. (2017). *Handbook of medical and psychological hypnosis: Foundations, applications, and professional issues*. New York, NY: Springer Publishing.

Elkins, G. R., Barabasz, A. F., Council, J. R., & Spiegel, D. (2015). Advancing research and practice: The revised APA division 30 definition of hypnosis. *American Journal of Clinical Hypnosis, 57*, 378–385. doi:10.1080/00029157.2015.1011465

Spiegel, H., & Spiegel, D. (2004). *Trance and treatment: Clinical uses of hypnosis*. Washington, DC: American Psychiatric Publishing.

Tellegen, A., & Atkinson, G. (1974). Openness to absorbing and self-altering experiences ("absorption"), a trait related to hypnotic susceptibility. *Journal of Abnormal Psychology, 83*(3), 268–277. doi:10.1037/h0036681

Yapko, M. D. (2011). *Mindfulness and hypnosis: The power of suggestion to transform experience*. New York, NY: W. W. Norton.

CHAPTER 5

FORMULATING HYPNOTIC SUGGESTIONS AND METAPHORS

Every person's map of the world is as unique as their thumbprint. There are no two people alike. No two people who understand the same sentence the same way ... so in dealing with people, you try not to fit them to your concept of what they should be.

—*Milton H. Erickson (1980)*

Introduction

Mindful hypnotherapy uses individualized hypnotic suggestions as well as standardized transcripts to facilitate clients' integration of mindfulness into their lives. Hypnotic suggestions can serve a wide variety of purposes depending on a client's needs and goals. Individualized hypnotic suggestions can be used to facilitate a hypnotic trance, focus a client's attention, and enable a client to shift thoughts, emotions, and behavior toward a state of greater well-being. Depending on the situation, these changes may include feelings of emotional tranquility and physical relaxation, changes in sensation, or even greater mindful awareness. Hypnotic suggestions can be expressed in a variety of ways in the context of mindful hypnotherapy, but there are certain principles that help distinguish effective hypnotic communication from ineffective hypnotic communication. The sources of these laws and principles are well known (Ewin, 2009), and there are several textbooks that cover the different laws and principles in greater detail (Elkins, 2017; Hammond, 1990). It is important to recognize that hypnotic suggestions may be formulated and delivered in a directive style, indirectly, in a permissive style, or with therapeutic metaphors.

This chapter presents the basics of formulating hypnotic suggestions, including principles such as pacing and leading and the use of reinforcement during hypnotic suggestions. The different styles of hypnotherapy as they relate to the delivery of hypnotic suggestions are discussed as well as the importance of therapeutic metaphors (or storytelling) in mindful hypnotherapy. Examples of hypnotic suggestions are also included to illustrate each principle.

Principles and Laws of Hypnotic Suggestion

Principles of hypnotic suggestion help to guide the wording and the delivery of hypnotic interventions. Effective suggestions require clinicians to be attuned with the client's wishes and goals, and they are a natural extension of a solid therapeutic alliance. When presenting hypnotic suggestions, it is important to establish rapport and a cooperative relationship (Gilligan, 1987; Hammond, 1990; Kane & Olness, 2004). During hypnotherapy, suggestions are not merely instructions or informational. Rather, they guide and facilitate therapeutic experiences, create positive expectancy, and at their best speak to the *heart and mind* of the client (Casula, 2017; Zeig, 2006).

PRINCIPLE OF PACING AND LEADING

During a hypnotic induction, it is important to attend to the environment and ensure that the client is in a comfortable position (sitting or reclining). At the beginning of a hypnotic induction, the mindful hypnotherapist changes the verbal and nonverbal communication to demarcate a transition into hypnotic experiences (Casula, 2017). One simple way to initiate an induction is to invite clients: to change their posture and behavior when they are ready to experience hypnosis. For example, the clinician might say

> When you are ready, I invite you to sit in a comfortable position. If you prefer, you can recline in the chair with your feet relaxed. If it is okay with you, your hands can rest on your thighs or the arms of the chair so that, when you are ready, you can focus your attention and soon your eyelids can close in a way that you can concentrate attention internally with a nonjudgmental noticing and accepting of whatever comes to you.

The therapist observes the client's breathing, muscle tone, and any movements, and can adjust the pace of hypnotic suggestions to match the client's responses. The therapist also begins to speak more softly and slowly with greater emphasis to key words. As the hypnotic induction progresses, usually the client's breathing becomes slower, more regular, and the body begins to relax.

During the hypnotic induction, the therapist should observe the client's breathing, posture, and responses. Careful observation allows therapists to notice nonverbal cues that indicate responses to suggestion and allows them to vary the pace of suggestions and pauses accordingly. For example, the mindful hypnotherapist may pace suggestions to match the client's breathing by delivering suggestions for deepening relaxation when the client exhales and pausing when the client inhales: As the first responses are achieved (e.g., eye closure, relaxation, or acknowledging experiences verbally), these responses can serve as a cue for the therapist to proceed to the next series of hypnotic suggestions. For example

> Just as you can notice that your eyelids close, so you can go on to a deeper and more relaxed state...able to notice and become aware of the sensations of breathing in...and breathing out...just noticing and observing...as you go deeper.

Skillful use of pacing and leading requires the therapist to adjust the timing of the suggestions based on careful observations during a hypnotic induction. For example, if a client does not appear to be relaxed, the therapist may allow more time, offer additional guidance for relaxation, or verbally check in with the client on the experience. Effective pacing and leading is a reflection of the hypnotherapist's capacity for empathy and connection with the client's experience. Even with careful observation, there may also be times where nonverbal communication is insufficient to communicate the nuances of a client's experience. In such cases, the hypnotherapist may ask the client to describe the experience verbally to pace and lead the client more effectively during the induction.

■ CLINICIAN NOTE

Principles and Laws of Hypnotic Suggestions

The principles and laws of hypnotic suggestion provide insights into how to formulate hypnotic suggestions for maximal effect. These principles have been developed over years by experienced clinicians and emphasize pacing and leading in delivering hypnotic suggestions, positively wording suggestions, and individualization.

PRINCIPLE OF POSITIVE LANGUAGE

Mindful hypnotherapy makes ample use of positive language throughout the intervention, and this becomes especially important during hypnosis. Suggestions are formulated to create a positive expectancy and convey positive goals consistent with mindfulness, as opposed to focusing on the experiences that the client would like to avoid or get rid of. This principle is expressed in the therapist's attitude of positive expectancy and in the positive wording of suggestions. Suggestions may be given such as the following:

> It is possible to be curious about your experience during hypnosis today...it is possible to see things from a new perspective...and allow them to unfold in their own time...as you soon feel more calm.

Negative suggestions are generally avoided, as they may be counterproductive and interfere with progress. For example, telling a person *not* to think about a pink elephant immediately conjures the image of a pink elephant in the mind. Similarly, suggestions such as "Try to not think about the pain" or "Don't be so tense" require clients to think about the very thing they are trying to avoid. Therefore, during hypnosis it can be useful to frame suggestions with positive language that conveys the same meaning, such as "You may experience thoughts of comfort and ease" or "You will notice a wave of relaxation that spreads through your entire body."

PRINCIPLE OF REPETITION

Hypnotic suggestions are more like planting a seed than hammering a nail. That is, hypnotic suggestions are usually delivered in a gentle manner, allowing clients to respond when they are ready. Clients' responses should be allowed to unfold in accordance with their own values and motivations rather than being clumsily forced by the therapist. Hypnotic suggestions are "like planting a seed" and then "allowing it to grow in its own time and way." Hypnotic suggestions are *not* repeatedly given as if the suggestion could be "driven" into the brain! Rather, the *principle of repetition* means that suggestions can be repeated a few times and in various ways such as through direct suggestions, metaphors, and implications. One of the many contributions of Milton Erickson was to demonstrate that direct hypnotic suggestions could be reinforced by weaving the same suggestion into metaphors and examples (Erickson, 1954; Hammond, 1990). The principle of repetition also applies when a therapist repeats suggestions over the course of multiple sessions to enhance their effectiveness. When used effectively, the principle of repetition can support and empower clients as they make positive changes in their lives.

PRINCIPLE OF INDIVIDUALIZATION

The principle of individualization is also attributed to Milton Erickson (Casula, 2017; Erickson & Rossi, 1979; Erickson, Rossi, & Rossi, 1976; Hammond, 1990). This principle recognizes that each individual is a unique human being with his or her own experiences, perceptions, memories, preferences, and personal qualities. The consequences of this principle extend beyond mere ideology: That is, this principle means that hypnotic suggestions can be optimized by tailoring your suggestions to the unique individual you are working with. There may be some clinical situations where the preferences of the client are very idiosyncratic and other times (such as when following a transcript) in which general suggestions are widely applicable to many people. However, even standardized transcripts can have built-in opportunities for the client's unique experiences to manifest. For example:

> As I suggest to you that you can go to a place where you feel calm and relaxed...it can be your own personal place...a place that is just right for you...your own personal place...where you feel safe and secure.

LAW OF PARSIMONY

The law of parsimony states that when given a choice, a simple and more direct route is generally preferred over a longer and more complex one. This principle acts as a reminder to stay focused on the client's goals and make sure that hypnotic suggestions are clear and meaningful. The words of a hypnotic induction hold no mystical power; they are merely tools designed to facilitate experiences. Avoid overwhelming clients with too many words, and don't encumber hypnotic inductions with overly complex metaphors.

LAW OF CONCENTRATED ATTENTION

The law of concentrated attention states that when an individual concentrates on an idea or a feeling, the idea or set of ideas tends to intensify and become more salient. For example, the feeling of one's feet inside the shoes may be mostly outside of conscious awareness; however, once the idea has been suggested and attention is concentrated on it, the sensations become realized. This law of suggestion is utilized throughout hypnotic inductions and interventions. It can be used to great benefit in clinical settings and it is an integral concept in mindful hypnotherapy.

Concentrated attention occurs whenever positive concepts and ideas related to mindfulness are introduced during a hypnotic induction. Some examples to illustrate this follow.

If the idea of *nonjudgmental awareness* is focused upon, it is more likely to be realized.

> As you enter a deep hypnotic state...you will find...that you are able to become more aware...of whatever is happening in the present moment...without judging...or trying to change the experience...just acknowledging whatever is happening...in the present moment...and letting it occur...observing without judging.

If an idea of *loving-kindness* is focused upon, it is more likely to be felt and experienced.

> Within this hypnotic state you may have the image...the memory of someone who was kind to you...loving...someone who treated you with loving-kindness...and it is possible for you to feel more of a sense of loving-kindness toward others...an attitude and feelings of caring, benevolence, friendliness toward yourself...and toward others.

Emil Coue was a famous French psychologist who often used the phrase "getting better and better...every day...and in every way" in his work, using the law of concentrated attention to enhance feelings of well-being and confidence.

LAW OF REVERSED EFFECT

The law of reversed effect primarily applies to activities or mind–body processes that cannot be *willed* or brought under full conscious control. The law of reversed effect, simply stated, is that "the harder one tries, the more one fails." The reality of this law can be demonstrated with the psychophysiology of sleep. If a person tries to will himself or herself into sleep, it is unlikely to occur. In fact, the harder a person "tries to go to sleep" by ruminating about sleep, worrying about sleep, and checking to "see if I am asleep yet," the harder it becomes to actually go to sleep! It is only by *letting go* that sleep can come more easily.

Humans have both a conscious mind and an unconscious mind, each with a different function. The conscious mind operates with rational thinking and voluntary action and using the voluntary nervous system. The unconscious mind operates as an experiential system of imagery, feelings, creativity, intuition, and automatic (nonvoluntary) responding

(Epstein, 1994). Within a hypnotic state, trusting in one's own experiences and self may come more easily. For example:

> Within this hypnotic state...you do not need to "try" to do anything in particular...just trusting your unconscious mind...and trusting in your own experiences...as is right for you at this particular time...letting go...and just noticing...and letting whatever happens, happen...easily and naturally...observing and noticing your own experience...without trying to do anything...a kind of a detached feeling...an openness to your own experience within hypnosis.

LAW OF DOMINANT AFFECT

The law of dominant affect (sometimes referred to as the law of dominant *effect*) states that a stronger emotion tends to replace a weaker emotion. Hypnotherapists can use this law to guide the client from maladaptive experiences toward more positive experiences through hypnotic suggestion. Mental images may be used to facilitate feelings of calmness and reduce stress. However, it is the *affective component of hypnotic suggestions* that gives the client more power and energy toward a desired effect. Hypnotic suggestions can be formulated to include words, images, and experiences with a robust emotional resonance. For example, the following suggestions for mountain imagery and curiosity include affective imagery that are underlined to highlight the law of dominant affect:

> As you go into an even deeper hypnotic state...you can experience being at a *very beautiful* place in the mountains...it is a place where you *feel calm*...and you are there with *someone you love* ...as you can feel the *peaceful emotions*...in this place...there is also a sense of curiosity...of what you may discover and learn...it is possible to learn much...in *the nature and beauty*...of being in the mountains...*surrounded by beautiful trees*...and aware of the *very good things*...about you...in this place you can *feel very good*...and follow your creative imagination...to discover more about...acceptance...patience...and a nonjudgmental attitude toward yourself...your thoughts...and toward others...there in the mountains...on *this beautiful day*...with *someone you love* and *who loves you*.

HYPNOTIC SUGGESTION AS A THREE-STEP PROCESS

The structure of hypnotic suggestions can also be conceptualized as a three-step process. The first step is the initial suggestion that *introduces an idea for what is going to happen* or may happen. It builds some anticipation and introduces an experience before it happens. The pacing should be such that it provides sufficient time for the client to acknowledge the initial suggestion for what is going to happen. For example:

> In a few moments I will begin counting some numbers, with each number that I count you can go deeper and deeper into this mental and emotional relaxation.

The second step in the process of hypnotic suggestion is to suggest that *it is now happening*. Mindful hypnotherapy is an experiential therapy in which the response to suggestion occurs in the present moment. This provides ratification of the suggestion as it is experienced and an awareness of it. For example, in the process of counting down toward greater relaxation during a hypnotic induction, the therapist might say:

> Now it is happening... five ... the number five ...deeper relaxed...now... allow all tension to be let go...so that you are now mentally and emotionally calm...nothing bothers...nothing disturbs...you are now just as relaxed... emotionally...and mentally...as is right for you...now.

The third step is to communicate a completion and validation (Elkins, 2014). As the client experiences the suggestion, he or she may be asked to nod the head "yes" to indicate the client is experiencing the suggestion. This allows the mindful hypnotherapist to pace suggestions and then to appropriately lead the client to other hypnotic experiences. For example:

> Number 10...Please nod your head "yes" as you feel emotionally and mentally calm...Very good. And as you remain deeply relaxed...mentally calm...emotionally relaxed...it is possible to go on to other experiences as well...Soon you will find that you become aware of...your breathing...in a gentle and appreciative way...noticing the sensations of breathing in and breathing out...gently and easily...your breathing is always with you...and can remind you to...remain calm...no matter what is happening around you...or how stressful situations may be.

Types of Hypnotic Suggestions

There are many different types of hypnotic suggestions that can be grouped into four primary categories: (a) direct suggestions; (b) permissive suggestions; (c) indirect suggestions; and (d) metaphors. In mindful hypnotherapy sessions these different types of suggestions may be integrated and all can be used to a certain degree. It is generally the case that more permissive and indirect suggestions and metaphors are used later in the hypnotic induction. In contrast, the suggestions presented initially in the hypnotic induction are more directive and guide the client toward experiences such as focusing attention and entering the hypnotic state.

Directive Suggestions

Directive suggestions involve direct wording for a specific experience or thought to occur. The wording for directive suggestions can be very straightforward, such as "Now I suggest you can experience a wave of relaxation spreading across your forehead, neck, and shoulders." Directive suggestions are clear and unambiguous. If the suggestions are fully acceptable to the client and resistance is low, then directive suggestions may be preferred. Examples of directive wording:

Now I suggest...

Soon you will notice...

This hand becomes...

The thought occurs to you...

You will be interested to find that...

Soon you will experience...

Now I want you to...

You are becoming...

You can observe in a detached manner...

Soon you will remember...

Finding that you are more open to experiences...

You will be able to observe without judging...

A positive feeling will occur to you...

As you focus on your breathing, you will become more calm and more relaxed...

Permissive Suggestions

Permissive suggestions are hypnotic suggestions that emphasize the concept of *choice*. In comparison to direct suggestions, permissive suggestions offer a variety of choices and options for responses. Permissive suggestions can decrease resistance and can allow the client to respond through several alternatives. For example:

> There are a variety of ways of deepening hypnosis...you may notice more of a relaxed feeling in your arms or legs...or you may feel more calm and peaceful...your thoughts might drift...just in your own way...going on to a deeper level of hypnosis.

Permissive suggestions may be preferred by some clients and can shift greater control to the client. If suggestions are overused and too many choices are presented, it may be confusing for the client. Therefore, it can be useful to integrate permissive and directive suggestions during a hypnotic induction. Some examples of wording for permissive suggestions are:

> You may want to begin by focusing on a spot on the wall or you may want to begin by closing your eyes.

> Your right arm may become lighter or it may become heavier as you experience a deeper level of hypnosis.

> It will be interesting to notice what images occur to you today...you may drift to the beach...or you may experience being in the mountain...or some combination of these things...whatever is right for you.

Indirect Suggestions

There are many different types of indirect hypnotic suggestions, many of which were identified by Erickson and Rossi (1979). Indirect suggestions present ideas without indicating that a particular response is desired. Some of the indirect suggestions we have found to be particularly useful in mindful hypnotherapy include stating truisms, stating not knowing, offering questions as suggestions, and using implications as suggestions. Examples of these are provided next.

TRUISMS

Truisms are statements of fact that fit within common experience (Hammond, 1990). Truisms are generally very acceptable types of suggestions and may relate to feelings, sensations, cognition, change, awareness, or other intentions. Some example wording for truisms are:

It is possible to notice things...

You may have a memory that is pleasant...

You could wonder...

You could be curious about...

You could be aware of...

There may have been time when you didn't know...

Feelings of comfort can be experienced ...

Time passes...whether we notice it or not...

There are sensations...

You could observe your thoughts...

Feelings change...sensations change...

NOT KNOWING

Indirect suggestions can include acknowledging that something is not yet known. These suggestions awaken the possibility of discovering, learning, and knowing in the future. Some examples of this type of suggestions are:

I really don't know if you would like to experience...

You may not know in what way mindful self-hypnosis may benefit you the most...

I wonder if you will go into a deep hypnotic state today...

I don't know what images you will find most peaceful...

You may not know what you will discover about yourself...

It is really not necessary to know why...

I don't know the best way of letting go of past worries...

Not knowing and not doing...can be valued as they lead to new understandings...and more flexible thinkin...

QUESTIONS AS SUGGESTIONS

Hypnotic suggestions can also be presented as questions rather than as direct statements. Questions can focus attention and introduce ideas and actions. Questions as suggestions do not challenge and do not define a particular response. Some examples of questions as hypnotic suggestions are:

Would you like to focus your attention on a spot on the wall?

Would you prefer that your eyelids close slowly or quickly?

Can you notice the space between your hands?

Can you imagine the space between your body and the ceiling?

Can you imagine comfortably floating in space?

Would you be willing to observe your thoughts without judging them?

Would you like to let go of some concerns?

Would you be willing to be more gentle with yourself and take better care of yourself?

Would you be willing to allow... ?

IMPLICATIONS AS SUGGESTIONS

Direct and permissive suggestions can be enhanced with suggestions that are worded as implications. For example, if direct suggestions are given for being at the beach, the experience may be enhanced by implying that the client can "hear the sound of the ocean" or "soon notice the warmth of the sand." These type of suggestions do not command certain responses but only imply that they may occur. This can facilitate the hypnotic state and dissociation as the client's experience moves from imagining to experiencing—from wishing to noticing the unfolding internal reality as it occurs. Some examples of implications are:

What colors do you see?

Notice the change in sensations in your right hand?

Did you take that step with your right foot or your left foot?

Which chair would you like to sit in to experience a deep hypnotic state today?

When you have the image, please let me know.

Would it be okay to have the pain bother you 50% less?

There could be a moment when you know you are letting go...

The deeper the relaxation, the deeper the response...

Notice whatever sounds that come to you...that you can observe in a deep hypnotic state...

Your practice of mindful self-hypnosis can be a source of expanding consciousness...

Metaphors as Hypnotic Suggestions

Metaphors are stories with meaning. They communicate ideas in symbolic terms or provide anecdotes to illustrate ideas. Metaphors can be incredibly useful and flexible tools in mindful hypnotherapy. They can be used to reframe problems, facilitate insight, prompt self-reflection, teach mindful ideas, or bypass resistance (Zeig, 1980). Metaphors use the language of the unconscious mind. They are symbolic and can have multiple meanings that are understood at a conscious or an unconscious level. They are certainly not unique to hypnotherapy, but rather have been used for millennia as an effective rhetorical device when teaching new concepts. In a modern context, metaphors are often found in storytelling, clinical interventions such as Acceptance and Commitment Therapy, and, of course, mindful hypnotherapy.

Metaphors can take different forms. For example, a metaphor may be an old saying such as "There is more than one way to skin a cat," meaning there may be more than one solution to a problem. Metaphors can be presented as illustrations from movies, books, or personal experiences. It is important to determine if the client has some familiarity with the book, movie, or story such that the client has a basis for relating. For example, the movie *The Lion King* teaches that in relating to a negative event in the past, one can "either run from it or learn from it" and that it is possible (and preferred) to live in the present instead of living in the past.

Mindful hypnotherapists can also create metaphors for their clients that involve *teaching tales*: metaphorical stories that seek to address some aspect of a client's concerns or areas for growth (Gordon, 1978; Hammond, 1990; Lankton & Lankton, 1983). The creation and use of metaphors is a creative process that can be honed over time as the hypnotherapist draws upon personal experiences and those of the unique client. A number of excellent examples of therapeutic metaphors can be found in a book by Ed Freedman, entitled *Freedman's Fables*. It is a wonderful resource for therapists of all kinds and may be a particularly helpful asset for new hypnotherapists.

A metaphorical story can have a powerful effect, especially if skillfully delivered. A hypnotic induction serves to lower conscious defenses, focus attention, and facilitate greater access to the unconscious processing of information. Therefore, it is generally recommended that therapeutic metaphors be delivered in the context of a hypnotic induction, following suggestions for a sufficient depth of hypnotic absorption and hypnotic state.

Summary

The development of skill in mindful hypnotherapy requires familiarity with both mindfulness practice and hypnotherapeutic techniques and formulating hypnotic suggestions. Hypnotic suggestions may be worded in a direct, permissive, or indirect manner. Indirect suggestions may be given through implication, questions, truisms, or queries. In addition, therapeutic metaphors and storytelling during hypnosis are an effective method of hypnotic communication. Familiarity with the laws and principles of hypnotic suggestion allows for greater creativity and helps clinicians to craft their own well-designed hypnotic suggestions consistent with mindful hypnotherapy.

REFERENCES

Casula, C. (2017). Laws and principles of hypnotic inductions. In G. Elkins (Ed.), *Handbook of medical and psychological hypnosis: Foundations, applications, and professional issues* (pp. 43–55). New York, NY: Springer Publishing.

Elkins, G. R. (2014). *Hypnotic relaxation therapy: Principles and applications.* New York, NY: Springer Publishing.

Elkins, G. R. (2017). *Handbook of medical and psychological hypnosis: Foundations, applications, and professional issues.* New York, NY: Springer Publishing.

Epstein, S. (1994). Integration of the cognitive and the psychodynamic unconscious. *American Psychologist, 49*(8), 709–724. doi:10.1037//0003-066x.49.8.709

Erickson, M. H. (1954). Special techniques of brief hypnotherapy. *Journal of Clinical and Experimental Hypnosis, 2*(2), 109–129. doi:10.1080/00207145408409943

Erickson, M. H., & Rossi, E. L. (1979). *Hypnotherapy: An exploratory case book.* New York, NY: Irvington.

Erickson, M. H., Rossi, E. L., & Rossi, S. I. (1976). *Hypnotic realities: The induction of clinical hypnosis and forms of indirect suggestion.* New York, NY: Irvington.

Erickson, M. H., & Rossi, S. I. (1980). *The collected works of Milton H. Erickson.* New York, NY: Irvington.

Ewin, D. M. (2009). *101 things I wish I'd known when I started using hypnosis.* Williston, VT: Crown House Publishing.

Gilligan, S. (1987). *Therapeutic trances: The cooperative principle in Ericksonian hypnotherapy.* New York, NY: Brunner/Mazel.

Gordon, R. (1978). Look! He has come through! *Journal of Analytical Psychology, 23*(3), 258–274. doi:10.1111/j.1465-5922.1978.00258.x

Hammond, D. C. (1990). *Handbook of hypnotic suggestions and metaphors.* New York, NY: W. W. Norton.

Kane, S., & Olness, K. (2004). *The art of therapeutic communications: The collected works of Kay F. Thompson.* Williston, VT: Crown House Publishing.

Lankton, S. R., & Lankton, C. H. (1983). *The answer within: A clinical framework of Ericksonian hypnotherapy.* New York, NY: Routledge.

Zeig, J. K. (1980). *Teaching seminar with Milton H. Erickson.* New York, NY: Brunner/Mazel.

Zeig, J. K. (2006). *Confluence: The selected papers of Jeffrey K. Zeig.* Phoenix, AZ: Zeig, Tucker & Theisen.

CHAPTER 6

HYPNOTIC ABILITIES

Measure what is measurable, and make measurable what is not so.
—*Galileo Galilei*

Introduction

All individuals have a capacity, if they so desire, to respond to hypnotic suggestions in some form. Like most human traits, a normal spectrum of variability exists in individuals' degree of responsiveness to hypnotic suggestion: Some respond more quickly or to a greater degree than others. This natural variability between people's response to suggestion is commonly referred to as *hypnotizability* or *hypnotic ability*, and due to the observable differences in responsiveness, it is possible to measure an individual's hypnotizability. There are a number of scales to assess hypnotic ability, including the Elkins Hypnotizability Scale-Clinical Form (EHS-CF) presented in Appendix A. However, we wish to acknowledge that although the assessment of hypnotizability is usually not necessary in mindful hypnotherapy (MH), it may be beneficial in some instances where deep trance ability is important or in predicting the response to mindful hypnotic suggestions. It is most useful to consider hypnotizability as a trait that may affect how quickly clients progress or may contribute to the depth of their experience of the hypnotic (mindful) state. It may also determine how much practice clients need with mindful self-hypnosis to achieve their therapeutic goals. This chapter explains the concept of hypnotic abilities and how it can relate to MH. Scales to measure hypnotizability are reviewed, and the clinical form of the EHS (EHS-C) is provided at the end of the book for clinical use.

Defining Hypnotic Abilities

The definition of *hypnotizability* is "an individual's ability to experience suggested alterations in physiology, sensations, emotions, thoughts, or behavior during hypnosis" (Elkins, Barabasz, Council, & Spiegel,

2015, p. 6). Several studies have shown that hypnotizability is normally distributed in the adult population (Elkins, 2014; Fromm & Nash, 1992; Hilgard, 1965; Woody & Sadler, 2016). It can be conceptualized as a trait (Bates, 1993; Heap, Brown, & Oakley, 2004; Woody & Sadler, 2016) that is relatively stable over time. Specifically, a landmark study by Piccione, Hilgard, and Zimbardo (1989) found test–retest coefficients ranging from .64 to .82 over 10, 15, and 25 years. As a trait, hypnotizability has been shown to exist across different cultures and countries (Bongartz, 1985; De Pascalis, Russo, & Marucci, 2000; Kallio & Ihamuotila, 1999; Lamas, del Valle-Inclan, Blanco, & Diaz, 1989; Laurence & Perry, 1982; McConkey, Barnier, Maccallum, & Bishop, 1996; Sapp & Hitchcock, 2001; Zachariae, Sommerlund, & Molay, 1996). Similarly, hypnotic abilities can be measured in a variety of languages, and scales have even been adapted for use with the hearing impaired (Bongartz, 1985; De Pascalis, Bellusci, & Russo, 2000; Matthews & Isenberg, 1995; Repka & Nash, 1995).

Hypnotizability Versus Depth of Hypnotic State

In defining hypnotizability, it is important to distinguish between hypnotic ability and depth of hypnosis (trance) during any particular time in a hypnotic induction. The experience of depth of the hypnotic state is partly subjective. The client's own sense of alteration in consciousness, absorption in imagery, experiential relaxation, involuntariness, and response to suggestions are all markers of the depth of hypnosis (Ludwig, 1966; Tart, Puthoff, & Targ, 1979). Individuals can be asked to rate their depth of hypnosis at any point during a hypnotic experience. However, it should be kept in mind that such ratings are subjective, and the basis for such ratings varies from person to person. People generally rate themselves as experiencing a deeper level of hypnosis if they discover they are able to respond to hypnotic suggestions and feel that their consciousness has been altered (Brown & Fromm, 1986; Tart et al., 1979). Thus, ratings of trance depth can provide relevant information within subjects, but less so between subjects.

Relevance to Clinical Practice

The assessment of hypnotic abilities can have broad practical utility beyond simply understanding whether a client has high, low, or average hypnotic ability. Some of the benefits of assessment involve acclimating a new client to hypnosis, tailoring the intervention to fit the client's abilities, and detecting signs of resistance before treatment begins.

In a clinical setting, some clients may feel nervous about the idea of using hypnosis and have questions about what they may or may not experience. Hypnotizability measures can be used in clinical practice as a concrete and nonthreatening way of demonstrating what a hypnotic induction feels like and gives them an idea of how hypnosis might be useful to them (Elkins, 2014; Woody & Sadler, 2016). Hypnotizability assessments include a hypnotic induction as a necessary part of the measurement process. This experience alone can familiarize clients with hypnosis and can address many of the myths or misconceptions that exist (Elkins, 2014). In addition, hypnotizability assessment can help new clients realize their innate capacity to change their experiences and perspective through hypnosis. In MH, hypnosis is also used to develop a greater awareness of the experiences that are unfolding naturally and to develop a different relationship with those experiences.

Clinicians who are new to assessing hypnotizability may worry that clients will be discouraged if they fall in the low end of the hypnotizability spectrum or may be concerned that such clients cannot benefit from hypnotherapy. In fact, research has shown that obtaining a lower score on a hypnotizability measure does not discourage clients from interest in hypnotherapy (Frankel et al., 1979). Even treatments like hypnoanalgesia produce similar results for mid- and high-hypnotizable individuals (Montgomery, DuHamel, & Redd, 2000). Furthermore, understanding clients' hypnotic ability can help clinicians to guide their treatment approach. For example, individuals who have a higher hypnotizability may benefit more *quickly* from hypnotherapy, while individuals in the lower range of hypnotizability might obtain the same benefit but need more sessions to do so (Elkins, 2017; Montgomery et al., 2000). Regardless of a patient's innate hypnotic ability, the information obtained during an assessment can be used to tailor future hypnotic sessions and can prompt deeper discussions about the experiences a client had during the assessment (Elkins, 2014, 2017; Woody & Sadler, 2016).

CLINICIAN NOTE

Utility of Assessing Hypnotic Ability

All people have some level of hypnotizability. Some are low, most are in the mid-range, and some are high. However, all are "hypnotizable."

Finally, if a hypnotic assessment is administered toward the beginning of a hypnotherapy intervention, it can potentially be useful in detecting the presence of resistance (Elkins, 2014). For example, a client who does not respond to simple direct hypnotic suggestions may benefit from more permissive or indirect suggestions. Clients who have difficulty relaxing or report that the experience was an unpleasant one may need more time to ask questions and get acclimated to the idea of hypnosis. Resistance during an assessment may also indicate that the therapeutic relationship needs to be developed further before the client feels comfortable enough to engage with hypnotherapy.

Development of Scales to Measure Hypnotizability

Bearing in mind the potential utility of assessing hypnotic ability, it is important to have a basic understanding of how this is accomplished. In the long history of hypnosis, the construct of hypnotizability has been measured in a variety of ways. The general approach to measuring hypnotizability is conceptually simple. The hypnotherapist completes a hypnotic induction and then assesses the degree to which an individual is able to respond to a set of hypnotic suggestions. The first scales of this type were created by Bernheim (1886/1964) and Liebeault (1889) in the late 1880s. Hypnotic depth was rated on a six-point scale, with "drowsiness" at the lower end and "profound somnambulistic sleep" at the higher end (Woody & Barnier, 2008).[1] In the 1930s, Friedlander and Sarbin (1938) developed a scale that clearly emphasized a standardized induction procedure, a standardized set of suggestions, and scoring criteria based on observable behavior.

In the late 1950s, Weitzenhoffer and Hilgard developed a new scale that included a pass/fail scoring scheme as well as additional items. Their work in this area resulted in two forms of their scale: the Stanford Hypnotic Susceptibility Scales, Forms A and B (Weitzenhoffer & Hilgard, 1959). These scales yielded a distribution of scores that was more normal (less skewed) than the distributions of scores on previous scales (Woody & Barnier, 2008). Weitzenhoffer and Hilgard then created the Stanford Hypnotic Susceptibility Scale, Form C (SHSS-C; Weitzenhoffer & Hilgard, 1962), to address the need for more difficult items on a scale (to distinguish individuals who have a high hypnotic ability from those with a *very* high hypnotic ability). The result was a reliable and valid scale that is scored from 0 to 12, with 0 being in the lower range and 12 indicating higher hypnotic abilities. The SHSS-C then became the gold

[1]Describing hypnotic depth in terms analogous to sleep reflected the theoretical understanding of hypnosis at the time. Today, hypnosis is understood to be an altered state of consciousness that is different from sleep.

standard for the measurement of hypnotizability and has been used in many research studies in clinical and experimental hypnosis.

The SHSS-C is valid and reliable, but takes about an hour to administer and score. Furthermore, some of the test items for the SHSS-C involve unpleasant experiences such as smelling ammonia and a suggestion that the subject is being pestered by a mosquito that may bite the person. If the hypnotic assessment is being used to acclimate clients to hypnotherapy treatment and allay the apprehension they may feel, this is less than optimal. Following the development of the SHSS-C, efforts were made to find ways to reduce the administration time. Examples of shorter scales include the Stanford Hypnotic Clinical Scale, Adults (Morgan & Hilgard, 1978–1979), the Stanford Hypnotic Arm Levitation Induction and Test (Hilgard, Crawford, & Wert, 1979), and the Carleton University Responsiveness to Suggestion Scale (Spanos et al., 1983). Despite increased efficiency, these scales are considered to have too few items psychometrically, so they have not been widely used by clinicians or researchers.

Elkins Hypnotizability Scale

The EHS (Elkins, 2014) was developed to address some of the limitations of previous hypnotizability measures. The goals for developing the EHS were (a) to be perceived as pleasant by clients, (b) to be brief, (c) to adequately test a range of hypnotizability, and (d) to have acceptable reliability and validity (Elkins, 2014). The EHS requires about 25 minutes to administer and score. Its scoring system is based on both observable behavioral responses and subjective experiences, and it uses ordinal instead of dichotomous scoring (Elkins, 2014).

Administration of the EHS starts with standardized introductory remarks followed by a standardized induction, which includes suggestions for relaxation and calmness. The EHS scoring takes into account a client's subjective experience, observed behavior, and the use of ordinal scoring. For example, the item on smelling a rose can yield a score from 0 to 2, with a score of 0 indicating no rose scent was reported; a score of 1 indicating a faint rose scent was detected; and a score of 2 indicating a distinct rose scent was detected (Elkins, 2014).

The EHS has been validated on 252 individuals recruited from outpatient clinical settings (Elkins, 2014) and 230 college students (Kekecs, Bowers, Johnson, Kendrick, & Elkins, 2016). In both samples, the EHS was found to have good reliability (α = .85 and .78, respectively). The test–retest reliability of the EHS is high (r = .93; Elkins, Johnson, & Fisher, 2012). The EHS has been shown to have strong correlations with the SHSS-C, ranging from .82 to .91, so it shows good convergent validity (Elkins, 2014; Elkins et al., 2012; Kekecs et al., 2016). In addition, these studies have indicated that the EHS is perceived as pleasant. On a 0 to 10 Likert scale, where 0 represents *completely unpleasant* and 10 represents *completely pleasant*, the mean pleasantness ratings were 8.97 in a clinical sample (Elkins, 2014).

Elkins Hypnotizability Scale–Clinical Form

A shorter version of EHS includes just the first nine items of the EHS. This shorter version of the scale is referred to as the Elkins Hypnotizability Scale-Clinical Form (EHS-CF) and is included in Appendix A. The EHS-CF has some advantages in that it is very brief, taking about 15 minutes to administer, and is designed to be used within a hypnotherapy session in a seamless manner. It can be administered at the beginning of a hypnotic induction and yields information about hypnotizability that is both reliable and valid.

The correlation between the full EHS and the shorter EHS-CF showed a very strong and significant relationship ($r = .962, p < .001$), indicating that the shorter EHS-CF provides a very good measure of hypnotizability. The EHS-CF is an essential skill to have in understanding hypnosis and providing hypnotherapy in clinical practice. It is easily administered and integrated into clinical practice but may also be used in clinical research.

CLINICIAN NOTE

EHS-CF

The EHS-CF transcript for administration and the scoring criteria are provided in Appendix A of this book.

The items on the EHS-CF are listed below in the order of their respective administration:

- Arm heaviness or immobilization
- Arm levitation
- Imagery involvement or dissociation
- Being able to smell of a rose, when no rose is present (positive hallucination)

Please refer to Appendix A for the transcript, protocol for administration, and scoring criteria of the EHS-CF. More detailed information on the EHS can be found in *Hypnotic Relaxation Therapy: Principles and Applications* (Elkins, 2014).

Summary

Hypnotizability is defined as "an individual's ability to experience suggested alterations in physiology, sensations, emotions, thoughts, or behavior during hypnosis" (Elkins et al., 2015, p. 6). Research has shown that most people have hypnotic abilities and most individuals can benefit from hypnotherapy, just as most people can benefit from mindfulness. However, some individual differences exist in the capacity for each person to focus attention, reduce peripheral awareness, and respond to suggestions. While it is not necessary to measure hypnotizability when providing MH, it may be useful in some situations to gain an insight into the client's hypnotic abilities. The Elkins Hypnotizability Scale-Clinical Form provides a clinician-friendly measure that can be integrated into the clinical practice of MH, if desired, and can be used to gain insight into the client's response.

REFERENCES

Bates, B. (1993). Individual differences in response to hypnosis. In J. W. Rhue, S. J. Lynn, & I. Kirsch (Eds.), *Handbook of clinical hypnosis* (pp. 23–54). Washington, DC: American Psychological Association.

Bernheim, H. (1886). *Hypnosis and suggestion in psychotherapy*. New Hyde Park, NY: University Books. (Reprinted 1964)

Bongartz, W. (1985). German norms for the Harvard Group Scale of Hypnotic Susceptibility, Form A. *International Journal of Clinical and Experimental Hypnosis, 33*(2), 131–139. doi:10.1080/00207148508406643

Brown, D. P., & Fromm, E. (1986). *Hypnotherapy and hypnoanalysis*. Hillsdale, NJ: Lawrence Erlbaum Associates.

De Pascalis, V., Bellusci, A. N. N. A., & Russo, P. M. (2000). Italian norms for the Stanford Hypnotic Susceptibility Scale, Form C. *International Journal of Clinical and Experimental Hypnosis, 48*(3), 315–323. doi:10.1080/00207140008415249

De Pascalis, V., Russo, P., & Marucci, F. S. (2000). Italian norms for the Harvard Group Scale of Hypnotic Susceptibility, Form A. *International Journal of Clinical and Experimental Hypnosis, 48*(1), 44–55. doi:10.1080/00207140008410360

Elkins, G. R. (2014). *Hypnotic relaxation therapy: Principles and applications*. New York, NY: Springer Publishing.

Elkins, G. R. (2017). *Handbook of medical and psychological hypnosis: Foundations, applications, and professional issues*. New York, NY: Springer Publishing.

Elkins, G. R., Barabasz, A. F., Council, J. R., & Spiegel, D. (2015). Advancing research and practice: The revised APA Division 30 definition of hypnosis. *American Journal of Clinical Hypnosis, 57*, 378–385. doi:10.1080/00029157.2015.1011465

Elkins, G., Johnson, A., & Fisher, W. (2012). Cognitive hypnotherapy for pain management. *American Journal of Clinical Hypnosis, 54*(4), 294–310. doi:10.1080/00029157.2011.654284

Frankel, F. H., Apfel, R. J., Kelly, S. F., Benson, H., Quinn, T., Newmark, J., & Malmaud, R. (1979). The use of hypnotizability scales in the clinic: A review after 6 years. *International Journal of Clinical and Experimental Hypnosis, 27*, 63–73. doi:10.1080/00207147908407547

Friedlander, J. W., & Sarbin, T. R. (1938). The depth of hypnosis. *Journal of Abnormal and Social Psychology, 33*(4), 453–475. doi:10.1037/h0056229

Fromm, E., & Nash, M. R. (1992). *Contemporary hypnosis research*. New York, NY: Guilford.

Heap, M., Brown, R. J., & Oakley, D. A. (2004). *The highly hypnotizable person: Theoretical, experimental, and clinical issues*. London, UK: Routledge.

Hilgard, E. R. (1965). *Hypnotic susceptibility*. New York, NY: Harcourt, Brace & Jovanovich.

Hilgard, E. R., Crawford, H. J., & Wert, A. (1979). The Stanford Hypnotic Arm Levitation Induction and Test (SHALIT): A six-minute hypnotic induction and measurement scale. *International Journal of Clinical and Experimental Hypnosis, 27*(2), 111–124. doi:10.1080/00207147908407551

Kallio, S. I., & Ihamuotila, M. J. (1999). Finnish norms of the Harvard Group Scale of Hypnotic Susceptibility, Form A. *International Journal of Clinical and Experimental Hypnosis, 47*, 227–235. doi:10.1080/00207149908410034

Kekecs, Z., Bowers, J., Johnson, A., Kendrick, C., & Elkins, G. (2016). The Elkins Hypnotizability Scale: Assessment of reliability and validity. *International Journal of Clinical and Experimental Hypnosis, 64*(3), 285–304. doi:10.1080/00207144.2016.1171089

Lamas, J. R., del Valle-Inclan, F., Blanco, M. J., & Diaz, A. A. (1989). Spanish norms for the Harvard Group Scale of Hypnotic Susceptibility, Form A. *International Journal of Clinical and Experimental Hypnosis, 37*(3), 264–273. doi:10.1080/00207148908414477

Laurence, J., & Perry, C. (1982). Montreal norms for the Harvard Group Scale of Hypnotic Susceptibility, Form A. *International Journal of Clinical and Experimental Hypnosis, 30*(2), 167–176. doi:10.1080/00207148208407381

Liebeault, A. A. (1889). *Le sommeil provoqué et les états analogues* [Induced sleep and analogous states]. Paris, France: Doin.

Ludwig, A. M. (1966). The formal characteristics of therapeutic insight. *American Journal of Psychotherapy, 20*, 305–318. doi:10.1176/appi.psychotherapy.1966.20.2.305

Matthews, W. J., & Isenberg, G. L. (1995). Hypnosis with signing deaf and hearing subjects. *American Journal of Clinical Hypnosis, 38*(1), 27–38. doi:10.1080/00029157.1995.10403175

McConkey, K. M., Barnier, A. J., Maccallum, F. L., & Bishop, K. (1996). A normative and structural analysis of the HGSHS: A with a large Australian sample. *Australian Journal of Clinical and Experimental Hypnosis, 24*, 1–11.

Montgomery, A. H., DuHamel, K. N., & Redd, W. H. (2000). A meta-analysis of hypnotically induced analgesia: How effective is hypnosis? *International Journal of Clinical Hypnosis, 48*(2), 138–153. doi:10.1080/00207140008410045

Morgan, A. H., & Hilgard, J. R. (1978 Oct–1979 Jan). The Stanford Hypnotic Clinical Scale for Children (SHCS: Child). *American Journal of Clinical Hypnosis, 21*(2–3), 148–169. doi:10.1080/00029157.1978.10403969

Piccione, C., Hilgard, E. R., & Zimbardo, P. G. (1989). On the degree of stability of measured hypnotizability over a 25-year period. *Journal of Personality and Social Psychology, 56*(2), 289–295. doi:10.1037/0022-3514.56.2.289

Repka, R. J., & Nash, M. R. (1995). Hypnotic responsivity of the deaf: The development of the University of Tennessee Hypnotic Susceptibility Scale for the Deaf. *International Journal of Clinical and Experimental Hypnosis, 43*(3), 316–331. doi:10.1080/00207149508409973

Sapp, M., & Hitchcock, K. (2001). Harvard Group Scale with African American college students. *Sleep and Hypnosis, 3*(3), 111–117. Retrieved from http://www.sleepandhypnosis.org/ing/Pdf/da1a0decbc6044e49263c90043725fe8.pdf

Spanos, N. P., Radtke, H. L., Hodgins, D. C., Bertrand, L. D., Stam, H. J., & Dubreuil, D. L. (1983). The Carleton University Responsiveness to Suggestion Scale: Stability, reliability, and relationships with expectancy and hypnotic experiences. *Psychological Reports, 53*, 555–563. doi:10.2466/pr0.1983.53.2.555

Tart, C. T., Puthoff, H. E., & Targ, R. (Eds.). (1979). *Mind at large: Institute of Electrical and Electronics Engineers symposia on the nature of extrasensory perception*. New York, NY: Praeger.

Weitzenhoffer, A. M., & Hilgard, E. R. (1959). *Stanford Hypnotic Susceptibility Scale: Forms A and B*. Palo Alto, CA: Consulting Psychologists Press.

Weitzenhoffer, A. M., & Hilgard, E. R. (1962). *Stanford Hypnotic Susceptibility Scale: Form C*. Palo Alto, CA: Consulting Psychologists Press.

Woody, E., & Sadler, P. (2016). What can a hypnotic induction do? *American Journal of Clinical Hypnosis, 59*(2), 138–154. doi:10.1080/00029157.2016.1185004

Woody, E. Z., & Barnier, A. J. (2008). Hypnosis scales for the twenty-first century: What do we need and how should we use them? In M. R. Nash & A. J. Barnier (Eds), *The Oxford handbook of hypnosis: Theory, research and practice* (pp. 255–281). Oxford, UK: Oxford University Press.

Zachariae, R., Sommerlund, B., & Molay, F. (1996). Danish norms for the Harvard Group Scale of Hypnotic Susceptibility, Form A. *International Journal of Clinical and Experimental Hypnosis,44*(2), 140–152. doi:10.1080/00207149608416076

SECTION II

MINDFUL HYPNOTHERAPY BY SESSION

CHAPTER 7

THE SESSION-BY-SESSION PROCESS OF MINDFUL HYPNOTHERAPY

Love, compassion, joy and equanimity are the very nature of an enlightened person. They are the four aspects of true love within ourselves and within everyone and everything.

—Thich Nhat Hanh (1999)

Introduction

In its standardized iteration, mindful hypnotherapy (MH) consists of eight sessions. These sessions are designed to unite a mindful perspective with hypnotherapeutic methodology so as to help clients make profound changes in their lives. The intervention is designed to gradually build clients' understanding of mindfulness and their expertise in self-hypnosis, with the end goal of self-sufficiency and inner transformation by the end of session 8 (Chapter 15). In this chapter, we lay out the "linear progression" of each session—that is, how each session builds upon the session(s) before it and leads logically into the session that follows. Furthermore, clinicians are encouraged to *think holistically* about the material they are working with and understand how the content of each session interacts with the concepts from other sessions. This holistic perspective can enable a clinician to foreshadow material from later sessions and weave small parts of it into earlier sessions when opportunities arise. An understanding of the intervention as a whole can also enable a clinician to help a client reflect on earlier sessions with fresh eyes as a greater understanding of mindfulness emerges. A clinician's holistic understanding of the intervention will emerge organically with practice, but some initial thoughts are presented for each session under the "holistic integration" headings.

Audio Recordings of Hypnotic Inductions

HOMEWORK ASSIGNMENTS

Transcripts for hypnotic inductions by session are provided in Chapters 8 to 15 (corresponding to sessions 1–8). The transcripts for MH may be individualized depending on client preferences, goals, progress, and culture. For example, some clients may have a preference for individualized mental imagery (imagery for a lake, mountains, beach, desert, specific location, etc.) for a pleasant and safe place. Other clients may find that they prefer a slower or more rapid induction. The transcripts provided in each chapter are lengthier than many clients will need. The decision to include lengthier transcripts was made so that new hypnotherapists will find it easy to selectively edit out passages (rather than needing to generate new material during an induction). Ideally, the lengthier transcripts included in this book will also provide ample material to spark new ideas when generating novel transcripts. Despite these considerations, rest assured that many clients will find a standardized recording of the transcripts as written to be fully acceptable and beneficial. It is important that clients be provided with audio recordings of the hypnotic inductions for their home practice. Therefore, it is highly recommended that therapists' audio-record their hypnotic inductions in the course of MH and provide clients with the recording for each session.

CLINICIAN NOTE

Audio Recording

Each session of MH relies upon daily home practice. These daily home practice sessions reinforce the concepts that were introduced during the session and give the client something to focus on during the week.

Templates for these recordings are provided at the end of Chapters 8 to 15 that fit each session of MH. Once these recordings are complete, they can be reused for each client. Alternatively, clinicians may choose to record a personalized script for clients.

The homework assignment for each week can include providing specific instructions for self-awareness, reporting on progress, and identifying areas of benefit. The homework assignment for each session includes instructing the client to practice mindful self-hypnosis using the audio recordings at least once per day. Our experience has been that some clients prefer an mp3 file downloaded to their phone or computer, while others may prefer a CD recording.

Using the audio recordings of the hypnotic inductions for guided mindful practice lays the foundation needed for subsequent self-hypnosis without use of those audio recording for home practice. As clients progress through the MH sessions, daily self-hypnosis practice is generally encouraged in addition to home practice of guided self-hypnosis using the audio recordings. Appendix B of this book provides the "Mindful Self-Hypnosis Daily Practice Log" for monitoring home practice of mindful hypnosis with or without use of an audio recording. A sample audio recording is provided at https://bcove.video/3VrKQo0 and gives an example of the pacing of hypnotic suggestions while following the transcript provided.

Session 1: Awareness of the Present Moment

LINEAR PROGRESSION

Most people who grow up in an icy climate learn to deal with the hazards of winter. Snow and ice can make the sidewalk slick, but if people walk carefully, distribute their weight evenly, and take small steps, they can often avoid slipping and falling when they know that they are approaching an icy patch. However, the hidden hazard of any frigid climate is so-called black ice—ice that has frozen in such a way that it is invisible. Every winter, this kind of ice can cause even the most seasoned individuals to slip and fall because they simply don't see the danger beneath them.

Similarly, the task of mental and emotional transformation is always challenging. However, it becomes nearly impossible if a client isn't even aware of what is transpiring within the phenomenology of their own experience. Session 1 of MH (covered in detail in Chapter 8) focuses on building clients' awareness of their present-moment experiences, and it acts as a foundation for the skills that will be built later in the intervention. On the slippery path to change, awareness provides traction for later sessions. Even by itself, awareness of the present moment can be a powerful experience for some clients. If they are used to navigating most of their life on "auto-pilot," this session can be a startling awakening that can produce either wonder or disquiet. In later sessions, this awareness is shaped into a particular *kind* of attention: one that is characterized by open curiosity rather than "clinging to" particular experiences and "pushing away" others.

HOLISTIC INTEGRATION

In session 1, clinicians can ease clients' transition into later material by looking for opportunities to foster clients' curiosity about the experience of being in the present moment. Each clinician may have his or her own ways of inviting clients' curiosity about their experiences. One example might be to ask the client to pay attention to something familiar with a degree of attentiveness that leads the client to discover something new about it. If there is a ticking clock in the room, many clients might assume that the ticking sound is uniform and the sound is instantaneous. With many ticking clocks, this is not the case. The sound is rhythmic, but its tone changes slightly with each tick. Oftentimes the "tick" is not instantaneous, but is made up of several, nested sounds (some low pitched, some high pitched) that unfold over the course of a fraction of a second. When a person discovers something unexpected amidst the mundane through the simple act of paying attention, interest is often piqued. This curiosity can lead a client more easily into the lessons of the next session, which deal with bringing curiosity to the experiences as they unfold. The lesson learned through discovering something unexpected amidst a mundane experience is often nonconscious, but can nevertheless help a client begin to think mindfully in preparation for sessions 2 through 8.

Session 1 can also connect well with sessions 5 and 8 in small and subtle ways. For example, exhibiting compassion and attentive curiosity toward clients in each session can foster the budding of clients' own compassionate curiosity toward their experiences. In this way, clinicians can act as a model for their clients in sessions 1 to 4 (and beyond) and invite them to explicitly follow suit with compassionate behavior toward themselves in session 5. Furthermore, an orientation toward fostering clients' curiosity and self-efficacy can help sow the seeds for session 8 (transition to long-term practice) even in the very first session.

Sessions 2 and 3: Nonjudgmental Awareness of Physical Sensations, Emotions, and Thoughts

LINEAR PROGRESSION

Sessions 2 and 3 (refer to Chapters 9 and 10 for these sessions) build upon session 1 by modifying the *quality* of the present-moment attention that a client has been practicing over the course of the past week. Since session 1 relates to a concept that is familiar to many people (i.e., the importance of living in the moment), session 2 can feel like the first true step into unknown territory for a client. One thing that will aid clients amidst this unfamiliarity is that they will have completed a week's worth of practice and may be discovering new things about their experiences in the present moment. Therefore, the process of bringing an open curiosity to those experiences may not feel like such a leap. Meanwhile, session 3 will build upon the content covered in session 2 by helping clients to understand that the *principle* behind session 2 (nonjudgmental curiosity toward the five senses) can be applied to thoughts and feelings—not just to what they can perceive with their five senses.

HOLISTIC INTEGRATION

Sessions 2 and 3 are an integral part of MH, insofar as they are accomplishing three distinct roles. The first role is that nonjudgmental attention can bring new *insight*. Nonjudgmental awareness accomplishes this by allowing clients to make nuanced observations about the way they are thinking, feeling, and experiencing the world. This insight is aided by the "nonjudgmental" aspect of mindful awareness, because experiences that are scary or unpleasant can nevertheless be observed with equanimity. This mode of observation helps to counteract some of the distortions and biases that can interfere with accurate self-observation.

The second role that nonjudgmental attention serves is that it allows clients to take *action* based on what they directly observe to be true. Clients who have a deep insight into their own thoughts and experiences are better equipped to make wise choices about their well-being. This insight-oriented action can take the place of clients basing their decisions on their pleasure-seeking, pain-avoidant instincts. For example, for a client with social phobia, the prospect of speaking to a stranger could be so scary that the person avoids doing so—even when the avoidance is harmful to the client. Nonjudgmental awareness can build a client's distress tolerance, potentially allowing the individual to speak to a stranger despite the distress this may cause. When self-compassion and compassion for others is introduced in session 5, nonjudgmental awareness can also empower clients to act compassionately based on the insight they develop through nonjudgmental observation.

The third role that nonjudgmental awareness holds in relation to MH as a whole has to do with transforming the internal landscape of subjective experiences. The way that clients *relate* to their experiences can change the experience that is being observed. To understand how this could unfold, imagine for a moment that we could peer into a person's mind as an external observer. What might we see as we gaze upon this internal landscape? In a person who is constantly at war with the inner experiences, conflict would be a common sight. We might visualize such a person fighting against those things that are unpleasant in the individual's life (adding fuel to an already raging fire). In contrast, a person who is beginning to treat the inner experiences with equanimity and open curiosity might produce a different tableau. The hardships and obstacles that arise in this inner landscape are met with calmness, investigated with interest, and ultimately overcome or adapted to while maintaining harmony within oneself. Thus, a person who is making a mindful transformation in his or her life is not just learning to observe the world differently; that is, the act of *observation* also changes the experiences that are being observed. Sessions 2 and 3, therefore, pave the way for session 5 by forging a less bellicose internal landscape.

Lastly, sessions 2 and 3 lay a foundation for session 6: mindful awareness of values. Sessions 2 and 3 help the client develop the capacity to face difficult emotions and physical sensations, and over the course of the intervention, these skills are honed and practiced. The burgeoning ability to face difficult emotions and discomfort is put to good use in session 6, because session 6 challenges clients to enact core changes in their lives despite the presence of emotional barriers and discomfort. Most people can readily identify changes they *should* make in their life to be a better person, to be more successful, or to care for themselves more consistently and kindly. In the broadest of terms, one of the most common obstacles to making these changes is a compulsion to gravitate toward physical and emotional comfort even if it conflicts with our values. Likewise, we tend to cease our march toward change and wellness when we come up against that which is uncomfortable. Sessions 2 and 3 give clients the tools needed to overcome these obstacles. Nonjudgmental awareness instills in clients the freedom to choose actions that are more frequently based on their values and less frequently commanded by their unthinking instincts and habits.

Session 4: Mindful Self-Hypnosis

LINEAR PROGRESSION

Session 4's place (Chapter 11) in the progression of understanding is twofold. First, this session teaches clients a new and important skill: self-hypnosis. By itself, the skill of entering a hypnotic trance at will would be as inert as a hammer without a nail. Paired with specific treatment goals and with mindfulness, however, self-hypnosis becomes a powerful tool. Learning self-hypnosis will empower clients to use self-suggestion to follow through with the more action-oriented sessions that follow, in session 5 and beyond.

■ CLINICIAN NOTE

Mindful Self-Hypnosis Daily Practice Log

An important component of mindful hypnotherapy is the client's home practice of mindful self-hypnosis between sessions. The Mindful Self-Hypnosis Daily Practice Log (Appendix B) provides a convenient means for clients to record their practice with ratings of relaxation and mindfulness as well as comments and reflections regarding feelings of mindfulness (nonjudgmental awareness of breathing, sensation, thoughts, feelings, self, compassion).

Second, session 4 gives clients a week to pause and reflect further on the mindfulness material they have covered so far, since no new mindfulness concepts are introduced. For many clients, the material covered to this point will probably seem different from the way they are used to seeing the world. For clients who are starting to feel lost amidst the novelty of MH, session 4 offers a concrete, stepwise instruction that doesn't layer any new complexity on top of the mindfulness material that was already covered. In terms of didactic instruction, clients are given a specific set of steps that can enable them to lead themselves into and out of a hypnotic trance at will.

On an experiential level, clients will nevertheless continue to build upon their mindfulness skills through self-hypnosis. The process of self-hypnosis involves paying close attention to the present moment, getting in touch with one's own experiences so as to be a kind and compassionate guide to oneself. Following session 4, clients are expected to continue to practice the concrete skill of self-hypnosis in the following weeks. While they practice, they will also be making self-suggestions for greater mindfulness and should become more confident in their ability to view their experiences nonjudgmentally.

HOLISTIC INTEGRATION

Session 4 has a great potential for synergy with other MH material. Self-hypnosis is a flexible tool that clients can use to deepen their experience of mindfulness, support themselves in making difficult life changes, and help themselves to practice more regularly through posthypnotic suggestions. Furthermore, session 4 relates to session 8 specifically, insofar as it gives clients a useful tool for directing their own practice when their time with an MH clinician ends.

Session 5: Compassion

LINEAR PROGRESSION

Session 5 (Chapter 12) continues to develop further insight for clients by bringing attention to the importance of compassion. It also draws upon the sessions that came before to enact healthy changes in clients' lives that are based upon a clear understanding of their needs. Session 5 makes use of sessions 1 to 3 by enabling clients to act despite physical or emotional discomfort. For clients who are in the habit of denying themselves comfort because of a rigid thought pattern or out of habit, session 3 allows them to recognize and confront these mental barriers if they interfere with genuine self-compassion. Meanwhile, session 4 allows clients to make use of self-suggestions to assist them in making mental, emotional, and behavioral changes in line with their new understanding of themselves.

Canny clinicians might also consider how they can lay an early foundation for session 6. For example, a clinician might invite a client to consider things such as:

- What kinds of compassionate actions and attitudes could help you to thrive?
- What *might* you be capable of if you didn't hold yourself back with self-flagellation and/or hostility toward others?

This line of thinking is congruent with session 5's main themes, but also intersects with session 6's orientation toward exploring one's values and acting in accordance with these values.

HOLISTIC INTEGRATION

While session 5 is *facilitated* by previous sessions, it also gives new meaning to previous sessions. Once clients begin to adopt a more compassionate view of themselves and others, they can meld this new sense of compassion with their nonjudgmental awareness. Nonjudgmental attention can become not just an act of curiosity, but an act of self-compassion. Clients can notice when they are battling against an unpleasant sensation or when they are trying to cling to something pleasant that is no longer there. Upon noticing their internal state of reactivity, mindful attention can be a means of self-care in the midst of distress.

Session 6: Mindful Awareness of Values

LINEAR PROGRESSION

Like session 5, session 6 (Chapter 13) is a blend of insight and action. This session acts as a platform for exploring clients' sense of meaning in life, their values, and the direction they would like to head in life if they were free from internal barriers. The session also invites clients to begin living with greater integrity as these values are uncovered. Using all of the varied tools and perspectives presented in sessions 1 to 5, clients are then in a strong position to forge a meaningful path of their own choosing.

HOLISTIC INTEGRATION

By session 6 of MH, many clients have experienced significant shifts in the way they experience themselves and the world. This inner change and the topics of session 6 may unlock new opportunities for insight as a client reflects on material from earlier in the intervention. For example, some clients may now see "present-moment awareness" (session 1) as an opportunity not only to observe their experiences, but also to savor the present-moment experience of being alive. Clients' nonjudgmental exploration of their experiences in session 2 may have allowed them to notice subtle pleasant sensations among predominantly unpleasant ones (and vice versa). After session 6, clients may begin to see this attentiveness to the nuances of their experience as a part of a much larger picture, enabling them to experience a sustained sense of meaning even amidst hardship and difficulty. Finally, session 6 presages session 8 by empowering clients to discover their own path forward, basing their decisions on their own values and their desire to live a rich life in accordance with those values.

Session 7: Integration of Mindful Hypnotherapy

LINEAR PROGRESSION

The intent behind session 7 (Chapter 14) is that it can be used flexibly to address a client's specific needs using the mindful hypnosis skills that have been introduced in previous sessions. Session 7 is an ideal time to help clients understand the concrete applications of mindfulness in their own lives if they are still having trouble connecting the material to their individualized treatment goals. For example, if a client has become more mindful in the context of an emotionally abusive relationship but doesn't see how this awareness can be used to change the situation, session 7 might focus on how to set appropriate boundaries or leave the relationship. MH can be used to help clients break free from habitual responses to abuse and help them tolerate the uncertainty that will inevitably unfold during this process.

If a client is having difficulty understanding or integrating material from one of the previous sessions, session 7 can also be devoted to a targeted, in-depth discussion of previous material. For example, some clients with anxiety and stress may still have ruminative thoughts that trouble them or panic attacks that are so intense that they can't seem to maintain an attitude of mindful acceptance toward them. Other clients may be *aware* of the acts of self-compassion that would help them, but are noticing that they consistently let these opportunities for self-compassion pass by without acting on them. Session 7 is an excellent chance to explore, discuss, and resolve these issues and answer clients' lingering questions.

HOLISTIC INTEGRATION

Session 7 can also be used to enhance clients' holistic understanding of mindful hypnosis. As clients gain practice with the disparate parts of mindfulness, they can develop an understanding of mindfulness as a single construct with multiple facets. Developing this perspective can help clients to apply their mindful hypnosis skills independently once treatment has come to an end. For example, this session could help clients understand how awareness of the present moment fits together with compassion, and how both of these themes fit together with non-judgmental awareness.

Session 8: Transition to Long-Term Practice

By session 8 (Chapter 15), the linear progression of the previous sessions and the holistic integration of MH converge. Over the course of the intervention, clients have been equipped with powerful new tools in the form of hypnosis and self-hypnosis. Their mindful attitude will enable them to "turn toward" difficult experiences, and the insights gained by careful, curious attention can allow them to make wiser decisions in their lives. These changes can be used to orient clients toward a life path that is guided by their own values rather than by blind instinct or rote habit. Therefore, the final step in MH is to help clients to recognize and acknowledge the transformation of the previous 7 weeks and help launch them into the future as the arbiters of their own destiny.

Summary

MH follows a process of linear progression and holistic integration to achieve mindfulness goals, values, and outcomes. An eight-session program of MH can be provided individually or in a group setting. Audio recordings of sessions are generally provided to clients for home practice between sessions. The last session provides an orientation to transition to long-term practice. The eight sessions of MH are presented in greater detail in Chapters 8 through 15 of this book.

REFERENCE

Hanh, T. N. (1999). *The heart of Buddha's teachings: Transforming suffering into peace, joy, and liberation*. New York: NY: Broadway Books.

CHAPTER 8

Session 1

RELAXATION AND PRESENT-MOMENT AWARENESS

We can make our minds so like still water that beings gather about us that they may see, it may be, their own images, and so live for a moment with a clearer, perhaps even with a fiercer life because of our quiet.

—*W. B. Yeats (1893/2011)*

Introduction

During the first session of mindful hypnotherapy, the most important goal is to establish rapport and a solid therapeutic relationship. Without these, any hypnotherapy intervention will be fraught with difficulty, and hypnotic inductions are likely to fail altogether. Secondary goals for session 1 are to orient clients to mindfulness and hypnosis and guide clients through their first hypnotic induction. Throughout this chapter, we provide examples of how these goals might be accomplished through clinical vignettes based on the experiences we have had with clients. Please note, as you read on through this chapter, that the goals for session 1 and beyond can be accomplished through the clinician's *own* therapeutic style, and therapists shouldn't feel constrained by the language or examples that we provide. Instead, the examples provided are meant to give a practical sense of how these concepts *could* be conveyed to real clients, and the post-vignette breakdown is meant to draw out salient points to keep in mind as you are working through each of the session's goals.

During the first session of mindful hypnotherapy, time management is important for therapists planning to use the standard eight-session model presented in this book.[1] During session 1, the therapist must complete a brief intake, orient the client to mindfulness and hypnosis, and complete a hypnotic induction. With experience and practice, most therapists should find that this becomes second nature, although when first learning this intervention it may create a greater sense of ease to reserve more time for the first session. This will allow a more leisurely pace for the session's myriad tasks until the process becomes more streamlined and familiar.

A clinician wishing to adhere more closely to the standardized mindful hypnotherapy (MH) protocol should have the materials required for session 1 on hand. These include the hypnotic induction script for session 1 and an audio recording of the hypnotic induction to provide to the client for home practice. If desired, the hypnotic induction can be recorded during the session on a smartphone or other recording device, provided that proper consent for recording is obtained. Take some time to familiarize yourself with the session content beforehand so that you can implement it faithfully and appropriately with whatever presenting questions and concerns the client has. For the best possible results, we recommend becoming familiar with the entire protocol prior to session 1. This will enable you to think strategically as a clinician, "foreshadowing" later sessions with conversations and examples that will fit well with the content that occurs later in treatment.

Introducing Mindfulness

Since there are many practices that people call "mindful" and many definitions for mindfulness, it is important to clearly establish a common lexicon with clients and let them know what *you* mean by mindfulness (or how the term is going to be used during treatment). The "true" meaning of mindfulness is an issue that may be of extraordinary importance in a religious or spiritual context and is an issue worthy of due consideration and respect. In a therapeutic context, it is merely important that each client understand what the therapist means when

---

[1]For situations where an expanded format is clinically preferable or indicated, the same concepts and goals would apply, but can be implemented at a slower pace.

speaking about mindfulness.[2] If the client engages in activities that are characterized by distraction or relaxation and this has been helpful for the client, it is generally of greater clinical utility to augment these with MH rather than replace them or get into a battle of semantics. The following vignette provides an example of how to introduce mindfulness within the context of MH session 1.

Therapist: *What do you know about mindfulness already? What have you heard?*

Client: *Well, in yoga sometimes we do "mindful breathing" at the end of the session.*

Therapist: *Excellent! What's that like? What do you do?*

Client: *Well, basically we lay still, relax, and just kind of tune out for a while and we breathe deeply.*

Therapist: *All right, have you had any other experiences with mindfulness?*

Client: *Well, sometimes I listen to mindfulness recordings through a smartphone app. They've got relaxing music, and guided imagery, and it's a great way to just think of nothing and let my mind drift.*

Therapist: *It sounds like those things have been really helpful to you in the past. If so, I encourage you to keep using them, but I'd like to give you another take on mindfulness that you can add to your repertoire of things to help you. There are a lot of different definitions of mindfulness, and a lot of different approaches you might take. The way I'll be talking about mindfulness involves a kind of curiosity and openness about the experiences you're having right here, right now. Those experiences may be physical (things you can see, touch, hear, and so on), or they might be thoughts or feelings. The main idea is that regardless of what's going on, you get in touch with those experiences, without trying to mentally cling to them or push them away. When you're being mindful, you aim to just "be with" your present-moment experiences without resisting them or wallowing in them.*

Client: *Huh. I was with you until you said that I don't resist experiences. Isn't that like giving up? I mean, there are some things in life that you should*

---

[2]By this vignette, the authors do not intend to establish that the framework for mindfulness we use is the most "legitimate," or to imply that yoga is characterized by distraction or relaxation and isn't a mindfulness activity (quite the contrary, actually). The example merely illustrates that a client may come in with a myriad of preconceptions about mindfulness or none at all, and it is important for a client and therapist to establish a common language to avoid misunderstandings.

resist, like systematic oppression or people who want to take advantage of you. The way you describe mindfulness sounds a lot like giving up.

Therapist: *Oh wow, I'm glad you brought that up! Mindfulness does involve a certain "acceptance" of your experiences as they are, but that's not the same as "giving up" or "accepting defeat." It's a matter of really opening your eyes and getting in tune with what's going on around you and within you. What you do with that insight is up to you. We're all pushed and pulled by our reactions to experiences, and mindfulness is one way to gain greater insight into what's going on and to have a greater degree of freedom in your actions.*

Client: *OK...what do you mean?*

Therapist: *Imagine that you want to go to a party, but you're feeling anxious because you don't know many people there. If the anxiety's really strong, you might decide to stay home because you can't stand to be that anxious, right?*

Client: *Right.*

Therapist: *In that case, your desire to avoid anxiety makes you stay home. If you could adopt a more neutral stance toward your anxiety, and accept that it is there, then you can decide to stay home or you can decide to go out, but the choice is yours. You're not compelled so strongly by your internal and external experiences that you have to change them. You can decide for yourself whether to change them, and you can choose the action that will help you to thrive, or the one that is most in line with your personal values.*

There are two important points to note about this vignette. First, this example client has heard of mindfulness, and the session provides an opportunity for psychoeducation regarding a common understanding of mindfulness. The client's description of yoga's approach to mindfulness may or may not be what was intended by the yoga teacher. Regardless, the therapist focuses on working with the client's description and experience to develop a different understanding for the purpose of the intervention.

The second important point illustrated in the vignette is that mindfulness is a categorically different way of experiencing the world and is easily misunderstood in the beginning phases of treatment. Although many clients will have no initial questions about mindfulness, therapists should be ready to answer difficult questions if they arise. Therapists using MH are encouraged to continue their own education and practice of mindfulness so that they can develop a nuanced understanding of the practice. This can help to answer challenging questions honestly and openly. Questions and challenges should be welcomed, as this will allow the therapist to directly address misconceptions and increase the client's understanding of mindfulness. After discussing mindfulness, the next task in MH is to review the concept of hypnosis and the many myths that surround it.

Introducing Hypnosis

Many clients are interested in hypnosis but may have limited understanding of the phenomenon or some misconceptions about it. Therefore, it is recommended that the clinician begin by asking the client about any prior experience with hypnosis or experience with self-hypnosis and discuss the use of hypnosis in counseling, psychotherapy, and medicine. As previously noted, hypnosis is defined as "a state of consciousness involving focused attention and reduced peripheral awareness" (Elkins, Barabasz, Council, & Spiegel, 2015). Focused attention and relaxation are commonly used methods of entering a hypnotic state, and the hypnotic state itself generally involves an increased awareness of internal experiences as peripheral awareness fades. During a hypnotic induction, the therapist guides the client through the process of focusing attention. When experiencing a hypnotic state, individuals can become more receptive to beneficial positive ideas and experiences.

For some clients, it may be helpful to provide them with a brief historical overview of hypnosis. Briefly, the history of hypnosis is often thought to have begun with Franz Anton Mesmer (1734–1815), a Viennese physician who practiced "mesmerism." However, hypnotic methods of *focused attention, altered states of consciousness,* and *suggestion* have been used for centuries and across cultures. Certainly, the methods of suggested focus of attention, relaxation, mental imagery, and suggestion of positive ideas predate Mesmer by thousands of years. For example, Muses (1972) provides a compelling narrative that trance induction techniques were used in ancient Egypt more than 3,000 years ago. The term "hypnosis" was coined by a Scottish physician by the name of James Braid (1785–1860). Braid initially thought hypnosis was like sleep, but eventually recognized that hypnosis was not sleep but rather a state of focused attention and receptivity to suggestion.

In introducing hypnosis, it should be emphasized that it is something that the client does, not something that is done to the client. However, it should be noted that hypnosis has sometimes been misrepresented in movies and stage hypnotist shows. Some of the more common questions or misconceptions that may arise in the first session are summarized next.

- ***Can everyone be hypnotized?***

  Although people vary in their hypnotic abilities, virtually everyone has the capacity to focus attention, become absorbed in the experience of hypnosis, and respond to hypnotic suggestions. It is true that some people respond more quickly than others, but with practice almost all people can achieve the same benefits from hypnosis. It just may take some people longer than others or more sessions.

- ***Is the hypnotic state the same as sleep?***

  No, hypnosis involves a state of focused attention. Persons may be relaxed, and appear to be asleep, but are not asleep. Sleep and hypnosis are completely different. However, in a deep hypnotic state with suggestions for relaxation, some patients may fall asleep.
- ***Will hypnosis make me do something I don't want to do?***

  No, the goal of hypnotherapy is to empower the client. It will help you achieve a hypnotic state and experience the things you want to experience. It is not a form of "mind control" or something that will make you do anything you do not want to do. On the contrary, it will help you do things you want to do but can't through conscious effort alone.

Although these questions can be very effectively addressed through psychoeducation, it is worth noting that *some* questions are best answered through direct experience rather than semantic understanding. It has been said that in a sense "all hypnosis is self-hypnosis"—meaning that hypnosis is an innate human capacity to experience focused attention and receptivity to positive suggestions rather than a special power that is granted from another person. *The goal of hypnotherapy is to empower the client* (Elkins, 2014). It is also important to understand that even when a client does not ask questions or challenge directly, misperceptions may still exist. Clear instruction and eliciting client feedback/reflection can help to dispel these misperceptions and deepen the client's understanding of hypnosis. The sample vignette illustrates some ways of introducing hypnosis.

Therapist: *Have you had any previous experience with hypnosis?*

Client: *No, I haven't had any personal experience with it. I'm interested to learn more about it, though.*

Therapist: *Very good. Let's start by talking about what hypnosis is and how it can be used for health and well-being. Hypnosis is defined as "a state of consciousness involving focused attention and reduced peripheral awareness." That means that during a hypnotic induction you are guided to focus your attention and then suggestions are given to help you achieve your goals.*

Client: *I've seen it at a stage hypnosis show in Las Vegas once. Is it different than that?*

Therapist: *That's right. Stage hypnotist shows are like "magic shows" that are designed for entertainment. Those shows are entertaining but promote misconceptions about hypnosis such as being controlled or acting in an embarrassing way. Those ideas have nothing to do with mindful hypnosis and helping you learn how to relax, focus attention, and learn self-hypnosis.*

Client: *So, I won't bark like a dog [laughing]?*

Therapist: *Right [laughing], no dog barking. Mindful hypnosis can include focusing on your breathing, suggestions to relax, mental imagery, and other suggestions. When you have listened to guided mindfulness recordings on an app, that could be considered as a form of self-hypnosis, or at least a state of mind that is very similar to what you may experience today.*

Client: *So, I won't be asleep?*

Therapist: *That is correct. When you practice hypnosis, you can be aware of the suggestions that I give you. It's true that some people use self-hypnosis at night to help them sleep better, and there is some research that shows that self-hypnosis can improve sleep quality and can help some people sleep better. But during a hypnotic induction you will be awake unless you want to go to sleep.*

Client: *Sounds good.*

Therapist: *Another thing you should keep in mind is that when you practice self-hypnosis with the audio recordings that I will give to you, you should practice only in a time and place where you can close your eyes and focus your attention. You should not listen to the recordings while you are driving or engaged in any activity that requires that you pay attention to what is going on around you.*

Client: *So you mentioned mindfulness before … how does the hypnosis and the mindfulness fit together?*

Therapist: *Mindfulness and hypnosis are complementary. Hypnotic inductions and practicing self-hypnosis can be a way to experience mindfulness and a way to deliver suggestions for greater mindfulness—for example, suggestions to focus your attention on your breathing; nonjudgmental experiencing of your thoughts, feelings, and sensations; or experience greater acceptance or more feelings of compassion.*

Client: *So hypnosis is kind of like a way to take it all in?*

Therapist: *Yes, with mindful hypnotherapy the goals are for both acceptance and change. You can experience present-moment awareness and mindfulness. Practicing with self-hypnosis and the home-practice audio can facilitate this process. Hypnosis can be thought of as a particular way of delivering mindfulness suggestions. Also, hypnotic inductions can include individualized* *suggestions to become more relaxed, less stressed, or reduce symptoms. Mindful hypnotherapy is goal directed, and suggestions are also focused on changing symptoms such as depression, pain, and anxiety. For example, there has been quite a bit of research showing that integrating hypnotherapy can be effective in reducing symptoms of pain, irritable bowel syndrome, anxiety, hot flashes, and other symptoms. As you practice mindful hypnosis, you may identify some additional ways it can help you, such as sleeping better like we just discussed!*

Client: *I think I understand. So you mentioned a hypnotic "induction"? How does a hypnotic induction work?*

Therapist: *Great question. During our hypnotic induction today, I will ask you to focus your attention on a spot on the wall. I will then give you suggestions to close your eyes and to relax. Suggestions will be given to deepen the hypnotic state and then I will give you some suggestions for mental imagery. Our theme for the hypnotic induction today is to experience present-moment awareness. We will talk some more about "present-moment awareness" before the hypnotic induction, but does that all sound OK to you?*

Client: *Yes, I'm looking forward to getting started!*

Hypnosis has a principle of "pacing and leading" (see Chapter 5) the client during a hypnotic induction, and this principle is just as important to integrate throughout the therapy session. In keeping with this principle, it will be important to gauge whether a client is sufficiently receptive to the MH approach to proceed. A client should have either a positive expectancy or a neutral curiosity about MH before proceeding, and ambivalence/resistance should be fully addressed prior to hypnosis. Further explanation or simple experiential mindfulness or hypnosis examples can be provided as needed to help address any significant ambivalence if it exists after the preparatory discussions.

Strategic Themes of Session 1: Present-Moment Awareness

Awareness of the present moment is the essential basis for the practice of mindful hypnosis. The surface-level rationale for this assertion is simple: To be nonjudgmentally aware of an experience in a mindful way, you must first be aware of that experience. Present-moment awareness is taught in the first session of MH so that it can serve as a scaffold for later mindfulness concepts. Fortunately, the importance of present-moment awareness is likely to be a familiar concept to many clients, even if they have not had prior experience with mindfulness. Idioms such as "stop and smell the roses" are common in Western culture, as are suggestions to "enjoy the moment" or "stop and take a deep breath" when life gets overwhelming. There seems to be an intuitively recognized truth across cultures that present-moment focus can be restorative: either a balancing force when life becomes hectic or a means to enhance the quality of a pleasant experience. The familiarity of this concept is an excellent place to start MH treatment because it takes mindfulness (a concept that is sometimes regarded as esoteric and mysterious) and makes it more accessible and intuitive.

Most clients will recognize the importance of present-moment awareness and will not question the ontological assertion that "experiences unfold in the present moment." During the first session of MH, the importance of present-moment awareness can be explained simply and in pragmatic terms. For example, a therapist might relate this concept to the client's own experiences of being daunted by all of the things that are waiting to get done (feeling overwhelmed by tasks that are not immediately at hand) or things that have happened in the past. Another approach would be to invite the client to reflect on how much time he or she actually spend paying attention to the present moment versus the future or the past. The therapist might then inquire about the impact of an excessive future/past focus and how this has led to feelings of being stressed or overwhelmed. If a client "buys in" to the idea of mindfulness and is willing to practice diligently over the course of treatment, the value of present-focused awareness will become self-evident.

Of course, some clients will be so skeptical or anxious about change that they will question whether focus on the present moment is valuable or even possible with their busy schedule. Therefore, in session 1 the therapist should screen for hidden or overt reservations about learning mindfulness and about adopting a present-focus specifically. If a client has reservations about incorporating present-focused awareness, these concerns should be addressed before proceeding with other tasks of MH. For anxious, busy, and task-driven clients, it may be helpful to make the case that even 5 to 10 minutes of present-focused awareness can help rest and restore the mind, enabling more *efficient* and *effective* mental activity during the rest of the day. For other clients with reservations, an appeal might be made by allowing them to expound on the pros and cons of making a life change. The status quo may have become untenable for many clients, but change is nevertheless a daunting endeavor that has its own risks and discomforts. If clients are willing to put aside a half-hour for formal practice and to integrate informal mindfulness into their day for just 8 weeks, this investment of time and energy may come to have a transformative effect on their life. Clients who experience a significant life change at the end of this time can decide for themselves whether continued practice is worth the benefits.

CLINICIAN NOTE

Experiential Learning

As an alternative or a complement to introducing present-moment awareness didactically, the *concept* of experiences unfolding in the present can be introduced with simple experiential exercises that are generally well received. For example, a clinician might ask a client to describe an unobtrusive object or sound in the room in robust detail (is the sound loud or soft? Near or far? Is it sharp? Warbling? and so on). To do this exercise successfully, clients will have to pay attention to their present-moment experiences so that they can describe their perception in detail. After clients have had a chance to "settle in" to this experience over the course of several minutes, the clinician should ask if they notice any difference in how they feel. Keep in mind that such an exercise may or may not result in a change in mood state. The main point of the exercise is to give clients a direct experience of what it is like to be in the present moment, as well as give them a concrete means of doing so.

Introducing Awareness of the Present Moment: Sample Vignette

The next vignette is a typical one based on the authors' experiences of using mindfulness with clients. In the example provided, the client is at least moderately receptive and has an appropriate degree of rapport with the therapist. Some clients will be less dubious about mindfulness or will be more insistent about the need to directly change symptoms, while other clients will be more receptive or will even have an experience of mindfulness through other activities such as meditation or yoga.

Therapist: *Mindful hypnosis practice starts with paying attention to what's going on in the "here and now." Most of us spend most of our time thinking about the future or the past, or we're lost in our imagination. In fact, most of us only pay enough attention to what's going on in this room in this instant to avoid bumping into the furniture! Is any of that sounding familiar?*

Client: *[Chuckles and nods] Yeah...I guess I spend a lot of time worrying about the future, thinking about all the things I have to do later, that kind of thing.*

Therapist: *Thinking about those things isn't bad! It's natural and sometimes it can be really helpful to plan for the future and reflect on important things. The problem is that so many of us spend so much time doing those things that we* *lose track of the life that we're living now. It's like this: The past and the future are like two heavy bags that you're carrying around with you wherever you go. There may be important things in those bags! Maybe it would be OK to put them down every once in a while and just rest for a moment in the present, though.*

Client: *OK, I think I understand. It would be nice to stop worrying, but it seems like I just can't stop.*

Therapist: *Well let's see what we can do to help you experience the present moment more fully. I think that what we do here can help you with that, but I just want to clarify that this mindfulness intervention isn't really designed to get rid of your unpleasant experiences like anxiety or sadness or pain. It's designed to help you to find peace and feel more "grounded," regardless of whether unpleasant experiences are present or not.*

Client: *Huh. Um…OK [ambivalently].*

Therapist: *We'll get into that a bit later, and I think with time it will start to make sense, but for now, I'd like to see if we can just carve out a bit of space for you in the present moment. That perpetual worry you mentioned before can feel like you're swimming around in an ocean, and if you're in it for too long, it can feel like you're drowning, struggling just to keep your head above the water.*

Client: *Mmhmm.*

Therapist: *If you can find an island to rest on, though, even for just a little while, it can really change the experience. If you rest for just a bit and focus on the present moment, you can go about the rest of your day feeling more focused, more productive, and more refreshed.*

Client: *That would be really nice. The problem is, every time I try to stop worrying, I can only get rid of those thoughts for a split second before I'm worrying about something else, or worrying about the same thing I was before! I'm willing to try, but I don't know if I can do it.*

Note in the preceding exchange that the client continues to move toward looking for a "fix" for worry and is oriented toward changing personal experiences. This will be the case in the substantial majority of clients, and it presents the therapist with an opportunity for an informal assessment of how much a client is embracing the mindfulness orientation to experiences.

Over the course of therapy, a client may move from statements such as this:

> I was really worried, and I just couldn't stand it! I wish this anxiety would *just go away*, because it's ruining my life. Every time it hits me, it just derails everything I want to be doing with my life and I just *have to* drop it all and *distract myself* to calm down.

to more calm, self-aware, and accepting statements such as this:

> I *noticed* that when I got worried, my stomach clenched up and I felt this urge rise within me that felt like I wanted to run away; but I was able to just notice that feeling and let it be. With time, it faded away all on its own, but at that point I didn't even care whether or not it did. It's just anxiety, and it doesn't need to control me.

Both mindfulness therapies and traditional hypnotherapy can reduce symptoms and distress. One of the primary differences between them is that in hypnotherapy, the aim is to reduce symptoms; distress then naturally fades away as a consequence of having fewer symptoms or reducing symptom severity. In mindfulness, the aim is to reduce distress (through changing a client's relationship with personal experiences). As a client's distress abates, the symptoms often begin to fade and lessen in severity owing to the reduced reactivity toward the client's own experiences. When a client is being mindfully aware of an experience as it unfolds, it is helpful to set aside the anticipation of what the experience *will* be like and what it *has* been like in the past, and to instead cultivate an open mind regarding what it *is* like in the present.[3] This present-centered attitude toward awareness helps reduce the distortions of an experience that come from pre- and post-experience bias and helps avoid overlooking details that would otherwise go unnoticed owing to the fixation on some aspects of the experience while ignoring others.

We recommend asking clients before and after hypnosis what their stress level is on a scale from 1 to 10. Collecting a quick measure of stress before and after hypnosis serves two purposes. First, it can help a therapist to track the client's overall response to hypnosis. This is useful information because it helps to monitor treatment gains and determine whether some changes need to be made to treatment along the way. The second purpose of tracking a client's subjective level of stress is that it can improve treatment gains. In most cases, a client will experience a greater degree of relaxation after a hypnotic induction than beforehand. This helps to demonstrate to the client in concrete terms that hypnosis is an effective intervention, which creates a positive feedback loop wherein the initial efficacy of MH will result in greater belief in the effectiveness of MH. Greater belief in treatment effectiveness can enhance the response and may

---

[3]If anticipation can't be set aside, a person can instead become mindfully aware of the thoughts, associations, and anticipation that arise about an experience.

also increase a client's compliance with following through with the home-practice element of MH.

Hypnotic Induction for Present-Moment Awareness

INTRODUCTION AND SETTING EXPECTANCY

During this session of mindfulness-based hypnosis, suggestions will be given for achieving a state of deep mental and physical relaxation. This will allow you to be more mindful and relaxed as a default state of mind...and you will also be able to enter this state of mind at will. Within this relaxed state, it will be possible to focus your attention on your breathing so that other things...concerns about the past and concerns about the future...fade for a time...into the background of your consciousness. Your level of stress will be reduced, and you can experience a greater sense of peace and calmness...and a greater mindfulness of your own inner experience...of relaxation...of breathing... focusing on the present moment.... If this is all right with you...now...please begin by just bringing your thumb and middle finger together so that you can notice the feeling of them touching... Either the thumb and finger of your right hand or your left hand...whichever one feels right to you.

FOCUS OF ATTENTION

Alright, now look closely at the thumb and finger...and begin by focusing your attention on the feeling of the finger and thumb as they are together...Notice the slight pressure of the very point where they touch...keeping your attention there...and concentrating on that...feeling...and as you do...soon allowing other things to begin to fade into the background...good. You can hear my voice...and as you concentrate, perhaps you can soon begin to feel more relaxed. Concentrate intensely now...so that other things are beginning to fade into the background. As they fade into the background...soon drifting into a deep hypnotic state.

EYE CLOSURE

Now just take a deep breath of air, hold it...hold...and now as you breathe out, letting all of the tension go and allowing the eyelids to close...good. Now let your hand and the fingers relax.

FOCUS ON BREATHING

Bring your attention now to your breathing...as you breathe in [on in-breath] and out [on out-breath]...noticing, more and more a relaxed feeling. Now take another deep breath of air, hold it, and as you release the air and breathe out...settling into a deeper state of hypnosis. Each time you breathe out...the mind and the body work together to achieve a deep state of comfort and relaxation.

SUGGESTIONS FOR RELAXATION

And with each breath, you will notice that you naturally can become more and more deeply relaxed...each breath allowing more and more tension to flow from your body...every muscle and every fiber of your body becoming so deeply relaxed...Breathing freely and deeply...and finding more and more comfort and calm feelings...and as you become more deeply relaxed, you're drifting into an even deeper level of hypnosis and mindfulness.

SUGGESTIONS FOR COMFORT

And as this relaxation becomes more complete. . .finding a feeling of comfort...feeling safe and secure. And as you enter a mindful state...peaceful feelings begin to arise and grow from within you...deepening your feeling of comfort and security. You may notice that the feeling begins now... growing...feeling calm and secure. Feeling so calm that nothing bothers or interferes with this feeling of comfort.

ALTERATION IN SENSATIONS

And from time to time, you may notice a floating feeling, drifting and floating as if you were floating on a cloud, more and more relaxed...as you drift into hypnosis...changes in sensations naturally occur...just noticing and accepting whatever feelings or sensations come to you. Your thoughts may drift from time to time...and yet when they do, you will find that you will soon become aware of the fact that they have drifted...and your thoughts soon return to the present moment...finding that your awareness always returns back to the present moment. And as you notice now whatever feelings and sensations are present...allowing those feelings and sensations to take you into a deeper level of hypnosis.

DEEPENING SUGGESTIONS

And as you hear my voice count from 10 to 1, with each number finding yourself drifting into an even deeper level of hypnosis.

[Count each number as the patient exhales]

Ten ...deeper and deeper relaxed...letting all the tension go from your forehead, face, neck, and shoulders.

Nine ...deeper relaxed...your neck goes limp, your jaw goes slack as all the tension drifts away.

Eight ...deeply calm and that wave of relaxation spreads across your arms and shoulders.

Seven ...your upper back and your lower back relaxed and calm.

Six ...deeper and deeper relaxed, halfway there, twice as relaxed...all of the tension drifts away and finding a feeling of peace.

Five ...deeper and even more calm...back, chest, and stomach relax.

Four ...arms, legs, and feet...that wave of relaxation spreads down your legs and into your feet.

Three ...a more peaceful state.

Two ...deeply relaxed.

One ...comfortably relaxed and able to notice just the present moment and accepting without judging...each thing that you notice.

SUGGESTIONS FOR PRESENT-MOMENT AWARENESS

And within this mindful...hypnotic relaxation...it is possible to experience things in a different way...than you usually do. Soon, you will find your full attention focused on the present moment...setting thoughts of the future and thoughts of the past aside for a time...able to effortlessly focus on the present moment...attending fully to each sight, sound, smell, sensation...thought and emotion...as they enter your experience...and then letting them go as new experiences continually arise...in the present. And...so awareness of your breathing can come to you again...effortlessly...automatically...allow yourself to trust your body...your breath doesn't need to be changed or controlled in any way...your body takes in the air it needs, when it needs it...and you can just observe as this happens, and become aware of the sensations...noticing your breathing...and the feelings of breathing in and breathing out...noticing the feeling in your chest...and going into a deeper hypnotic state...noticing the coolness of the air as you breathe in...and the feeling of "letting go" as you breathe out...and drifting...drifting into a deeper hypnotic state...so that the past and the future...they...fade more and more into the background...fade more and more...and possibly, fade to the point where the only thing that remains in your awareness...is the present moment...and noticing...just noticing...automatically...effortlessly...your breathing.

SUGGESTIONS FOR IMAGERY AND AWARENESS

And...within this state of hypnotic relaxation...it is possible for images to come into your mind...images...that allow you to focus on the experiences that you have, and soon you will be able to become aware...a beautiful flower...perhaps a rose... or it may be a different flower...you may notice color first...or the feeling of being in a flower garden...certainly a pleasant... relaxing place...where you can see a...flower...Just allow it to come to you...nothing you need to do...just drift deeper relaxed and...you might want to take a deep breath of the flower...and the relaxation becomes more complete...relaxed...and comfortable.

As you go on further...notice that you have less stress...and a greater feeling of well-being...finding that you can experience being in a peaceful place where you notice and experience everything that is there...every sensation, and as you pay attention to these things, notice that your mind is becoming more and more focused...more and more able to really notice the nuances of each experience...and allowing yourself to become curious about each new experience...as you allow the image of a flower to come to you.

SUGGESTED EXPERIENCE OF A FLOWER

Now...notice which kind of flower you begin to see and experience...Notice each petal of that flower...Notice the color...the texture...the smell...whatever comes to you...as you can experience a beautiful flower...whatever you notice.

SUGGESTED AWARENESS OF CHANGE

And as you notice these things in exquisite detail while the experiences are present...other sensations...images...thoughts may occur...as they naturally do...It is possible to observe and notice these images...as they are allowed to just pass on by...letting them go as you notice other images and experiences...and other ones after that...as each image or sensation emerges...allowing it then to pass as you remain grounded in the present moment. [Pause 10 seconds]

POSTHYPNOTIC SUGGESTIONS FOR AWARENESS OF PRESENT MOMENT

And as you do, you...more and more...every day...will become able to achieve awareness on the present moment...whenever you would like...and your mind will feel clear, and It will be easy to redirect your mind...to the present...your mind is steady and focused...like a rock in the midst of a gentle stream. The water passes over the rock in a stream, as thoughts pass by...Just like a rock in a gentle stream, you can be aware of thoughts and experiences as they pass by...and let them go without resistance when they pass. [Wait 10 seconds]

REINFORCEMENT OF RESPONSE TO SUGGESTED PRESENT-MOMENT AWARENESS

Now you are more and more fully in the present moment...finding an even greater sense of calmness...in the present moment there is a stillness...and perhaps you will begin to notice...a deep sense of serenity and relaxation that lies in the stillness of the present moment. You can be so much more completely relaxed and fully aware of experiences as they occur and fade away. Feeling serene...and deeply peaceful. Very good...and as you are aware of these positive feelings... just nod your head...yes...and they become more a part of you...sinking deeply into your being...able to be accessed any time you wish.

ALERTING

In a few moments, it is possible to begin returning to conscious alertness...Returning to conscious alertness in your own time and your own pace...in a way that just feels about right for you today... Feeling very good, normal, with good sensations in every way as you return to full conscious alertness...and every day...a greater sense of mindfulness...now...returning to conscious alertness as I count from the numbers 4 to 1...now 4...3...2...1.

Posthypnotic Inquiry, Assigning Homework, and Closing the Session

The period immediately after the hypnotic induction is an ideal time to ask about a patient's experiences during hypnosis. During this process, it is helpful to ask the client to rate his or her level of stress on the 0 to 10 scale immediately after the hypnotic induction. As with many things in life, communication is key, so inquiring about a client's experiences will help the therapist to gain insight into how the client responds to hypnosis. The clinician may consider asking about the client's subjective experiences during hypnosis, the degree to which the client was able to experience present-moment awareness, and which parts of the induction resonated or did not resonate with him or her personally. If the therapist is experienced with hypnosis and comfortable modifying hypnotic inductions, this information can help to introduce changes into future hypnosis sessions by altering the inductions we have provided in this book according to the client's preferences.

Finally, the therapist can bring the session to a close by giving the client the home-practice audio for the session along with a reminder to practice with it at least once per day and to record the practice session using the Mindful Self-Hypnosis Daily Practice Log (Appendix B), including ratings of relaxation and mindfulness as well as comments and reflections regarding feelings of mindfulness. It is very important to emphasize daily practice. For example:

Therapist: *I am going to give you a recording of today's hypnotic induction. Would you like to have that as a CD recording or emailed to you as an MP3 file that you can download to your phone? It is important that you practice mindful hypnosis every day as we discussed.*

Client: *Yes, if you can email it to me I, can use my phone to listen to it in the afternoon. I have a good set of headphones.*

Therapist: *Great! Yes, please be sure to practice with it at least once every day between now and our next appointment. You can listen to it in the morning, afternoon, or night—whatever works best for you. Each time please record your practice using the Mindful Self-Hypnosis Daily Practice Log. It will give you a way to track your experience of relaxation and mindfulness as well as to record comments and reflections regarding feelings of mindfulness. This will help to guide your future sessions as we record your progress and help you be aware of positive changes and areas to focus on in future sessions.*

Mindful hypnosis is similar to exercise, in a way. Exercising once per week is probably healthier than being completely sedentary, but more regular exercise will produce more dramatic results. Likewise, clients who are interested in creating significant and dramatic changes in their stress level will usually find that daily practice with the practice audio will support them in making these changes.

Summary and Closing Thoughts for Session 1

For most people (clinicians included), the mind can be like a pendulum swinging wildly back and forth from the future to the past (spending very little time in the present, at the nadir of the "swing"). Session 1 roots a client's understanding of mindfulness in this simple, powerful acknowledgment. What's more, it gives the client a glimpse into an alternative way of experiencing the world. During meditation or hypnosis, the mind can gradually slow its "swing," spending more and more time focused on the present and becoming less prone to jumping to the future or the past. In the deepest state of hypnosis or meditation, it is possible for the mind to become very still indeed, focused only on the continually emerging present.

Developing the capacity to experience the present moment restores a kind of balance to everyday life. The majority of a client's life may still be spent thinking of the future or the past, but the ability to experience the simplicity of the present moment during a portion of the day acts to temper the mind's frenetic pace and channel the mind's energy into more goal-directed thought. At the beginning of this therapeutic journey, persons trying to focus on the present moment might be surprised at just how chaotic and restless their thoughts usually are. Distractions arise almost immediately, as though conjured from a mind that doesn't *want* to sit still or is unused to doing so. This is normal, and with time, most people find that the mind begins to settle and become less restless. With practice, a person might find that it gradually becomes easier and more enjoyable to experience the present moment and that fewer mental and physical distractions arise during the attempt.

After being introduced to mindfulness and hypnosis and engaging their interest in treatment, most clients will be ready to experience hypnosis for themselves. This part of the session is an opportunity to merge a client's budding *intellectual* understanding of mindfulness with the lived *experience* of mindful hypnosis. We recommend using the mindful hypnosis script either in part or in its entirety. Once you have familiarized yourself with the script as it is written, you may find that personalizing the hypnosis script to the client's unique needs may enhance treatment gains beyond a strict adherence to the script. For example, in the script for session 1, we use the experience of seeing a flower as a means of deepening focus and relaxation, and increasing the depth of the hypnotic trance. If a client told you beforehand that a trip to the beach with family was a cherished memory, you might decide to use the imagery of a beach or other individual preferences of the clients.

REFERENCES

Elkins, G. R. (2014). *Hypnotic relaxation therapy: Principles and applications*. New York, NY: Springer Publishing.

Elkins, G. R., Barabasz, A. F., Council, J. R., & Spiegel, D. (2015). Advancing research and practice: The revised APA Division 30 definition of hypnosis. *American Journal of Clinical Hypnosis, 57*, 378–385. doi:10.1080/00029157.2015.1011465

Yeats, W. B. (2011). *The Celtic twilight: Faerie and folklore*. New York, NY: Dover Publications. (Original work published 1893)

CHAPTER 9

Session 2

MINDFUL HYPNOTHERAPY AND NONJUDGMENTAL ACCEPTANCE OF SENSATIONS

Seek not to have that everything should happen as you wish, but wish for everything to happen as it actually does happen, and you will be serene.

—*Epictetus*

Introduction

Mindfulness interventions are predicated on the idea that suffering is amplified when there is a strong resistance or attachment to particular experiences. Therefore, one of the core components of mindfulness interventions such as mindful hypnotherapy (MH) is helping clients to develop a nonjudgmental attitude toward their experiences. Session 2 is intended to open the client's eyes to the possibilities of nonjudgmental awareness by fostering curiosity and openness to physical experiences. The session invites the client to attend to physical experiences that are relatively innocuous (such as breathing, mild pleasantness, or mild irritation), but encourages the client to pay attention to these experiences as though it were the first time ever experiencing the sensation. With practice and experience, this mindful attitude can also be used with more intense and unpleasant experiences, and it can even be used to mindfully notice thoughts and emotions (as discussed in Chapter 10). A *beginner's mind* helps to generate an attitude of openness toward experiences, and a sense of curious wonder helps to displace a judgmental attitude toward experiences. Together, these attitudes aid clients in experiencing nonjudgmental awareness for themselves.

In session 2 of MH, the task of the therapist is to solidify client investment in mindfulness and create a foundational knowledge of mindfulness as a unique approach to experience. Relating mindfully to the five senses is important in its own right, insofar as it can provide a *grounding* experience during times of stress and create a greater awareness of the somatic components of stress and wellness. Mindfulness of the five senses introduces the idea that the sensations that we experience as physically unpleasant needn't be reacted to with distress. In terms of positive psychology, this session can be an opportunity to cultivate a sense of interest, curiosity, and awareness of bodily sensations regardless of their valence (pleasant, neutral, or unpleasant).

Session 2 is also crucial in that it provides a kind of stepping stone between present-moment awareness (which many clients find accessible, somewhat familiar, and immediately useful) and mindfulness of thoughts and feelings (which is often more challenging and far less familiar). For many clients, unpleasant sensory experiences are easier to relate to mindfully, whereas unpleasant thoughts and feelings are regarded as more *personal*, a more quintessentially human experience, and hence more difficult to relate to with equanimity. Mindfulness of sensory experiences can create a new cognitive framework that can then be used as a template for mindfulness of thoughts and feelings.

Experienced practitioners of mindful therapies should certainly draw upon their experience to introduce these familiar mindfulness concepts in their own words. For those new to mindful therapies, the prospect of explaining mindfulness to clients can be a daunting experience despite understanding the underlying principles. In this session's agenda and at the end of the chapter are several suggestions for explaining key aspects of mindfulness, and the explanations provided throughout this chapter can be used with clients as well.

These transcripts are not exhaustive, but rather are meant to supplement and hone the clinician's working knowledge of mindfulness principles. In addition, it should be noted that many of these explanations are geared toward clients who are at least somewhat psychologically minded and open to learning. Explanations for mindfulness should be adapted to fit the therapist's own style and should be phrased in a manner that is accessible to the individual clients.

Strategic Themes of Session 2: Mindful Hypnotherapy and Nonjudgmental Acceptance of Sensations

The second MH session is designed to enhance the individual's depth of hypnotic relaxation and further the goal of nonjudgmental acceptance. There is a synergy between these two goals that goes above and beyond either approach on its own. Deepening a client's ability to experience hypnotic relaxation provides a safe and receptive state of mind in which a client can explore new behaviors and experience a greater degree of symptom reduction. Meanwhile, introducing nonjudgmental acceptance enables a client to begin cultivating a new relationship with experiences that will be the basis for a significant and lasting change. In session 2, the strengths of hypnosis and mindfulness become more closely entwined, and in our experience, the benefits of this union are seen within just a few weeks. However, before these new goals are implemented in session 2, it is important to review the home practice and answer any questions regarding the content from session 1. The new content will take root more deeply if the foundational material from session 1 is solid and firmly established.

Review Home Practice

In a feasibility study of MH, adherence to home practice was exceptional, with the average person practicing six times per week in addition to practicing "informal" mindfulness during the course of daily activities. These results may not be typical in an outpatient setting, however, and it is important to help a client to engage in frequent practice to support change. A review of a client's mindful hypnosis practice using the Mindful Self-Hypnosis Daily Practice Log (Appendix B) should be completed. Discussing a client's ratings of relaxation and mindfulness and comments and reflections regarding feelings of mindfulness can help reinforce practice and give insights into how to individualize the session to best meet the client at his or her level of progress.

It is very important to emphasize daily practice. As discussed in the previous chapter, the importance of home practice might be compared to physical exercise. The health benefits of going to the gym once per week for 30 minutes *may* be noticeable, but the changes in physical fitness will almost assuredly be small. Similarly, clients can expect to change only slowly or not at all if they do not practice or integrate mindfulness into their daily lives between sessions. Just like developing a regular exercise routine, a client can expect to notice substantial benefits over the course of only a few weeks or months of regular practice, and if regular practice is maintained over a long period of time, these benefits can be profound indeed. During each session, the therapist should review adherence to home practice, as well as explore interesting experiences (if any) that emerged during home practice and discuss any obstacles to practice that came up.

A clinician who is still developing a familiarity with mindfulness and MH may find that the entirety of his or her cognitive resources are devoted to delivering the *content* of MH faithfully while giving little attention to the *process* of how this content is delivered. Although this is expected and developmentally appropriate, a therapist can subtly reinforce a client's shift toward a mindful approach by *delivering* the content of MH mindfully. For example, it may be tempting to criticize a client's lack of adherence to home practice since home practice is so important to progress. Harsh criticism may feed into a client's own lack of self-compassion, however, which will run counter to the aims of session 5 (compassion for self and others). In contrast, if a therapist is genuinely curious about the obstacles to home practice, and proffers home practice as an act of self-compassion and self-care, this attitude of open, compassionate curiosity can serve as a model for the client and enhance the effectiveness and ease of learning in later sessions of MH.

Home practice can be difficult for clients, just like any change in a person's normal routine. Some suggestions that may be helpful are provided here, but a therapist delivering MH is encouraged to draw upon preexisting clinical skills to support this daily practice and behavior change. One way a client may begin to develop a regular practice is to think of it as mental hygiene. Even when a client is stressed, overwhelmed, traveling, or busy, most still find the time and energy to brush their teeth and shower/bathe. Clients might be encouraged to think of home practice in the same way: something they find time and energy for regardless of life's circumstances and something that is skipped only in the most exceptional circumstances. Other suggestions might include:

- Linking daily practice to another daily activity (such as practicing every day immediately after dinner or before breakfast).
- Asking a close friend or family member to check in and ask if they have done their daily practice until practice becomes habitual.
- Adopting a stance of acceptance toward mental/emotional resistance. It's OK to be resentful about practicing instead of doing something more "fun." Notice and explore this resistance as you shift activities from entertainment or preestablished habits and toward the daily MH practice. This last approach may be difficult for some clients in the early stages of MH but may help to reinforce and foreshadow later sessions.

Discuss Specific Stressors

A discussion of specific stressors is helpful for several reasons. First, it helps to gather information that is useful in personalizing the MH intervention. A thorough understanding of the specific stressors in a client's life can help to give examples of mindfulness that are salient to a client's life and are culturally relevant. For example, a therapist might start with a discussion of a client's self-ratings of stress over the course of the week or ask follow-up questions if a client says that ruminative thoughts or a busy life interfered with the client being able to follow through with the homework. A therapist can model mindfulness and turn obstacles to their advantage by exploring sources of stress with curiosity and openness. The therapist's own nonjudgmental curiosity is likely to be met with a greater willingness on a client's part to share his or her stressors. Furthermore, it helps to deepen rapport and foster a collaborative working relationship between a therapist and a client.

The exploration of life stressors is also an opportunity to sow the seeds for the new information that is intended to be presented later in this session (nonjudgmental awareness of physical sensations). The therapist can do this by inquiring about the physical sensations that are associated with stress or stressors. For example, a client may be able to describe a sense of muscular tension, a tightness in the throat, or a sensation of heaviness in the chest. Keep in mind that "nonjudgmental awareness of physical sensations" includes an awareness of *all* of the five senses, not just tactile sensations or proprioception. Therefore, the therapist may find opportunities to inquire about the stressful sights, sounds, smells, or tastes if these are part of a client's milieu of stressful experiences.

Nonjudgmental Awareness

Nonjudgmental awareness is the first truly radical concept that is introduced in MH. It is a powerful, counterintuitive shift in perspective that is the key to all future sessions. For both clients and therapists who are new to mindfulness, *nonjudgmental awareness* can be a confusing term. In short, it means to be aware of present-moment experiences (as described in Chapter 8) while letting go of emotional resistance to those experiences. For each of us, there is an instinctual denial or fighting against experiences that are unpleasant. For example, if I stub my toe, I'm likely to have a cognitive and emotional reaction that might sound like this: "Ugh! I hate this pain in my toe! I wish it would go away! Maybe if I tune it out and pay attention to something else, I won't be so aware of it." This emotional rejection of the unpleasant experience and an emotional *need* to have my experiences be other than they are is called resistance, and it is the opposite of what we try to cultivate with nonjudgmental awareness. On the other side of the spectrum, when my alarm goes off at 5 a.m. and I am feeling cozy beneath the covers, I want to *stay* cozy beneath the covers and go back to sleep. It is normal and natural to want to cling to pleasant experiences. The emotional clinging to pleasant experiences and the emotional *need* to retain pleasant experiences is another form of judgmental awareness. Both resistance and clinging are opposites of nonjudgmental awareness.

Nonjudgmental awareness means cultivating a genuine interest in your experiences, whether pleasant, unpleasant, or neutral. Clinicians who are already familiar with mindfulness may have no further need of explanation, but for those who are new to mindfulness (whether they are therapists or clients), this description of nonjudgmental awareness raises quite a few questions. For example, are we recommending that clients shouldn't avoid hurtful or dangerous situations, and just accept them as they are? Should we just grit our teeth and endure what we must when unpleasant experiences occur? How does this "nonjudgmental awareness" help, and how would we accomplish it even if it *does* help? This chapter addresses these questions and others later, but first it is important to explore some of the things that nonjudgmental awareness *doesn't* mean.

Nonjudgmental awareness does *not* mean:

- **Losing perspective on whether an experience is harmful or helpful**

  Nonjudgmental awareness often allows a person to *better* distinguish harm from nonharm. In essence, this shift in perspective empowers a person to see the difference between something that is pleasant but harmful versus something that may be unpleasant but helpful. For example, indulging in an addictive habit can be pleasant in the moment but harmful in the short or long term. Engaging with experiences with open curiosity (i.e., nonjudgmentalness) can make the distinction between pleasantness and harm clearer.

- **Being *tough* and *having discipline*, or *gritting your teeth and bearing it***

  Nonjudgmental awareness means genuinely being OK in the midst of unpleasantness and genuinely being OK when something pleasant goes away. Toughness and discipline can be very positive qualities and needn't be discarded. However, gritting one's teeth implies a degree of resistance to experience that is antithetical to the state of nonjudgmental awareness. Although it is instinctual to mentally and emotionally resist unpleasant experiences, this attitude toward experience often enhances the perception of suffering rather than alleviates it.

- **"Giving up" (in the fight against injustice, against life's challenges, and so on)**

  Mindfulness often involves a dialectic between seeing an experience as it is, with acceptance, *and,* if appropriate, making changes in one's life so that the experience can be transformed into a healthier one in the present and/or future. For example, a person might be nonjudgmentally aware of the anger that social injustice provokes internally, accepting the feeling just as it is without pushing it away or clinging to it. This acceptance does not prevent that same person from taking action to make the world a better place.

- **Pretending or deceiving yourself**

  Nonjudgmental awareness isn't a matter of pretending that pain doesn't hurt, pretending that pain is pleasant, or pretending that you want more pain in your life. Nonjudgmental awareness helps us let go of some of our instinctual reactivity. In doing so, people are often able to observe their experiences with greater acuity and nuance. By letting go of our preconceptions and reactivity, we are often able to see things much differently.

CLINICIAN NOTE

Nonjudgmental Awareness

While the seeds of nonjudgmental awareness can be taught didactically, experiential exercises can be even more effective in conveying this complicated concept. The hypnotic induction that occurs in the second part of session 2 provides this experiential exposure to the concept. However, at the therapist's discretion, this can be supplemented through traditional meditation or other experiential exercises such as the *itch* exercise.

With these common misconceptions of nonjudgmental awareness in mind, how does one actually effect a shift toward nonjudgmental awareness? As previously stated, judgmental resistance to experiences is an instinctual trait, one that helps us to survive hostile conditions by driving us away from harm and toward pleasure with the force of an emotional engine (e.g., hate, fear, pleasure, comfort). Fortunately, human beings are also inherently curious. Curiosity is an irresistible imperative in some people and a subtler drive in others. Regardless of the innate strength of curiosity, it is a quality that can be fostered in all people, and it is the quintessential trait that can lead to greater freedom from the instinctual drives. When a person is *curious* about an event, there is an emotional inclination toward discovering more about a phenomenon while simultaneously letting go of preconceptions. This *discovery* orientation toward experiential phenomena acts as an antidote and an antithesis to both clinging and resistance. Thus, curiosity is the essential tool of transformation that can allow a person to discover nonjudgmental awareness.

The Itch Exercise

No formal induction is required for the *itch exercise* experience. For about 80% to 90% of clients, this exercise can fast-track their intuitive and holistic understanding of mindfulness and of nonjudgmental awareness. In addition, it will impart an understanding of how mindfulness can be helpful in their life. *However*, with the most resistant clients, this exercise will actually produce *greater* distress and may leave them feeling reluctant to explore mindfulness further. Therefore, we recommend trying this exercise yourself first and using it with clients at your own discretion based on your clinical judgment. The exercise does not typically produce distress beyond the frustration of an itchy nose (which clients can scratch at any time if they want to "opt out"), so for most clients the risk is minimal.

1. Get consent and buy-in for trying an experiential exercise.

   Therapist: *OK, during the next two minutes, you might notice an itch somewhere on your body. No matter how much it itches, DON'T SCRATCH during this exercise. Do you understand? No matter how much it itches, DON'T SCRATCH! OK. Do you notice an itch anywhere on your body? If no itch arises, the exercise can be modified.* Ask the client to sit absolutely still and notice any slight ache or discomfort in the body and focus on that instead, adapting the rest of the exercise to attend to whatever sensation has arisen.

2. Bring attention to the "itch" sensation and increase awareness.

   Therapist: *OK, now that you've got your itch...what does an itch FEEL like? What do you notice?*

   Client: *Huh. What do you mean what does it feel like?*

   Therapist: *Well, for most people, the first thing they notice is the urge to scratch it. To make it go away. I'd like you to put that to the side for the time being, though, and focus on the sensation ITSELF. Not just what it makes you want to do. Is it cool? Warm?* [Client response]. *Do you notice that it's in a big area or a small area?* [Client response]. *Good, and if you REALLY pay attention, can you notice the very boundary where it transitions from being an itch to not being an itch?* [Client response]. *Is it EXACTLY the same from moment to moment, or do you notice it getting more intense, less intense, moving, or changing?* [Client response]. *Are there any other sensations you can notice about it, like tingling, numbness, or pain? Really allow yourself to get curious about the sensations. It might be the first time you've ever paid attention to what an itch actually FEELS like.* [Client response]. *Excellent, now I'll be silent for the next 30 seconds or so to let you* *notice anything else about what an itch feels like. Really see if you can pay close attention, and cultivate a curiosity about the sensations, whatever they may be.*

3. Bring the exercise to a close. In doing so, allow the client to scratch the itch if he or she would like and inquire what it was like to pay attention to the itch. Many clients report that the itch faded or went away entirely as they paid more and more attention to it. Others may report that the itch was still there but it did not bother them as much. Clients who report *increased* psychological distress that builds throughout the exercise rather than abates may benefit from a gentler introduction to nonjudgmental awareness—that is, cultivating a genuine curiosity about neutral or pleasant sensations. The itch exercise's focus on unpleasant sensations is useful only insofar as it demonstrates quickly and efficiently that nonjudgmental curiosity can result in reduced psychological distress, which is counterintuitive to many people, as the more common assumption is that paying attention to unpleasant sensations makes them "worse."

Sample Vignette

Following is an example of how a client *might* respond after the therapist explains the basic concept of nonjudgmental awareness.

Client: *Oh yeah, I do that* [nonjudgmental awareness] *all the time.*

Therapist: *All right! So, this is already sounding familiar to you.*

Client: *Oh yeah, for sure. It's a great way to relax at the end of the day, or on a weekend.*

Therapist: *Could you describe what you do a bit more, when you're tuning into your senses nonjudgmentally?*

Client: *Sure. Let's see ... well yeah, for example, the other day, I had one of those days at work where everything just went wrong! I won't bore you with the details, but by the end of the day I was just a bundle of knotted muscles and stress. So, when I got home I just cracked open a beer, turned on my favorite TV show, and just tuned it all out.*

[Describes using distraction and nonpathological alcohol use to escape discomfort rather than mindfulness]

Therapist: *And did that help?*

Client: *Well, yeah, for the most part. I mean, there were times when my mind wandered back to the way my boss yelled at me or my back started hurting too much to ignore it, but I think it helped to take the edge off.*

Therapist: *Well, that's sounds like it was at least a partial fix, and for the most part you were able to tune things out. It sounds like that's been helpful to you in the past, yet you also mentioned last week how overall you still find yourself really stressed out. I want to clarify an important point though: When you choose to practice mindfulness, it means paying MORE attention to things. Not so much tuning out, but tuning in, even to unpleasant things like pain or discomfort.*

[Validating the useful part of current coping techniques, and clarifying the unique approach of mindfulness as a primary, supplementary, or replacement coping tool]

Client: [Looks confused and skeptical]

Therapist: *I know, it sounds absolutely crazy, but bear with me. What if at some point in your life there was a pain or distress so intense you couldn't distract yourself from it? If you're in that situation, you might be thinking to yourself: "I wish this pain would go away, I hate it, I can't stand it, it's so bad." You'd be between a rock and a hard place, right? You want to distract yourself, but you can't. You want to get rid of it, but you can't. You can't stand it, but it's with you anyway. If you continue to think that way about your pain, if you continue to react that way to your experience, do you think that that will make the pain better or worse?*

Client: *Well, worse probably, if I can't make it go away and I can't ignore it.*

Therapist: *I'd agree. So, here's the thing: There are a lot of coping techniques that can help you distract yourself from discomfort and pain or make them go away. For everything else, mindfulness can help you to feel okay even when you're in pain, anxious, sad, or something else.*

Client: *Great, that sounds pretty good.*

Therapist: *Wonderful. Now, it might take a little practice to be mindful with the really intense stuff, so let's start by practicing mindfulness with more neutral sensations just to introduce the basic idea. If you can learn how to be genuinely open, curious, and attentive to neutral sensations and mild discomforts, that mode of awareness can also help you to feel a baseline level of well-being even if more intense pain or emotional distress happens during the course of your daily life.*

[Therapist continues with an experiential exercise in mindfulness of neutral sensations or proceeds to hypnosis script for session 2]

As a final note on nonjudgmental awareness, therapists should keep in mind the evolutionary purpose of our instinctual, judgmental awareness of experiences. This instinctual perspective is meant to be a biological shortcut that defends against the most simple and primal threats to our well-being. Therefore, if clients are in a situation where there is a persistent threat to their physical well-being, it may be the case that their instinctual (judgmental) responses will serve their well-being more effectively than mindfulness will. For example, if a client lives under the threat of physical violence, this should obviously take priority in therapy. Otherwise, the therapist will be attempting to dismantle defenses that are still essential to the client's well-being. In most cases, the stressors of modern life are more complicated and are several steps removed from these more primal threats. Therefore, the instinctual stress response that is so well suited to "fight or flight" is less useful than the mindful approach we are implementing in MH.

Hypnotic Induction for Nonjudgmental Acceptance of Sensations

Before beginning the hypnotic induction, it is helpful to ask clients to rate their stress level (0–10 scale) for comparison after the hypnotic induction has been completed. We recommend using the script provided at the end of the chapter as a basis for a hypnotic induction, though the therapist may improvise modifications to the script as he or she sees fit. Notice that in the script provided, the key elements are the following:

1. Building an awareness of the present moment
2. Deepening the hypnotic state, allowing the client to be simultaneously relaxed and attentive
3. Inviting the client to bring an open curiosity to physical experiences, regardless of whether they are pleasant, unpleasant, or neutral

INTRODUCTION AND SETTING EXPECTANCY

During this session of mindful hypnosis, suggestions will be given for achieving a state of deep mental and physical relaxation. Within this relaxed state, it will be possible...to become more aware of the physical sensations of your body nonjudgmentally. As this happens, your stress will become less and you can experience a state of serenity in the present moment...and a greater mindfulness of all aspects of your internal experience...of relaxation...of breathing...focusing on the present-moment sensations of your body as they come and go... If this is all right with you...now...please begin by resting the palm of your hand against your mid- or upper chest...either the right hand or the left hand, whichever feels right to you...and keeping your eyes open for the time being. Just notice the rise and fall of that palm against your chest as you breathe in and out...and over the course of this gentle rise and fall, perhaps you will begin to notice the sensations in your hand or arm...or feel the sensations in your chest as it fills with air...or you may notice the slight weight of your hand upon your chest. You might also choose to switch your attention between these sensations.

As this transpires and you become more aware of the sensations in your body as you breathe, you will soon find your attention settling into the present moment...very similar to what you have experienced this past week as you have become more and more aware of the present moment.

And if you were to notice your attention settling into the present moment now...that focus...that grounding...would allow you to deepen your experience of mindfulness...you could allow yourself to observe the sensations of your body. During this session whatever you notice as you become more mindful of your senses is OK...the sights or sounds or physical sensations of your body needn't be changed...they are fine just as they are. You may find that during the course of hypnosis today...more and more you will be able to observe your senses nonjudgmentally...letting go of judgments about which sensations you want to be present and which you don't want to be present...instead just becoming aware of what sensations are present...and accepting them just as they are... As this happens, you will experience a deep sense of peace, relaxation, and serenity.

EYE CLOSURE

Now if your attention has wandered...it might be pleasant to allow your attention to drift back toward your breath for a moment...breathing freely and deeply...easily and steadily...and as you continue to breathe you may find yourself settling more and more deeply...and when you are ready, your unconscious mind will allow the steady rhythm of your breathing to carry you into a hypnotic state...the slow, steady rhythm of your breathing will carry you...ever deeper into hypnosis. With each breath, you will feel more and more relaxed...every muscle and fiber of your body unwinding...relaxing...its weight supported completely by the chair...and you will know that you are entering a hypnotic trance when your eyelids begin to feel tired and heavy... noticing now, more and more a relaxed and heavy feeling...the steady rhythm of breathing making your eyelids heavier, and heavier until they close all by themselves...[when the subject has closed his or her eyes] very good.

FOCUS AND NARROWING OF ATTENTION

Now settling more and more into the present moment...and as your focus on the present moment becomes more complete...perhaps noticing now [timed with in-breath] both the in-breath...[timed with out-breath] and the out-breath...as they occur. As you breathe, you may find that your breath is made up of many stages...and as your focus narrows, it would be possible and even natural to become aware of each part of the process of breathing as it happens...more and more focused on each stage of the breath...perhaps becoming aware of the sensations at the very beginning of the in-breath, the middle of the in-breath, and the end...as your lungs are filled with air...and noticing the unique sensations that occur at each point in the out-breath... Each breath is unique...nuanced...if your attention were to waver, you might miss something interesting about your breath...something you never noticed before. And as people focus on their breath with this level of detail...unwavering...they sometimes find that there is a whole universe of interesting and ever-changing sensations. As they observe these sensations as they come and go...there is no desire to attend to anything else...and everything else except my voice fades to insignificance...in the background of awareness.

Now as you focus more and more...on each sensation as it comes...it may be possible to find a point of absolute focus and stillness...in the present moment... as you allow this awareness of your breathing to carry you into a deep relaxation...everything else fading into the background...relaxed and serene.

BLENDED SUGGESTIONS FOR FOCUS AND RELAXATION

In the state you are entering now, your mind will be capable of discerning things clearly and effortlessly...as they occur. You will be completely relaxed, calm, and deeply peaceful. Mental clarity and relaxation will exist as one state of mind within you...as you become more and more mindful.

Your breath is carrying you to this state of mindfulness now...as you breathe in and out...becoming more and more mindful with each breath. Relaxed and aware... As you breathe in...your mind will become more focused...more clear...without any willful effort on your part... Each and every in-breath allowing your mind to become more focused on the present moment...and able to respond to each suggestion with ease.

And with each out-breath, your body will become more and more relaxed...and your mind will become more at ease...as you breathe out and your body relaxes, peaceful feelings will arise...mind and body relaxing together...more and more deeply relaxed with each and every breath. Muscles unwinding...tension draining...completely at ease in the present moment. More and more noticing a feeling of "letting go" and noticing your muscles loosening...every muscle and every fiber of your body becoming so deeply relaxed.

With each breath, you find yourself becoming more focused on the physical sensations of breathing...[on in-breath] in...[on out-breath] and out...as you breathe in, focusing more completely on the sensations of breathing...as you breathe out, relaxing more completely...breathing freely and deeply...and letting yourself become absorbed in this deep, relaxed awareness. Your mind is clear and peaceful...completely at ease. And finding more and more comfortable and calm feelings. So deeply relaxed now that it would take too much effort to even try to open your eyelids...and this is a good feeling that allows you to relax even deeper ...and as you go deeper relaxed, you're drifting into an even deeper level of hypnosis. Feeling so calm that nothing bothers or interferes with this feeling of comfort....

SUGGESTION THAT DRIFTING THOUGHTS WILL RETURN

And from time to time your thoughts may drift...minds do this sometimes...but in this mindful state you are in, you will notice when your thoughts begin to drift...and when you notice, your thoughts will gently and effortlessly return to the present moment...and back to a nonjudgmental awareness of what is going on in your body at the present instant. Whenever this happens...you will find that as you return to nonjudgmental, present-moment awareness of the body...you will sink into an even deeper level of hypnosis...and a deeper state of mindfulness.

DEEPENING SUGGESTIONS

Now you may or may not be aware of this...but deep inside of you is a place of complete and utter serenity...a place of calmness and relaxation...where your mind is at ease, and nothing troubles you...where your thoughts are clear like a cool mountain lake...still, and serene...not burdened by the slightest care... this may be something that you have felt before...or something that you have yet to discover...but you might find it pleasant to journey inward toward that place within you now...and as you hear my voice count from 10 to 1, with each number finding yourself settling into an even deeper level of hypnosis...deeper toward that place of complete mental and physical relaxation within you.

[Count each number as the patient exhales]

Ten...setting your cares aside now as you embark on this inner journey...you needn't worry about losing track of them...they will be safe, and right where you left them if or when you choose to pick them up again.

Nine...feeling a sense of relief...relaxing...your body leading the way on this journey by becoming very relaxed...muscles unwinding...tension that you didn't even know you were carrying is now drifting away...bringing a sense of deep relief.

Eight...deeply calm...number eight and already so deeply relaxed...and you may begin to notice a warmth or tingling sensation in your body, as it relaxes even further.

Seven...and now a sense of profound calmness begins to blossom...unfolding...effortless, like a flower to the sun...and as you feel this, you might realize that mental and physical relaxation is not something that you do...it is a process of letting go...of not doing...even if just for this short while...like holding a ball in your hand...if you want to send the ball toward the ground...you needn't throw it, or exert effort or do anything...just the opposite, in fact...the only thing you need to do is let it go.

Six...halfway there, and already so profoundly relaxed...letting go of struggles and cares...letting go of any tension...letting go and simply being...in the present moment.

Five...perhaps at one time it took effort to calm your mind and body from its busy-ness...but now you are effortlessly still and serene...settled so deeply into the present moment...that to direct your mind to the past or the future or other things would require effort, and you would prefer not to try.

Four...allowing your mind to settle...becoming still and calm...profoundly peaceful.

Three...deeper and more calm...no worries in this special moment.

Two...almost there...deeply relaxed, nothing bothers and nothing concerns... and perhaps it would be OK...with the final number I count...to let go of even the smallest vestige of tension or worry...to settle into complete and utter stillness and serenity...peaceful and content...or perhaps you will prefer to be very calm but not take that last step...trusting now that whichever your mind chooses is the right choice for you in this moment...what you truly need.

One...at the final step of your own inner journey...comfortably and deeply hypnotized...resting in the present moment...your thoughts uncluttered...still...and calm.

SETTING SESSION GOAL AND POSTHYPNOTIC SUGGESTION

And as you are there...soon you will find your full attention focused upon what is going on in your body right now. You will be able to notice each sensation easily...without judging each experience as good or bad. Instead, you may discover an open curiosity about each experience...regardless of whether it is physically pleasant, physically unpleasant, or physically neutral.

When your mind attends closely to each of the experiences entering your awareness...without judging it as good or bad...you will notice that you become more relaxed...and more able to cope with stressors as they arise. The more mindful you are in your daily life...the less distress you will feel.

SUGGESTIONS FOR NONJUDGMENTAL AWARENESS OF BODY SENSATIONS

Now as you are sitting there, so relaxed...you may find yourself becoming curious about what being relaxed actually feels like...curious about the sensations that are going on in your body...moment by moment...and you may be curious about how these sensations change. Allow your mind to explore the sensations of your body now. It may be possible to notice sensations of warmth or coolness...if so, where do you notice yourself feeling warm or cool? Where is the feeling most pronounced?...where does the feeling begin or end? Does the feeling stay constant, or can you...perhaps...notice slight changes in the intensity or location of the warmth or coolness from moment to moment?

[Wait 5 to 10 seconds to allow the client to notice these things]...and as you pay attention to these things, notice that your mind is becoming more and more focused...more and more able to see things as they are...and not just as you expected them to be. Really noticing the nuances of each experience now...and allowing yourself to become curious about each new experience as it unfolds moment by moment...not taking them for granted.

And now allowing that same attentive curiosity to drift back toward the sensations of breathing...now noticing your breath, and what it feels like to fill your lungs with air...noticing what it feels like as your chest expands with your breath, and deflates...[wait at least one full breath]...allow your attention to shift to the sensations as air passes through your throat...[wait at least one full breath] you may also notice the change in warmth or coolness at the tip of your nostrils as you inhale and exhale [wait at least one full breath]. Whatever you happen to notice going on in your body is OK...just allow yourself to notice it in detail...and pay attention...to how it actually feels. If whatever sensations you notice in your body feel slightly pleasant...allow yourself to notice the pleasant sensation while it is present...and think to yourself..."this pleasant sensation is fine just as it is"...and gently let the pleasant sensation go when it passes...If whatever sensations you notice in your body feel slightly unpleasant...allow yourself to notice the unpleasant sensation while it is present...and think to yourself..."this unpleasant sensation is fine just as it is" ...and gently let the unpleasant sensation go when it passes... If whatever sensations you notice in your body feel neither pleasant nor unpleasant...allow yourself to notice the sensation while it is present...and think to yourself..." this sensation is fine just as it is"...and gently let the unpleasant sensation go when it passes. Maybe it would be OK to just allow yourself to fully accept, without judgment, whatever sensations are arising in your body...accepting them just as they are...without judging them as "good" or "bad"... without trying to push them away or cling to them...just accepting them as they are...as you focus on the present-moment experiences that are arising in your body. In a moment I will pause...and during this pause I would like you to just notice the sensations in your body...just notice them as they come and go...and accept them just as they are...

Therapist Note: Wait 10 seconds before proceeding.

SUGGESTIONS FOR SERENITY

As you become mindful of sensations as they occur in your body...accepting them just as they are...you may notice a deep feeling of peace and serenity that comes from this practice.

When you dwell in the present moment...when you accept your experiences just as they are...your mind can begin to settle into a restful attention...calm...focused...and serene...noticing sensations in your body with a nonjudgmental awareness.

REINFORCEMENT OF RESPONSE

Very good...now if you were able to experience nonjudgmental awareness of your body's sensations...just nod your head...good...and your mind will become more and more capable of experiencing sensations from your body nonjudgmentally...and you will find yourself engaging in nonjudgmental awareness of your bodily experiences frequently on a daily basis...you will be able to be access this state of mind any time you wish...and each time you do so, you will find yourself feeling relaxed, peaceful, and refreshed.

Therapist Note: Insert individualized suggestions here, if applicable and if not interspersed throughout.

____

____

____

____

____

POSTHYPNOTIC SUGGESTIONS

Soon I will guide you out of this hypnotic state toward conscious alertness... but before this occurs, I would like you to maintain this state of relaxed, mindful awareness a little longer. During this next week you will experience a nonjudgmental awareness frequently during the day...both when you practice with the mindfulness recordings and on a regular basis....and you will find it easier and easier to experience nonjudgmental awareness of bodily sensations in the present moment...touch, hearing, sight, smell, and taste...becoming aware of the experiences as they come and go, with acceptance...you will also find that nonjudgmental awareness of your body will allow you to care for yourself better...and you will find it easier and easier to return to a present-moment awareness...of the sights, sounds and sensations around you and within you...in times of stress, returning to a nonjudgmental awareness of the body will calm you...allowing you to reclaim the same peace, serenity, and deep relaxation that you feel right now...the same relaxed, focused awareness you have felt during the hypnosis session today. These feelings will ground you and empower you...allowing you to function with more efficiency, less stress, and less distress in your daily life.

ALERTING

In a few moments, it is possible to begin returning to conscious alertness. Returning to conscious alertness in your own time and your own pace, in a way that just feels about right for you today...feeling very good, normal, with good sensations in every way as you return to full conscious alertness...returning to conscious alertness as I count from the numbers 4 to 1 now...4...3...2... 1.

Posthypnotic Inquiry, Assigning Homework, and Closing the Session

Again, collecting stress ratings before and after hypnosis can be useful information for the therapist. It is very important to provide the client with an audio recording of the hypnotic induction from session 2. *The homework assignment should include clear instructions to practice with it at least one time per day.* As previously noted, this can be in the form of a CD or audio file. It is very important to emphasize the importance of daily practice of self-hypnosis and to record the practice using the Mindful Self-Hypnosis Daily Practice Log (Appendix B).

Also, the posthypnotic inquiry serves as a means of keeping the lines of communication open between the client and the therapist. If a client experienced a different way of relating to his or her experiences, give the client permission to share this moment of wonder and curiosity. Seeing and experiencing the world in a new light is the core transformative experience that enables the powerful treatment gains that are possible with MH. If a client experiences difficulty, obstacles, or some degree of disconnect with what the therapist communicates about mindful hypnosis, this is important information as well. In this case, the therapist should collaborate with the client to find ways of either clearing these obstacles or cleverly turning the obstacles to the client's advantage.

For example, in traditional mindfulness practice, sometimes people find that when they are trying to focus on the sensations of breathing, their back starts to hurt from sitting in a meditative posture. If the pain is strong, this can seem like an obstacle to successful mindfulness practice. In such cases, meditation teachers often recommend shifting one's attention from the breath to the back pain, noticing what it feels like with nonjudgmental curiosity. In this case, what was once an obstacle to successful mindfulness practice has *become* the mindfulness practice. We recommend the therapist using inventiveness and flexible thinking to use every so-called *failure* or *obstacle* to an advantage. There will come a point in the session where the client has a basic grasp of what nonjudgmental awareness entails. When the client's most pressing questions about nonjudgmental awareness have been answered, there will come a point where the client's understanding is better served by having a direct experience of nonjudgmental awareness.

Summary and Closing Thoughts on Session 2

The concept of nonjudgmental awareness is crucial to mindfulness. This first encounter with nonjudgmental awareness can feel like a leap of faith for clients, but when clients are actually able to experience it for themselves, it opens up a whole new frontier of possibilities in therapy. We have found that starting with nonjudgmental awareness of physical sensations makes the client's introduction to nonjudgmental awareness slightly easier, versus jumping directly into nonjudgmental awareness of thoughts or emotions. Once a client grasps the concept of nonjudgmental awareness, this exact same perspective can be flexibly applied to any experience, whether physical, mental, or emotional. Throughout this session and beyond, therapists should use their clinical skills to make the key concepts as clear and accessible as possible, using their own words and experiences to guide the session.

CHAPTER 10

Session 3

NONJUDGMENTAL ACCEPTANCE OF THOUGHTS AND EMOTIONS

The phenomena contemplated are distinct from the mind contemplating them.

—*Dan Goleman (1980)*

Introduction

There is a common adage that "simple" and "easy" are two very different things. Mindfulness of thoughts and of emotions are excellent examples of this distinction. Conceptually, these concepts are quite simple: Pay attention to the thoughts and emotions that are transpiring in the present moment, and do so with an attitude of openness, curiosity, and compassion. Being mindfully aware of thoughts and emotions usually takes time and practice, however. Furthermore, it often takes a great deal of courage to be mindfully aware of thoughts and feelings. Some clients have been avoiding intense thoughts and feelings for years, and the idea of "turning toward" them is daunting, to say the least. Nevertheless, many clients find that when they finally notice their thoughts and emotions mindfully, the experience is different than they might have thought.

When a client has avoided difficult thoughts and emotions for a long period of time, the situation is very similar to seeing a frightening shadow on the wall. The shadow is "real" insofar as it isn't a figment of our imagination. The shadow has a shape. It may move and loom larger, and take the shape of our worst fears. The shadow is also *caused* by something that is quite solid and real. Despite all of these facts we can acknowledge about the shadow, the object casting it may bear little resemblance to the shadow itself. Generally speaking, the solid object is smaller than the shadow it casts, and looking at it in the light is not nearly as intimidating. Similarly, when clients avoid their experiences, fight their experiences, and judge their experiences, they often feel far greater distress than when they are simply able to "be with" and notice their experiences with compassionate attention. Some may find that this mindful attitude comes naturally, while others may find it more difficult. Regardless, the concept of mindful attention is identical whether it is used to attend to physical experiences or mental ones. Since the client will already have practice with mindfulness of physical experiences (session 2), this should put the otherwise daunting task of mindfulness with mental experiences within reach.

During session 3 of mindful hypnotherapy (MH), your two main goals as a therapist will be to (a) solidify the client's understanding of the material covered so far and (b) help the client "bridge the gap" between mindful awareness of the physical senses and mindful awareness of thoughts and emotions. Take time at the beginning of the session to review mindfulness of the five senses. Answer any questions a client may have, and try to emphasize those parts of a client's dialogue that convey an accurate understanding of what mindful awareness means. As part of this process, it can also be helpful to explore any initial benefits and discoveries clients are making about themselves, their experiences, and the impact (if any) these discoveries are having on stress.

Although time management is important during any therapeutic session, this investment of time exploring the previous week's theme will lay the groundwork for the new material. If clients truly understand mindful/nonjudgmental awareness, they *already* have all of the skills and understanding they need to be mindfully aware of thoughts and emotions. Metaphorically, this process is like learning to ride a bike on flat pavement and then learning to ride a bike on hilly terrain. The latter is more challenging, but the basic skill set needed for the endeavor already exists. By taking a bit of time to review the previous session's "lessons learned," you can build the client's sense of self-efficacy.

CLINICIAN NOTE

Leading by Example

As you explore potential changes in your client, do so with an attitude of open, engaged curiosity about your client's inner world.

If your client is not seeing benefits by session 3 or says that the practice has been difficult, it may be tempting to see this as an early sign of failure. If you are fearful and reactive about your client's progress (or lack thereof), it invites your client to adopt the same judgmental attitude toward his or her experiences.

If you are mindful and "present" as you explore your client's experiences, it invites the client to adopt the same attitude.

Review Home Practice

As with all sessions of MH, take some time to review the client's experiences with the homework during the week and the Mindful Self-Hypnosis Daily Practice Log (Appendix B). If you're not careful, it can be easy to get sucked into the "crisis of the week." Sometimes, a concern will have to be addressed and MH will need to be put aside. Examples include, but are not limited to, a client feeling suicidal, a death in the family, a substance-abuse relapse, or another critical event that requires immediate attention. It is appropriate to trust your clinical skill and instinct in deciding whether the MH protocol needs to be set aside to attend to other important issues. However, with noncritical events, look for opportunities to weave a client's weekly stressors and crises into the structure of MH.

Client: *Man, you would not BELIEVE the day I had at work on Tuesday! First, my boss came into my office looking really serious and told me that...[goes on to describe a difficult but nonurgent work situation]...and after THAT the copier broke down, so...*

Therapist: *Bob, if I could jump in for a moment, you mentioned that your boss "chewed you out" for making a mistake on that report. When he was criticizing you, how did you feel? I mean, what did you notice specifically?*

Client: *Well I guess I felt really hurt and embarrassed, and kind of angry, too, because...*

Therapist: *When you say hurt, embarrassed, and angry, it makes me curious what those things felt like in the moment. It's really hard when we're experiencing those kinds of emotions, but I'm tempted to bring some of that mindful, open curiosity to the experience. What did you notice in your body as you were experiencing those things?*

Client: *Huh. I don't know...I guess my face got hot! It felt like my throat and chest were tight, like it was hard to talk.*

Therapist: *Interesting, OK. So as you were feeling all of these unpleasant emotions, there were also physical sensations going on in the moment. Did you feel like you wanted to escape those feelings in the moment? Or make them go away?*

Client: *Well, yeah, of course! But I was stuck there with my boss; what could I do?*

Therapist: *Exactly. So, this is the kind of situation we were talking about last week and we'll continue to talk about today in terms of trying to resist our experiences when they're unpleasant...[continues to review how last week's material relates to the situation, and uses this as a bridge to discuss nonjudgmental awareness of thoughts and feelings].*

In the vignette, there is a choice point for the therapist. The client–therapist pair could easily have spent time discussing what happened in the meeting and what the client should do about this work situation. The therapist could have been supportive but nondirective, allowing the client to vent about his difficult day. In some circumstances, these interventions could be appropriate, but in this case, the therapist has decided that it's in Bob's best interest to steer the conversation toward MH topics. This is the approach we would recommend unless it is contraindicated according to your clinical judgment (e.g., maybe the client had previously mentioned that "If I make one more mistake at work, my boss said I'm going to be fired"). It is also important to note that even though the therapist in the vignette is steering the client toward a discussion of MH topics, he or she relates the discussion to the concrete issues and experiences that are important in the client's life.

Another thing to notice in the vignette is that there will often be an opportunity to seamlessly integrate the content from the previous week(s) with new content that is introduced. In the previous example, Bob starts by describing a situation that engenders some strong emotions. The therapist acknowledges these emotions, but starts building upon the client's nascent awareness of physical sensations first.

What did clients notice about the sights, sounds, and physical sensations at a particular moment? If these sensations are emerging in the present moment as they retell the story, can they bring a curious mindful awareness to the sensations? If they notice heat in their face as they tell the story, which part of their face feels most hot, or least hot? This kind of review will help clients feel a greater sense of expertise and mastery of the basic concept of nonjudgmental awareness, which can then be used as a bridge to explore the meaning of nonjudgmental awareness of thoughts and feelings. As the previously described session goes on, the therapist could return to the situation the client described (being criticized), but review the thoughts and emotions of the moment in more detail.

Strategic Themes of Session 3: Nonjudgmental Awareness (of Thoughts and Emotions)

Although session 3 may *feel* as though it is introducing a new concept, the ability to experience nonjudgmental awareness of thoughts and feelings is a natural extension of the concept introduced in the previous session. The core message that clients have to learn and experience for themselves is that all of their experiences (physical, mental, and emotional) can be regarded with curiosity, openness, and interest. By regarding their experiences with this nonjudgmental attitude, clients gain a greater freedom in their lives. They are less controlled by their experiences, because they no longer *have* to change their experiences to escape from intolerable suffering. If clients are able to engage with their experiences with open curiosity, they will be able to:

- Observe the experiences with greater clarity and with greater attention to subtle nuances.
- Choose for themselves what, if anything, they would like to do about these experiences.

When the concept of nonjudgmental awareness is applied to emotions, this simply means engaging with the emotions arising in the present moment with an attitude of curiosity. For example, if clients are feeling sad, they can bring a compassionate attentiveness to their sadness. Rather than trying desperately to deny their sadness or attitudinally "turn away" from their sadness, they can allow themselves to regard their sadness with openness. What does it feel like? What is their instinctual desire when they are focused on the sadness? Does the sadness become more intense or less intense from moment to moment and over the course of 5 minutes of mindful attention? Oftentimes, clients experience an initial spike in emotional intensity as they mindfully pay attention, followed by a gradual decrease. However, when exploring such issues with clients, it is important to direct their efforts toward the process of being mindful rather than the end goal of symptom reduction. Symptom reduction is excellent when it happens, and it is often a beneficial side effect of being mindful, but an overeagerness to change an experience often reflects reactive, judgmental awareness of the experiences that are actually present in the moment. Therefore, a greater effort to extinguish an unpleasant emotion often results in greater distress.

Mindful awareness of thoughts operates on an identical principle to mindful awareness of emotions or sensations. The goal when being mindful with thoughts is to become aware of the process of thinking and less caught up in a mindless train of thoughts. Thinking is what brains *do* and it's a wonderfully helpful process that helps us plan for the future and reflect on the past. However, when practicing mindfulness of thought, individuals should try to notice when they get lost in their thoughts, acknowledge the thought process they were just involved in, and bring an attentive curiosity to which thoughts might be unfolding in the present moment.

The first several weeks of treatment involve teaching these concepts and allowing clients to practice and experience mindfulness for themselves. Clients can facilitate this transformation by practicing every day with their home audio recordings and by looking for opportunities to informally practice mindfulness throughout the day. This informal mindfulness practice does not require an induction or "meditating" per se. Instead, it means that throughout the day, clients take some time to notice what they are experiencing in the moment and pay attention nonjudgmentally. For example, a client may notice that he is feeling anxious about an upcoming meeting as he walks from his car to the office. Upon noticing that he is feeling anxious, the client can bring a gentle curiosity to the experience: How does *this* experience of anxiety feel? Is there any feeling of the anxiety getting more intense or less intense from one moment to the next? Or does the anxiety remain absolutely constant? The posthypnotic suggestions integrated into the scripted hypnotic induction provided can help clients attend to their formal and informal mindfulness practice, and allow them to experience mindful awareness more easily and often.

CLINICIAN NOTE

Normalizing Difficulties

In practice, it is very difficult to be simultaneously thinking and *aware* of the process of thinking. Therefore, you might normalize this process for clients by assuring them that it is normal to get lost in a train of thought (to be thinking without being aware that you are thinking).

Remind your clients to be patient and kind with themselves, and simply recommit themselves to mindful attention *when* their mind wanders (not *if* their mind wanders).

Encourage clients to bring their curiosity to their thoughts, emotions, and sensations often throughout the day when their attention is not needed elsewhere. If a client is exceptionally busy, this busyness is sometimes viewed as an obstacle to being able to engage in informal mindfulness throughout the day. If a client raises this objection, remind the client that these moments of informal mindfulness can last as long as several hours or be as short as a single breath. This reminder can help clients who are thinking too rigidly about needing to set aside vast swaths of time. For other clients, their resistance to practicing has more to do with an unacknowledged fear of paying attention to their experiences during a stressful and hectic day. Stress is unpleasant, so if clients are new to nonjudgmental awareness, they may fear the emotional consequences of paying attention to it. Clients may also have fears about the consequences to their performance if they "slow down" to pay attention to their experiences even for a moment. In our experience, exploring clients' reservations about practice is an excellent opportunity to help them experience mindfulness more deeply.

As with previous sessions, make sure that you leave time in session 3 for a hypnotic induction and posthypnotic inquiry. In session 3, it is often useful to practice mindfulness of emotions by asking a client whether he or she would be willing to bring to mind a mildly or moderately stressful experience during hypnosis. It is important to seek permission beforehand so that you can maintain good rapport and a collaborative relationship with the client. Choosing the experience beforehand can also help you guide a client through the hypnotic induction in a way that feels safe and supportive. Finally, this pre-hypnosis discussion can help you to steer the client away from bringing extremely stressful experiences to mind during the hypnotic induction. Without a doubt, mindfulness *can* be applied to very stressful experiences. However, with clients who are still very new to mindfulness, it is often more beneficial to practice with less-intense experiences until they can develop a greater facility with mindfulness. Once clients have gotten in the habit of mindfully attending to their experiences, their mindful outlook can be flexibly applied to a great range of experiences, including those that are extremely unpleasant.

Hypnotic Induction for Nonjudgmental Acceptance of Thoughts and Emotions

Note: A singing bowl, chime, or bell is required to complete this script as it is written. An instrument of this sort can be useful as an auditory focus of attention, and a hypnotherapist may supplement another sound or use an alternative means of focusing attention mindfully. If you choose to use a singing bowl, chime, or bell, have this tool at hand and ready to use. Also, it is helpful to ask the client to rate his or her level of stress on the 0 to 10 scale prior to hypnotic induction.

CLINICIAN NOTE

Inductions Using Sound

For those clinicians who do not have a singing bowl, chime, or bell, consider that many free meditation apps have these sounds programmed in.

An auditory focus can also be just about anything, so don't let a lack of specialized equipment limit you.

INTRODUCTION AND SETTING EXPECTANCY

During this session of mindfulness-based hypnosis, a hypnotic induction will be completed and suggestions will be given for achieving a state of deep mental and physical relaxation. Within this relaxed state it will be possible...to become acquainted with your thoughts and feelings mindfully. Just as things that you sense through your body can be regarded mindfully—accepting them just as they are without needing to judge them as good or bad...in the same way you will be able to experience thoughts and feelings mindfully.

It is a process in which you will discover a sense of inner peace and stability...that comes from seeing thoughts and feelings for what they really are...just thoughts and feelings. When you have a thought, you will be aware that you are having a thought...and what the thought is telling you can be regarded dispassionately. Feelings can be regarded mindfully, too...noticing what you are feeling...but even more so noticing that you are feeling...without getting caught up in the feeling. The feeling itself holds no truth or falsehood...it needn't be clung to or pushed away...it just is...and you will notice your thoughts and feelings nonjudgmentally...letting go of judgments...letting go of distress.

HYPNOTIC INDUCTION WITH SUGGESTIONS FOR RELAXATION AND EYE CLOSURE

You may begin by allowing your body to relax, discovering a sense of ease, and clearing your mind...you might begin this process by taking a series of three deep breaths...and you may find that as you relax...so deeply...your eyes may begin to get heavy...and you may allow your eyes to close whenever it feels most natural to you... now taking a deep breath, and holding it for a moment...hold... and as you exhale, allow all of your muscles to relax...unwinding...tension draining from your body...and when you're ready, take another deep, deep breath...and hold...and now exhaling all of your cares and worries...perhaps feeling lighter as your burdens pass from you...a sense of ease settling deeply into your being...and in a moment...your final deep, deep breath will carry you into the present moment...becoming deeply mindful and present even more easily than you have in the past...effortlessly. Breathing in now for the third time...and hold...and as you breath out, entering the present moment...leaving concerns of the past and the future behind.

AUDITORY FOCUS AND NARROWING OF ATTENTION

In a moment, you will hear a tone...and this tone will at first be clear and eventually become softer until it disappears. When the tone sounds...you will focus on it so intently...that everything else begins to...fade...into the background...easily focusing on how the tone changes from moment to moment...attending closely to each nuance of the sound...and allowing each of these things that you notice to pass easily from your awareness as you attend to what is happening now with the next sound...focusing more and more on the present moment. When the sound starts to fade, you will find your mind becoming more and more focused on the fading sound...as the sound becomes fainter and fainter, you will pay closer and closer attention...more and more focused...and when the tone can no longer be heard, your mind will be as focused as it is capable of being...as focused as you allow it to be. I will stop talking while this tone sounds, so that you can focus fully on the sound of the [singing bowl/chime/bell]...and when I speak again your mind will be in a deep state of focus ...able to easily respond to each suggestion that I give.

[Wait 5 seconds, then ring the bowl/chime/bell.]

[If you are using a tool that can sustain a sound like a singing bowl, produce the sound for 10 seconds before allowing it to fade. Wait 5 seconds after the tone is no longer perceptible before continuing the script.]

DEEPENING SUGGESTIONS

...and soon allowing yourself to sink deeper into hypnosis...journeying inward...toward a place of complete and utter serenity...a place of calmness and relaxation...where your mind is at ease, and nothing troubles you...where your thoughts are clear like a cool mountain lake...still, and serene...not burdened by the slightest care...this may be a familiar place...and you may find it pleasant to journey inward toward that place within you now...and as you hear my voice count from 10 to 1, with each number finding yourself settling into an even deeper level of hypnosis...deeper toward that place of complete mental and physical relaxation within you ...

[Count each number as the patient exhales.]

Ten...setting your cares aside now as you embark on this inner journey...you needn't worry about losing track of them...they will be safe, and right where you left them if or when you choose to pick them up again.

Nine...feeling a sense of relief...relaxing...your body leading the way on this journey by becoming very relaxed...muscles unwinding... tension that you didn't even know you were carrying is now drifting away...bringing a sense of deep relief.

Eight...deeply calm...number eight and already so deeply relaxed...and you may begin to notice a warmth or tingling sensation in your body, as it relaxes even further.

Seven...and now a sense of profound calmness begins to blossom...unfolding...effortless, like a flower to the sun...and as you feel this, you might realize that mental and physical relaxation is not something that you do...it is a process of letting go...of not doing...even if just for this short while...like holding a ball in your hand...if you want to send the ball toward the ground...you needn't throw it, or exert effort or do anything...just the opposite, in fact...the only thing you need to do is let it go.

Six...halfway there, and already so profoundly relaxed...letting go of struggles and cares...letting go of any tension...letting go and simply being...in the present moment.

Five...perhaps at one time it took effort to calm your mind and body from its busyness...but now you are effortlessly still and serene...

settled so deeply into the present moment...that to direct your mind to the past or the future or other things would require effort, and you would prefer not to try.

Four...allowing your mind to settle...become still and calm...profoundly peaceful.

Three...deeper and more calm...no worries in this special moment.

Two...almost there...deeply relaxed...nothing bothers and nothing concerns...and perhaps it would be OK, with the final number I count...to let go of even the smallest vestige of tension or worry...to settle into complete and utter stillness and serenity...peaceful and content...or perhaps you will prefer to be very calm but not take that last step...trusting now that whichever your mind chooses is the right choice for you in this moment...what you truly need.

One...at the final step of your own inner journey...comfortably and deeply hypnotized...resting in the present moment...your thoughts uncluttered...still...and calm.

SETTING SESSION GOAL AND POSTHYPNOTIC SUGGESTION

And as you are there...that deep calm and focus you feel will allow you to become aware of thoughts and feelings...without being caught up in them...you will become mindfully aware of your thoughts and feelings...and this experience will pave the way for being mindful of thoughts and feelings in your daily life...day by day becoming more mindful toward thoughts and feelings...day by day becoming more mindful...and feeling relaxed, calm, and capable...whatever thoughts, feelings, or sensations you encounter in your daily life.

SUGGESTIONS FOR NONJUDGMENTAL AWARENESS OF THOUGHTS

And soon something very interesting is going to happen...it is possible to be thinking with one part of your mind...and yet with another part of your mind to be observing yourself thinking...aware of each thought as your mind drifts...letting each thought come and go... allowing the thoughts to be just as they are...nonjudgmentally...The thoughts are like leaves drifting past you in a gentle stream... each leaf is a thought...you can just notice the thoughts drift by without getting caught up in them...whether you have thoughts wondering, "Am I doing this right?"...or thoughts about what you need to do later...or thoughts about how useful this session will be for you...or any other thoughts drifting by...those thoughts are fine just as they are...you can notice them nonjudgmentally...their content is unimportant...they are just thoughts, and you can see them for what they are...and in a moment you will hear a tone and I will be silent to allow you to observe this process of mindful thinking...observing the thoughts as they come and go like leaves on a stream...each thought is a leaf...coming and going in its own time...noticing now where your mind goes as I am silent.

[Ring the bell, chime, or singing bowl, and pause 20 seconds or until the sound is inaudible.]

Good...and whatever you noticed is just fine...just continue to rest in a relaxed, mindful state...peaceful and serene...focused on my voice and on what is happening in the present moment.

SETTING EXPECTATION FOR MINDFULNESS OF FEELINGS

And perhaps it would be acceptable...to soon explore a new aspect of mindfulness...mindfulness of feelings.

Feelings can be pleasant or unpleasant...and although it is natural to gravitate toward pleasant feelings and away from unpleasant ones ...there may be a time in your life when unpleasant feelings are present whether you want them to be or not...during this exercise you will be able to experience unpleasant feelings...and still feel a sense of peace...just like thoughts can be experienced nonjudgmentally...drifting by like leaves on a stream...feelings can be experienced the same way...you will feel unperturbed, deeply peaceful, and steady...regardless of the emotions that come and go...they will blow through your body like winds blowing through an empty house.

MINDFULNESS OF FEELINGS

[The next section asks the client to bring to mind a stressful time. Use clinical judgment in how and whether to do this. If mindfulness of stress is contraindicated at this time, consider skipping the section or substituting a script for mindfulness of a positive emotion, without getting caught up in it.]

Now in a moment I'd like you to bring to mind a time during this past week when you felt stressed...either mild stress or moderate stress

...and when you bring that scene to mind soon...you will experience the feelings of that moment in a different way...mindfully...and this will enable you to experience stress mindfully in the future...If at any point during the exercise you wish to disengage...you may do so easily...focusing on your breath...peaceful and relaxed...and if that would be OK with you, just nodding your head yes.

[Wait for nod, and skip to the next section "Posthypnotic Suggestion," if approval is not obtained.]

Good...and it is possible to observe feelings without being caught up in them...to observe them nonjudgmentally as they come and go...like clouds drifting in the sky...forming...and dissipating...some clouds may look solid and formidable...but in reality all clouds are insubstantial...they form and they dissipate as they drift by...when you bring a mildly or moderately stressful event to mind, your feelings will be like drifting clouds...you will observe them nonjudgmentally...noticing as they come and go...without getting caught up in them...

Good...now as you allow your mind to drift to a time during this past week when you felt mild-to-moderate stress...it is important to realize that you will feel steady and in control...and you may let the scene go and return to this room, mindfully aware of your breathing...at any time you wish...now at your own pace, allow this mildly or moderately stressful time to come to mind...the image will become clearer and clearer...to the point where now you begin to notice the sights...sounds...and sensations...as though you were right back there...and as this time becomes clearer...clouds forming and dissipating as they drift by...you become gradually and mindfully aware of the feelings you felt at the time...although the feelings are the same, your reaction to those feelings is different isn't it? As you become aware of the way your body responds during stress...you recognize that stress is nothing to be afraid of...you will remain calm and unperturbed as the stressful feelings pass through you...observing the feelings peacefully and mindfully without being affected by them...watching them, like you might watch clouds form and dissipate on a sunny day...drifting past...and as the feelings drift past you and begin to dissipate...recognizing that you have the power to face stressful and unpleasant feelings without fear...if you choose to... you can observe them mindfully...nonjudgmentally...allowing them to pass over you and through you...and fade away. Stress will become less and less for you...and you will be able to encounter stressful events with a steady mind and heart...empowered and able to feel without being overwhelmed...whenever you choose to do so.

POSTHYPNOTIC SUGGESTION

Soon I will guide you out of this hypnotic state toward conscious alertness...but before this occurs I would like you to maintain this state of relaxed, mindful awareness a little longer. During this next week you will experience a nonjudgmental awareness of thoughts and feelings frequently during the day...both when you practice with the mindfulness recording and on a regular basis ... and you will find it easier and easier to experience nonjudgmental awareness of thoughts and feelings in the present moment...observing thoughts as they come and go...drifting by like leaves on a stream...observing feelings without being swept away...just watching them form and dissipate like clouds drifting by...observing and accepting your thoughts and feelings just as they are...nonjudgmentally...this awareness will ground you and empower you...allowing you to face difficult thoughts and feelings with greater ease...freeing you to live your life in the way that you think is best for you.

ALERTING

In a few moments, it is possible to begin returning to conscious alertness. Returning to conscious alertness in your own time and your own pace, in a way that just feels about right for you today...Feeling very good, normal, with good sensations in every way as you return to full conscious alertness...soon you will hear a tone that will signal for you to return to conscious alertness. When that tone sounds, you will begin to gently return to alertness...gradually opening your eyes as the sounds fades...and when the sound can no longer be heard, your eyes will be open. You will be fully awake and alert, in your normal state of wakefulness. Ready now? Returning to alertness with the sound of the tone...

[Ring bell, chime, or singing bowl.]

Posthypnotic Inquiry, Assigning Homework, and Closing the Session

After the hypnotic induction is complete and the client has been re-alerted, it is helpful to ask the client to rate the level of stress on a 0 to 10 scale. Also, once the client has been re-alerted, it is useful to follow up with a posthypnotic inquiry. This will allow you to learn more about the client's experiences and use this information to guide your clinical intervention. As always, look for opportunities to model mindfulness during your inquiry by allowing your own genuine curiosity to lead the way. If clients experienced their thoughts and emotions in a different way than they usually do, what was that like for them? What did they experience? If clients did *not* experience their emotions in a different way than they usually do (or if they found themselves reacting against unpleasant experiences), what was that like for them? In cases when clients maintain their typical judgmental attitude toward experiences, what did they notice as they were mentally "pushing against" their thoughts and feelings? If they didn't experience any strong emotions at all or if they were not aware of thoughts, explore these experiences with open curiosity. Sometimes clients will report an uneventful experience or a "bad" experience, and by conducting a mindfully inquiry, you can invite those clients to look a little deeper and shift their reactive attitude toward their experiences.

As always, close the session by providing the client with an audio recording of the hypnotic induction for this session and encouraging the client to practice with it every day during the week. At clients' discretion, they may also feel free to practice with any of the audio from previous weeks, as long as they practice with the session 3 hypnotic inductions for the majority of days during the week. It is common for clients to develop preferences for certain hypnotic inductions and find others to be less stimulating. Allowing clients to personalize their MH home practice (within certain parameters) can help keep clients engaged and allow them to have a greater sense of agency in their own path to greater wellness. It is very important to also remind clients to continue to record their practice using the Mindful Self-Hypnosis Daily Practice Log (Appendix B).

Summary and Closing Thoughts for Session 3

The aim of the third session is to facilitate a greater degree of nonjudgmental awareness of thoughts and feelings. Although mindful awareness of thoughts and feelings can be a difficult endeavor for clients, the task can be made less daunting by keeping in mind that the skill is no different than the one introduced in session 2. You can help your clients by starting with a thorough review of session 2 and helping them feel more confident about the meaning of nonjudgmental awareness. Once this is accomplished, therapists might consider highlighting the somatic components of emotions and how these sensations can be noticed mindfully. Finally, clients can apply this attitude toward mindful awareness of thoughts and emotions. With sufficient preparatory work, session 3 can feel like a logical next step rather than an insurmountable obstacle.

In each session of MH, the hypnotic principle of pacing and leading should be kept in mind (please refer to Chapter 5). Throughout the intervention, the therapist is leading a client into a new territory, an ever-greater mastery of mindfulness, and an ever-growing insight into its applications. However, it is important to be patient with your clients and allow time for their understanding to take root. It would be unrealistic to expect clients to immediately understand nonjudgmental awareness on a cognitive level *and* to be mindfully aware of all their experiences in a single week. Understanding mindfulness and putting it into practice takes time, even when using hypnotherapy. In our experience, it often takes several weeks for the seeds of understanding to take root. Anecdotally, clients who are engaged with treatment and practicing dutifully tend to report a shift in their experiences around weeks 4 to 6. For example, a client who has been very reactive toward his or her anxiety in the past might report that the following:

> You know, a funny thing happened last week. I started to get anxious and worried like I usually do, but as things were starting to really ramp up, I just kind of...noticed...it. I don't know, I noticed that my breathing was getting faster, and my heart was speeding up...but I was still OK, you know? I realized that it's *just anxiety*. Whatever anxiety is capable of doing to me, it's already doing it. I just observed it, and let it be. Eventually it went away on its own, but at that point I didn't even need it to. I was going to be OK either way.

Of course, more subtle shifts in attitude and ability are often perceptible prior to sessions 4 to 6, and sometimes these changes take more time. In addition, the shift in insight described previously does not happen on its own. Instead, it is the result of diligent practice and engaging with the MH treatment. Session 4 is a deliberate change in topic to allow more time for clients to practice what they have learned thus far. The treatment shifts from a focus on "understanding mindfulness" to a focus on "understanding self-hypnosis." The clients will continue to practice mindfulness during the week for home practice, but they are given a chance to figuratively "catch their breath" from the fast pace of learning that occurred in sessions 1 to 3.

REFERENCE

Goleman, D. (1980). A map for inner space. In R. N. Walsh & F. Vaughn (Eds.), *Beyond ego* (pp. 141–150). Los Angeles, CA: Tarcher

CHAPTER 11

Session 4

SELF-HYPNOSIS AND MINDFUL HYPNOTHERAPY

The greatest discovery of my generation is that a human being can alter his life by altering his attitudes of mind.
—William James (1890/1950)

Introduction

The focus of this chapter is on enhancing clients' understanding of self-hypnosis. Mindful self-hypnosis may be accomplished with or without audio recordings. Up to this point (session 4), mindful hypnotherapy (MH) has involved providing audio recordings of hypnotic inductions, asking the client to "practice self-hypnosis using audio recordings," and tracking progress on the Mindful Self-Hypnosis Daily Practice Log (Appendix B). Practice using the audio recordings is very beneficial. However, the benefit can be enhanced by teaching clients how to also experience self-hypnosis without use of audio recordings. This is "true" self-hypnosis, as it is fully self-directed, and learning this skill is the primary aim of session 4. As clients learn this new aspect of self-hypnosis—that is, self-hypnosis *without needing to use audio recordings*—it can further enhance the benefits from use of the audio recordings of hypnotic inductions that are usually provided at the end of each session.

Learning and practicing self-hypnosis with and without audio recordings has a number of benefits and can enhance the progress of MH. Self-hypnosis without audio recordings can be used in a very flexible manner. For example, clients can use it to achieve a hypnotic state and reinforce mindful suggestions and goals. In addition, the practice of self-hypnosis without audio recordings can be long (i.e., 20–30 minutes or longer) or very brief (i.e., 1–5 minutes). With the brevity of self-hypnosis, it can be practiced more frequently (such as 3–4 times a day), thereby further enhancing the benefits of audio-recorded and therapist-delivered mindful hypnosis. It is important to emphasize that self-hypnosis practice does not replace audio-recorded or live sessions, but provides an additional tool for supporting and increasing progress. Self-hypnosis can be very empowering as it gives greater control to the client and hypnotic suggestions can be self-directed.

Strategic Themes of Session 4: Learning Mindful Self-Hypnosis

As clients progress in MH, they become more familiar with their own personal preferences for hypnotic inductions and more engaged in the overall process of MH. Most clients learn self-hypnosis easily after they have practiced mindful hypnotic inductions with audio recordings for several weeks. The advantages of adding self-hypnosis are that clients can practice mindful self-hypnosis as often as they like, when they need it, and for as long as or as brief as circumstances may dictate. The experience of self-hypnosis is very similar to guided or audio-recorded hypnotic inductions. In fact, it has been said that "all hypnosis is self-hypnosis," meaning that hypnosis is something the client experiences and learns to do, rather than something that is "done to the client."

During session 4, the client's progress is reviewed and areas of emphasis for self-hypnosis practice are identified. After the review of home practice is completed, self-hypnosis is introduced. Most clients welcome the instruction in self-hypnosis and are receptive to learning self-hypnosis practice. It is often useful to include a guided hypnotic induction with suggestions for self-hypnosis practice. During this induction, the client can be provided with psychoeducation about the structure of a hypnotic induction as it is taking place. If several hypnotic inductions are given during a single session, this can also be a useful way to teach. In each induction, the hypnotherapist can give less and less explicit instruction, gradually allowing clients to lead themselves by through the hypnotic experience.

Review Home Practice

As you review the client's Mindful Self-Hypnosis Daily Practice Log, it can be helpful to ask: "How often have you practiced with the audio recordings during the past week?"; "What did you find most helpful about the practice with the audio recordings?"; "Did you try to enter a hypnotic state on your own, without the use of the recordings?" This can provide a very good opportunity to learn about your client's experience with mindful hypnosis practice to date and to suggest the idea of self-hypnosis as an option.

It is also important to inquire about stress and your client's progress. Asking clients to report on how well they are coping with stress, reducing anxiety, and responding to the sessions and audio recordings can provide essential information and help guide the session. Identifying their experiences, likes and dislikes, can help to identify focus for self-hypnosis practice.

Introduce Self-Hypnosis

It is important to communicate to the client that the goal of session 4 is to learn the steps and process of self-hypnosis. Self-hypnosis is introduced as a method that can enhance progress and empower the client with greater control. This is illustrated in the following exchange between the therapist and the client.

Therapist: *During this session, you will learn self-hypnosis. In a sense, all hypnosis is self-hypnosis because a hypnotic state is something that you create within yourself; it is not something that is done to you. The integration of self-hypnosis into MH can be empowering because it gives a greater sense of control and ease of practice. Self-hypnosis refers to the experience of hypnosis through your own ability. Once you learn self-hypnosis, you will be able to integrate it into your daily practice.*

Client: *So, I will learn how to do hypnosis on my own, without using the audio recording?*

Therapist: *Yes, that's right. A self-hypnosis session can be as long as or as brief as you would like it to be. It can be very useful to enter a hypnotic state and respond to self-generated suggestions toward mindfulness in your own time and in ways that are best for you.*

Client: *I like the idea of self-hypnosis. It is something that we are going to cover today? How can I learn self-hypnosis?*

Therapist: *Great question! The best way to learn self-hypnosis is through practice and experience. Therefore, I will guide you through integrating self-hypnosis. Once you learn self-hypnosis, you can continue to practice with your other audio recordings just as often as you would like but also you can integrate the practice of self-hypnosis. This can be beneficial, as this combined practice often brings the most positive results.*

CLINICIAN NOTE

Self-Hypnosis

Learning self-hypnosis is a process that begins with the use of hypnosis audio recordings. It then includes psychoeducation about self-hypnosis and the 10 steps of mindful self-hypnosis. However, to fully learn self-hypnosis, it is essential that the client practice self-hypnosis without use of any audio recordings so that unassisted self-hypnosis is learned. Unassisted self-hypnosis can be very brief (5–10 minutes, and this can be very empowering for the client.

Mindful Self-Hypnosis Instructions

As self-hypnosis is explained to the client, it is important to answer any questions and to review the steps toward self-hypnosis. During this session the client should also be given instructions with the steps for practicing self-hypnosis. These instructions can be provided as a handout, as follows:

I. Focus of attention: Roll your eyes upward and focus on a spot.

II. Allow eyelids to close: Take a deep breath of air, and as you exhale, allow your eyelids to close.

III. Awareness of breathing: Now, focus on your breathing and with each breath of air, as you breathe out...relax. Aware of breathing in...and...breathing out...relaxing...deeper and deeper.

IV. Suggestions for relaxation: Now, notice a wave of relaxation that spreads from the top of your head down to your feet...across your forehead, neck, shoulders, arms, back, chest, stomach, legs, and feet. Every muscle and every fiber of your body...more and more completely relaxed.

V. Deepening the hypnotic state: Deeply relaxed...letting go of all tension...letting go of all judgmentalness...aware of your own experience...as unimportant things fade into the background.

VI. Mental imagery for a safe place: Now, with one part of your mind, going to another place. A place where you are safe and feel secure, calm and at ease. Going to that place now...where you find comfort. That place may be walking down a cool mountain path, or another place...aware of all the beauty around you in this safe and good place.

VII. Suggestions for awareness: And there...mindfully observing your own experience...aware of the present moment. You can become more aware of your breathing...feelings...or thoughts...the present moment...any sensations...feelings...or thoughts...nonjudgmentally...noticing and being aware...without trying to change or alter...just noticing and being aware of the present moment...as it unfolds.

VIII. Awareness of mind: You may notice thoughts that arise...just nonjudgmentally observing the thoughts as they arise. Just noticing...without judgment.

IX. Nonjudgmental awareness of the present moment: Now, aware of your breathing...more at peace within yourself...as you experience mindfulness.

X. Return to conscious alertness: And, now gently and easily returning to conscious alertness, in your own time and your own pace...In a way that pleases you...now.

After giving the client time to look over the instructions, the therapist should then identify the 10 steps for self-hypnosis and answer any questions. The following transcript illustrates an example of this discussion.

Therapist: *OK, so please look over the instructions on self-hypnosis. Do you have any questions?*

Client: *Will we have a hypnotic induction today?*

Therapist: *Yes, in our hypnotic induction today I will guide you through the 10 steps of self-hypnosis. I will also give you an audio recording of the session, so you can practice and learn how to do self-hypnosis. With practice you will be able to remember and complete the 10 steps without needing the audio recording.*

Client: *That makes sense.*

Therapist: *OK, so just to review the 10 steps of self-hypnosis and then we will go on to your hypnotic induction. First, a focus of attention. Second, suggestions for your eyelids to close. Third, suggestions for awareness of your breathing. Fourth, suggestions for relaxation. Fifth, deepening the hypnotic state. Sixth, mental imagery for a safe place. Seventh, suggestions for awareness...of breathing...of feelings...sensations... thoughts. Eighth, awareness of your mind—its tendency to analyze, critique, plan, judge. Ninth, nonjudgmentally observing and be absorbed in your awareness of the present moment. Tenth, return to conscious alertness.*

Hypnotic Induction for Learning Self-Hypnosis

After the steps to self-hypnosis have been reviewed and the handout provided, a hypnotic induction can be completed with suggestions for self-hypnosis practice. The client's personal goals for self-hypnosis practice can be discussed as well as any questions. Also, asking the client to rate his or her level of stress on the 0 to 10 scale before the mindful self-hypnosis practice is recommended.

Self-hypnosis can be learned through practice and experience. You can review the steps of self-hypnosis by referring to your handout. Also, during today's session I will guide you through the 10 steps of self-hypnosis. As you practice these 10 steps, you will learn self-hypnosis. You can also continue to use your other audio recordings of mindful hypnotic inductions. However, you can now integrate the practice of self-hypnosis without the use of audio recordings as well. This can be very helpful as you can practice self-hypnosis as often as you like and this can bring the most positive results.

"First, Focus of Attention"

Now, we will begin the process of learning self-hypnosis. There are 10 steps. Begin by first finding a comfortable place to sit or lie down with good support for your head, neck, and shoulders. It is important to be in a comfortable and resting position in which you can best experience relaxation and a hypnotic state and respond to suggestions for mindfulness.

Now, one, focus on an object, a light, or a spot. Focus on an object or a feeling of your choosing...You might even just focus on your breathing...Focus intently so you allow other things to fade into the background more and more...absorbed in that focus of attention...the beginning of a hypnotic state...and as you allow this to occur...so...also allowing your eyelids to close.

"Second, Allowing Eyelids to Close"

Now, bring your attention to your breathing...notice breathing in and breathing out...and as it feels right for you...as you exhale, allow your eyelids to close. As you allow the eyelids to close...this serves as a cue to begin to drift into a very calm and deeply relaxed state, letting all tension go, drifting deeper and deeper relaxed.

"Third, Suggestions for Awareness of Breathing"

Your breathing is always with you...sometimes in your awareness and sometimes outside your conscious awareness...but for this time...bringing your attention to the sensations of breathing in and breathing out...as you are more aware of your breathing...other things fade into the background...more and more...just aware of the sensations of breathing in and breathing out...the coolness of the air in your nostrils as you breathe in...the feeling of letting go...as you breathe out...you can always bring your awareness to your breathing...fully aware...noticing your breathing...without controlling it...just nonjudgmentally observing your breathing...and drifting deeper. . .relaxed.

"Fourth, Suggestions for Relaxation"

Now, notice a kind of a wave of relaxation that spreads from the top of your head to your feet. Drifting deeper and deeper relaxed... Every muscle and every fiber of your body becoming more and more relaxed...There is no need of any tension...no need of any concerns...just drifting deeper and deeper relaxed.

That wave of relaxation spreading, like a cool breeze across your forehead and your face. And an awareness of breathing. With each breath of air drifting deeper and deeper relaxed. That wave of relaxation now spreads from the top of your head, across your face, and into your neck so that you can begin to go limp and relaxed, your shoulders can become deeply relaxed. That wave of relaxation...now can spread into your arms...allow them to go limp and relaxed. Allowing that wave of relaxation to now...spread into your back...your upper back and lower back...relax.

So now...your chest and stomach, relax; and just aware of your breathing...breathing in and breathing out...every breath taking you deeper and deeper relaxed...emotionally relaxed...physically relaxed.

That wave of relaxation spreading now...into your legs and feet, the legs go limp...relaxed...no need for any tension...no tension...no stress...every muscle, every fiber of your body, more and more completely relaxed.

"Fifth, Deepening the Hypnotic State"

Now, going into a deeper hypnotic state...in which you will be able to respond to each suggestion just as you would like to respond...achieving a mindful state...awareness of the present moment...relaxed...nonjudgmental awareness...and deeply relaxed...

Other things...unimportant things...fade further into the background...so that you are even more aware of your own experience...aware of breathing in and breathing out...aware of any sensations that arise...any images that arise...just observing and noticing as you go even deeper...relaxed. Entering a deeper hypnotic state as you now drift even more relaxed...in every way...letting go...of all tension...letting go...of all judgmentalness...letting go...of worries and concerns...and drifting deeper and deeper into this hypnotic state...your own hypnotic state of focused attention and awareness of the present moment.

"Sixth, Mental Imagery for a Safe Place"

Now, within this hypnotic state...it is possible to feel safe and secure...Mental images of being in a safe and secure place...a peaceful place where you can let go...feel at ease...and have a greater degree of mindfulness...nonjudgmental awareness...Just notice whatever images of being in a safe place come into your consciousness.

A safe place...such as if you were walking down a path that leads you to a beautiful waterfall....Walking down a cool mountain path...there are beautiful trees...along the path...notice each step that you take...the feeling of walking...notice the trees...and the beauty all around you...the sunlight as it filters through the branches of the trees...and up ahead is a beautiful waterfall...perhaps you can hear the sound of the waterfall...or perhaps you will see it...first...so that now...you have come to a lovely place...it is peaceful here...the waterfall cascades down...down...into a lovely pool of water.

You might be sitting there...perhaps on a rock...overlooking the pool of water...notice the water as it cascades over the waterfall...and drift into a deeper hypnotic state...notice the pool of water...it is calm...peaceful...here...and so...you may feel more calm and peaceful here...You are in a safe place...a peaceful place...a calm place...within your own experience.

"Seventh, Suggestions for Awareness"

And here...mindfully observing your own experience...notice your breathing...notice as you breathe in...that you are breathing in...notice as you breathe out...that you are breathing out...each breath...bringing calmness...aware of the present moment...no worry about the past...no worry about the future...just aware of this beautiful, wonderful moment...breathing in and breathing out...drifting deeper and deeper relaxed...aware of the beauty and wonder of each moment...You may feel a smile come to you...as you are aware of the beauty and wonder of each moment.

And aware of each sensation and feeling as it arises...nonjudgmentally aware...just observing and noticing...you might notice the movement of your chest as you breathe in and breathe out... you might notice the temperature of the air around you...or you might notice the calmness and relaxation in whatever way...it comes to you.

"Eighth, Awareness of Mind"

You may also notice thoughts that arise from the mind...You can observe these thoughts...as they arise...just nonjudgmentally observing the thoughts as they arise...The mind creates thoughts...some are pleasant...the mind may drift to memories...it may analyze...or anticipate plans...and that is all right...but for now...just observing any thoughts as they arise from the mind...form and then recede...just watching and observing any thoughts that arise from the mind...the way you could watch clouds drift across the sky.

Observing any thoughts the way you could lay down on a recliner...outside and look up at the clouds in the sky...white puffy clouds...and just watch them drift across the sky...feeling calm and peaceful...nonjudgmental...just noticing and accepting the presence of each thing as it comes into your awareness.

"Ninth, Nonjudgmental Awareness of the Present Moment"

So that now...again aware of your breathing...and aware just of the present moment...more at peace within yourself...and aware of your own experience...noticing any sensations, feelings...whatever comes into your awareness...thoughts or memories that can be observed...mindfulness...as I am silent for a few moments...as you experience... mindfulness.

[Silent for 30 seconds to 1 minute.]

"Tenth, Return to Conscious Alertness"

Very good...In a few moments returning to conscious alertness...Each time you practice self-hypnosis, you find it easier and easier to enter a very deeply relaxed state...and finding through this practice of self-hypnosis that you become more mindfully aware of the present moment, more aware of each thing...thoughts...sensations...feelings...as they arise within and around you...stress becomes less...as you are more calm...more aware...more at ease ...every day...The ten steps of self-hypnosis will become a part of your awareness and integrated into your lifestyle...and practice of mindfulness-based hypnotherapy...in ways that you find most helpful for yourself.

Now...just very gently and easily...returning to conscious alertness...no hurry...no rush...just being gentle with yourself...now and every day...and for now...just gently returning to conscious alertness...as your eyelids open...return to conscious alertness...you might stretch your arms and back...return to full conscious alertness...fully alert...relaxed...and more mindful...a deeper understanding of mindfulness in your daily experience.

Posthypnotic Inquiry, Assigning Homework, and Closing the Session

After the hypnotic induction is completed, it is helpful to ask the client to again rate his or her level of stress on the 0 to 10 scale. Also, after the hypnotic induction has been completed, it is very helpful to ask the client to then complete a self-hypnosis experience with just the "Self-Hypnosis Instructions" as a guide and minimal prompts. Allow about 5 to 10 minutes for the client to go through a self-hypnosis practice before concluding the session. The posthypnotic inquiry can be focused on exploring the client's experience and any questions.

It should also be emphasized to the client that the response to self-hypnosis should feel effortless. It is important that the client experience self-hypnosis as occurring easily and without struggle. Self-hypnosis suggestions are best experienced as positive ideas and can be allowed to occur, rather than being forced.

The session can conclude with the homework assignment. The client should be provided with an audio recording of the hypnotic induction for learning self-hypnosis and the Mindful Self-Hypnosis Daily Practice Log. The client can be asked to practice self-hypnosis without the recording at least twice per day. The practice of self-hypnosis without the recording can be very brief (i.e., 5–10 minutes or less).

Summary and Closing Thoughts for Session 4

As self-hypnosis is integrated into MH, it is possible that clients may be more able to adopt a mindful approach to whatever arises in their experience (thoughts, feelings, sensations). Mindful self-hypnosis can help clients feel more grounded in present-moment awareness, and can help them regard their experiences nonjudgmentally. With self-hypnosis practice, becoming aware of present-moment experiences can be transformative and can enhance the ability to cope with stress. As clients practice mindful self-hypnosis, they may feel more calm and aware of everyday experiences (aware of the sensations of walking, feeling of the sun on the face, coolness of the air, breathing sensations, and so on). As these things occur, the practice of self-hypnosis is reinforced and may become more frequent. This hypnotic induction recording for learning self-hypnosis can be used until the practice of self-hypnosis becomes well learned and easy for clients to do without the recording.

REFERENCE

James, W. (1950). *The principles of psychology*. New York, NY: Dover Publications. (Original work published 1890)

CHAPTER 12

Session 5

MINDFUL HYPNOTHERAPY FOR COMPASSION

If compassion is imagined as a beautiful dove, then wisdom is its wings. Compassion without wisdom never takes off.
—*Ajahn Brahm (2005)*

I have learned many things. Among them, that we can apparently endure anything . . . eventually; that the moment is always precious because it will never return; that time is really the only true commodity; and that we are being incredibly foolish when we take relationships for granted, focus on negative things like hatred, racism (any kind of "ism" really), malicious gossip, or the negative judgment of others.
—*Hugh Riley, PhD (Personal communication)*

Introduction

Compassion is an attitude with tremendous potential for healing and for transforming one's actions. Compassion's potential to transform the world for the better means that many people have come to think of compassion as a moral imperative. "Good" people *should* have compassion for others, and if they don't act compassionately, they are "bad" or evil. Furthermore, in Western culture, compassion is implicitly understood to be an outward-bound characteristic. Good people have compassion for *others*. Compassion for oneself is often regarded as unimportant at best and narcissistic at worst. This session is an opportunity to examine and perhaps challenge some of these unspoken assumptions about the role of compassion. The result of this process is that clients unlock the profound healing potential of compassion for themselves and for the people around them. Throughout the session, the therapist can help expand clients' view of compassion from an exclusively moralistic, one-way street to a broader view that encompasses both themselves and others.

Strategic Themes of Session 5: Compassion for Self and Others

Session 5 often proves to be an emotional turning point in mindful hypnotherapy (MH). Clients who are progressing well often start to grasp the concepts introduced in the first several sessions and may be implementing mindfulness spontaneously in their daily life. For clients who are doing exceptionally well, this new understanding will sometimes manifest as novel changes in perspective, affect, or action that demonstrate a convergence with a mindful perspective on life.

In the early stages of MH, even clients who are doing well and starting to notice changes may still be thinking of mindfulness as a "neat trick," a cognitive exercise, or a purely utilitarian activity. For these clients, session 5 can be an opportunity to open the door to the affective and meaningful aspects of mindfulness through practicing self-compassion and compassion for others. Look for opportunities to lead the way by letting your own compassion and concern for a client's well-being show in your facial expression, in your tone of voice, in your attentiveness and attunement to the client, and in other ways.

The previous sessions have laid the groundwork for clients' transformation by beginning to change the way they relate to their own experiences. Clients may be more receptive to novel ways of thinking and behaving, and their attentive curiosity toward their own lives and experiences presents new opportunities. In this session, the core theme is to invite clients to use their newfound ability to see their experiences clearly and to act on what they think is *best* rather than what they feel compelled to do by habit or instinct.

For most clients, it will be helpful to foster independence by encouraging them to decide for themselves which acts of self-compassion are right for them and which acts of compassion might be appropriate. As a therapist, you can offer support by laying out a novel conceptualization of self-compassion and giving some examples to make it clear what you mean. However, proscribing specific self-compassionate activities for clients to enact during the week may bypass the need for them to "tune in" to their own needs as they emerge. It is important to nurture clients' capacity for self-examination and self-attunement as a guide for their compassion and self-compassion. Doing so will allow clients to transition more easily to self-directed practice.

In this session, the overall concept of compassion is subdivided into two categories: (a) compassion for self and (b) compassion for others. Clients often struggle with one or the other concept differentially, finding one easy to apply in their own lives and the other more difficult. During this session, both facets of compassion should be given attention and consideration for how they might be integrated more fully into the client's life. However, the therapist should spend greater time with whichever facet is lacking most in the client's life. Alternatively, a therapist may choose to emphasize the facet of compassion that has the greatest potential to change the client's life for the better.

Review Home Practice

At the beginning of session 5, check in with your clients about their home practice during the week and review their Mindful Self-Hypnosis Daily Practice Log. This is an opportunity to foster their eventual transition to self-guided practice, since self-hypnosis allows for customizing a client's experience even beyond what you are able to provide in-session. Session 5 is also an excellent opportunity to check in on a clients' experiences of stress. As you inquire about their recent experiences with stress or anxiety, be sure to orient the conversation toward their relationship with their emotions, not just the content of what they are experiencing. If clients describe hints of a novel relationship with their experiences, or describe feeling less emotional distress in their lives, this is good progress.

As the client's understanding of mindfulness begins to take root in the second half of the MH intervention, it is more important than ever that the therapist listen attentively for any distortions in mindfulness that are apparent in a client's words. As discussed in earlier chapters, it is easy for clients to conflate "mindfulness" with "relaxation" because the former often leads to the latter. Similarly, it is common for clients to assimilate the "mindfulness" you have been discussing during MH with the way they had been thinking of "mindfulness" prior to treatment. For example, prior to MH some clients think of mindfulness as a process of "tuning out," or not doing anything. Others think of mindfulness as a state of mind where a person is not *aware* of any of the unpleasant experiences that are arising because they are "beyond" them. Remember that a person's attitude toward his or her experiences is important. If a person is hyperaware of the physical experience of pain because of fear of what that pain may mean or is afraid that the pain may get worse, this is not mindfulness despite the person's attentiveness. Attentiveness caused by fear of experiences indicates the presence of a strong resistance to experiences that is antithetical to mindfulness. Therefore, keep alert for these subtle or overt distortions and kindly correct them when they arise.

Introduce Compassion

When transitioning to the new content introduced in session 5, it is helpful to get a sense of a client's current experience of compassion for self and others. Some clients will already have an excellent attentiveness to self-care, and their attitudes toward themselves and others may already be very kind. For these clients, session 5 may be an opportunity to let these qualities shine and rededicate themselves to these compassionate behaviors and attitudes. You can also invite these clients to bring a new awareness to how self-compassion and compassion for others impact their lives. Perhaps they might even notice a new and synergistic relationship with the mindfulness material that has been taught thus far in MH.

Much more often, however, clients acknowledge that they have a harsh or critical attitude toward themselves. Other clients feel as though they are very compassionate toward themselves, but experience frustration and anger when interacting with others. Some clients struggle with both compassion for themselves and compassion for others. In any of the cases where a client struggles with kindness or self-kindness, the goal will be to open the client's eyes to viewing compassion as a means to thrive. It is not just a moralistic issue, but instead a quality that opens up new possibilities and reduces a client's experience of suffering. Once you have established which areas of compassion/self-compassion a client struggles with most, you can use this information to guide your conversation during the rest of the session.

Therapist: *Another potential source of stress and distress in people's lives comes from a kind of ... lack of compassion, or lack of empathy for oneself or others. Some people find that they forgive others easily and treat them with kindness, but they have trouble finding the same love and empathy for themselves. Other people have more trouble forgiving others, and the anger and frustration builds up inside to the point that it's hurting them and stressing them out. Is any of this sounding familiar?*

Client: *Well, more so the first one. Like I was talking about a few weeks ago, with my job, I just feel like I push myself so hard and it stresses me out because I'm afraid that even that might not be good enough. You know? I* *know it's kind of nuts because I've never or almost never gotten that feedback from my boss, but...well...*

Therapist: *Mmhmm...go on.*

Client: *Well, I don't know; I guess I'm afraid of not being good enough so I push myself harder.*

In this short exchange, the therapist is able to normalize the experience of harshness toward oneself or others. He or she uses language that frames these attitudes as causing internal harm. If a person is angry and frustrated with people all day, this may be a difficult experience for the people around them, but it is *also* a difficult experience for the angry and frustrated person! Similarly, a client may struggle with self-compassion, but this doesn't make him or her a bad person. A useful metaphor might be imagining that day after day, Maria stubs her toe on the coffee table on her way out the door. Even if it happens every day, we wouldn't think of Maria as evil or bad. Still, her actions are causing consistent pain and harm, and it might be a good idea to move the coffee table to a location that's out of the way.

Barriers to Self-Compassion

In broaching the subject of self-compassion, you may wish to begin by exploring clients' barriers to self-compassion and inviting them to become curious about this themselves. Clinicians are encouraged to find their own voice, style, and methods of navigating the discussion of barriers to self-compassion. Some common barriers and counterpoints are discussed later, but any discussion that leaves clients open to the importance of self-compassion and curious to see what positive impact it can have on their lives will be equally effective.

One of the barriers clients commonly experience is worrying that the only thing driving them to success is a fear of failure. When client have this attitude, they may think of harshness toward themselves as a way to keep this fear of failure alive. Clients who operate under this assumption might be invited to consider whether other emotions might potentially drive them to succeed—for example, the desire to accomplish their goals, to be happy, or to have a positive impact on the world through their success. Positive emotions and values can be a motivating force that can take the place of an overreliance on unpleasant emotions such as fear of failure, self-loathing, or harsh self-judgment. If clients are familiar with the idea of "the carrot or the stick," this can be an easy way to point out that there is more than one motivating force that can lead them toward success. Some clients get so used to using the metaphorical "stick" that they forget the "carrot" even exists.

Another barrier to self-compassion is related to the one discussed previously. It is a commonly held belief that harsh criticism is a necessary and integral part of having high standards. Some clients worry that if they don't berate themselves for failing to reach their goals, they will stagnate and become unmotivated. Such clients might be invited to consider that if harsh criticism is what leads to success, why not berate a friend in the same way when that person fails? The "high standards" barrier to self-compassion is a fallacy. If a person is aware that he or she has fallen short of his or her goals, it is entirely possible to be mindfully aware of this, to treat oneself with compassion, and encourage oneself to take corrective actions. These attitudes can stem from a deep sense of love for oneself and a desire to see yourself succeed.

Still other clients may feel that self-compassion is the same thing as egocentrism and that compassion is a zero-sum game. These clients may argue that all of their energy, resources, and time should be devoted to helping others; anything less is a selfish failure of discipline. In this case, a client might be invited to reflect on whether this view is internally consistent. The orientation toward helping others is certainly laudable, yet, even if this is a person's highest ideal, is a lack of self-compassion the best way to help others? Typically, a well-rested person is more capable of helping than an exhausted one, and a person who treats himself or herself like "worthless trash" sets a poor example for other people. In contrast, a person who feels physically and emotionally energetic will have the resources to be able to respond to others' needs. Some clients will expect that other people will care for them even when they do not care for themselves, yet who is in a better position to see and attend to the client's needs than the client himself or herself?

Following is just one example of how the discussion of barriers could play out with a typical client:

Therapist: *Speaking of self-compassion, you mentioned that you failed a calculus test today. When people struggle with self-compassion, it's common to think to yourself, "Wow, Jacob, you are such an idiot! I can't believe you didn't study more for that test. At this rate, I wouldn't be surprised if you flunked out of college, and it would be your own damn fault."*

[Notices the client wince.]

I mean, for some people, that's an exaggeration, but for other people that's really what they think to themselves. Does any of that sound familiar?

Client: *No, no, you're right, actually. I think that kind of thing to myself all the time, but who doesn't, right? I think it's pretty common to be your own worst critic.*

Therapist: *You're right that it's pretty common, but I wonder whether it actually makes sense. If harsh criticism is what helps people to thrive, why not tell that to your best friend when she fails a test? Can you imagine rubbing that in someone's face right after the person fails an exam? Do you think the person would feel motivated to study after you say something like THAT?*

Client: *Well, no. I guess the person would feel pretty discouraged.*

Therapist: *Do YOU feel motivated when you tell yourself you're an idiot who will never succeed?*

Client: *No.*

Therapist: *So how might you help your best friend to do well, especially if she didn't study enough? Maybe something like "I'm so sorry that you failed the exam, that's really hard! I believe in you, though, and I think you can do better next time. Tell you what, why don't we go to the library after class and study together?" How would your friend feel then? Motivated to study more?*

Client: *Yeah, for sure.*

Therapist: *And that motivation to do better came from encouragement, love, and support. Jacob, I see that you've been struggling for a long, long time with this harsh inner voice of yours. It's like a lead weight that you carry on your back all the time. On the whole, you've been fairly successful in school despite that harsh weight dragging you down. I wonder what you might be capable of if you treated yourself with love, support, and compassion.*

Self-Compassion as a Gift of Love

When a client is feeling receptive to the general idea of self-compassion, this is an excellent opportunity to explore what self-compassion actually *means*. A useful metaphor to use with clients is thinking of self-compassion as a gift that they can give themselves. What makes something a good gift versus a bad gift?

- A good gift is one that meets the person's needs or interests.
  - A gift certificate to a steakhouse would make an excellent gift for someone who loves steak. It would make a poor gift for a vegetarian.
- A good gift is one that demonstrates love and care.
  - Though not gifts in the conventional sense, kind words for a friend who is struggling, a sympathy card for someone who has lost a loved one, and inspiration for a person who is feeling unmotivated would all make excellent "gifts" of love.

- A good gift is one that doesn't harm the recipient.
  - It would be inappropriate to give a kitten to someone who is deathly allergic to cats.
- A good gift is one that helps the recipient to thrive.
  - Ice cream is delicious, but would make a poor gift to someone who was recently diagnosed with diabetes or someone who is trying to lose weight.

Similar to some of these examples, a gift of self-compassion requires a person to bring a careful, mindful attentiveness to his or her inner state and needs. In some cases, loving oneself may mean "easing up" and not being so critical or self-punishing. For example, a person may notice that he has been working very hard and sleeping very little. In this case, the person may decide that today, a gift of self-compassion means sleeping in for an extra hour instead of working out like he usually does. In other cases, it may mean actually doing something the person has been putting off because he will feel a greater sense of ease and well-being once the thing is done. For example, someone who has been sleeping too much and feeling lethargic may decide that even though he feels sleepy, he will get out of bed today and work out because he knows that he will feel more energized for the rest of the day. A gift of self-compassion could mean a student taking a 15-minute study break when she has been working very hard. It could also mean doing that paper she has been procrastinating over, because this gift will help the student to be free of the anxiety she has been feeling.

In essence, a gift of self-compassion is not "good" or "bad" in all circumstances. A good gift requires attuning yourself to what you actually need to thrive and feel cared for, and then loving yourself enough to follow through with giving yourself this gift.

■ CLINICIAN NOTE

Teaching Compassion

Affective attunement to the client is important throughout mindful hypnotherapy. This quality may be especially important during session 5 in allowing clients to become attuned to themselves and relate to themselves compassionately.

Therapist: *I'd like you to consider something for me, and take this question seriously: If you truly and deeply loved yourself in this very moment, what gift would you give yourself?*

Anything within your power to give—what might that be? What would help you to thrive? What would allow you to feel genuinely loved by yourself, and give you exactly what you need?

Client: *[Looks thoughtful]...huh, I guess I could really use a nap right now.*

Therapist: *A nap! Tell me more about where that gift is coming from.*

Client: *[Discussion ensues, exploring the client's harsh internal voice, resulting in driving the self so hard that the client's work begins to paradoxically suffer]*

Therapist: *All right. I'd like you to continue to ask yourself this question at least once per day in this next week. Heck, you might consider doing it every day for the rest of your life, but let's start with the week and see what impact that has.*

Client: *OK*

Therapist: *In asking the question, I'd like to point out that the answer isn't always obvious; you have to really get in touch with yourself and consider the gift carefully. For example, you might set your alarm for 5 a.m. so you can exercise before work. However, if you have been missing sleep due to a long work schedule, the best, most compassionate gift you could give yourself on that day might be an extra hour of sleep. On another day, the best, most compassionate gift for yourself might be to get out of bed even though you don't feel like it, because you know that you will feel wonderful and energized for the rest of the day if you get a run in. For that matter, there may be times where the best gift you can give yourself is to face a project that you have been putting off, because facing the temporary unpleasantness of work will rid you of anxiety about the task and allow you to relax about it. You see what I mean? Compassion doesn't necessarily mean that you "slack off," and it doesn't necessarily mean you push yourself harder. You have to really get in touch with what you need to thrive, and consider the best gift that you can give yourself in the moment. A gift of deep and genuine love. A wise gift, stemming from an intimate and mindful knowing of yourself.*

Client: *Oh, wow! That's kind of neat, I like that. I've never considered before that a gift to myself might be to face something I've been procrastinating.*

Therapist: *Exactly. It's the gift of freedom from anxiety and dread. Be careful with that thought, though, because if you're not careful, it may just turn into another way to hold yourself to an impossible standard or be harsh with yourself. Keep the asking of the question genuine and compassionate: "If I love myself, what gift would I give myself right now?"*

Client: *All right, I'll give it a try.*

Compassion for Others: Barriers and Letting Go of Anger

Like self-compassion, compassion for others can be a healing and transformative process. For individuals who experience a lack of compassion for others, it is very commonplace for them to realize that if they had greater compassion for the people around them, the people around them would feel better. However, clients who struggle with compassion sometimes fail to realize that anger and ill will toward others actually hurts themselves as well. Anger and vindictiveness can be deceptive emotions because they can often *feel* empowering. Sometimes, anger *is* an appropriate feeling. Angry responses to a situation can stem from a sense of moral justice or rightness. Nevertheless, it is an emotion that takes its toll when it is sustained for long periods of time and when anger is chronically present. When clients are caught up in the powerful feelings that anger engenders, they can lose sight of the harm that this inner harshness can do them, even though it is directed at others. Similarly, these clients sometimes lose sight of the good and healing experience that compassion can engender in themselves.

For such clients, it is important to acknowledge the purpose of anger and invite them to explore when it has outlived its usefulness. There is an oft-quoted line whose attribution is difficult to trace: "Holding onto anger is like drinking poison and hoping that the other person will die." Oftentimes, anger is an emotional response that arises when a person feels threatened, disrespected, or wronged. Anger arises as a protective force that compels a person to act to correct the situation. However, sometimes anger and frustration can be misplaced, or can develop into a habitual disposition. In these cases, clients might see the value in letting go of their anger.

Individuals who are reluctant to adopt a compassionate disposition sometimes fear the consequences of doing so. For example, they might think that if they are not angry, they will not act to defend themselves (or others) from harm. Just as with self-compassion, a therapist might engage in a kind of Socratic dialogue with these clients. They might consider whether they could *choose* to act to correct unjust and unsafe situations because of their values rather than being *compelled* to act by anger. Other clients may be reluctant to let go of anger because they equate "letting go" with "forgiveness" or condoning some act that has transpired in the past. For these clients, it will be important to separate the emotion of anger from the evaluation of the past act. The act of compassion (or at least, freedom from ill will) can set a client free from the destructiveness of his or her own anger.

Asking Too Much (or Too Little)

Strategically, it is important to keep the timeline for treatment in mind as you are working with a client. If a client has suffered extraordinary harm due to another person's actions, the client may understandably hold deep-rooted feelings of resentment toward that person. In cases like this, asking a client to give up this resentment and heal his or her wounds in a few weeks may constitute a breach of empathic attunement. Similarly, a client may have a deep-seated self-loathing that may benefit from multiple sessions focused on self-compassion, not only one. By the same token, a client who grew up with a dearth of people who showed the client love may need help in fostering these feelings for self or for others. If you have time in your treatment setting to adapt MH, introducing a few more sessions focused on compassion could help you meet the specialized needs of clients like these. Conversely, if you are constrained to the eight-session model, we recommend asking your clients to go only as far into compassion for self and for others as they are willing to go. In this regard, you must use your own clinical skill and instincts to make sure that you do not ask too much *or* too little of your clients.

Hypnotic Induction for Compassion for Self and Others

When clients have come to a point where they would like to try to find greater compassion for themselves and others, the next logical question is "How?" The hypnotic induction can start a client along this path, by creating a kind of scaffold for self-compassion. During the induction, a client begins by bringing to mind an individual who is easy to love and gradually expanding the circle of this love to include self and others. This kind of progression is common in self-compassion meditations, and other varieties of self-compassion meditation will be rich sources of inspiration if you would like to personalize the hypnotic induction to your clients. Also, asking clients to rate their level of stress on the 0 to 10 scale before the hypnotic induction for compassion begins is recommended. since it may help to highlight the personal benefits of compassion.

INTRODUCTION AND SETTING EXPECTANCY

> This session of mindfulness-based hypnotherapy is directed toward expanding your experience to include feelings of compassion and loving-kindness. Becoming more aware of feelings of compassion and loving-kindness toward yourself and toward others can be a transformational experience. Compassion for yourself means to treat yourself with kindness and consideration with gentleness

and understanding. It may mean forgiveness or letting go of hurts or criticisms. Compassion can then be extended toward others. Loving-kindness is related to compassion. Loving-kindness has the qualities of openness, empathy, and caring, loving feelings. As loving-kindness is extended toward others, fears and resentments diminish. Within a hypnotic state, it is possible to become more aware of compassion and loving-kindness toward self, others, the world, nature, and the universe, however you conceptualize these things to be.

Now, before you begin the hypnotic induction...please find a comfortable place to sit or lay down with good support for your head, neck, and shoulders... setting aside any distractions so that you can become fully present...and focus your attention, entering a deep hypnotic state.

FOCUS OF ATTENTION

During this session, I would like you to begin by extending one of your arms straight out in front of you. This extended arm represents several things...It represents your expanding your experience of mindfulness to encompass compassion and loving-kindness...first toward yourself and then toward the world. It is also an object to focus your attention... Focus your attention on a part of your extended hand. Concentrate on that part of your hand...allow other things to fade into the background.

As you concentrate there...the arm and the hand can begin to lower...the arm and the hand can feel heavier and heavier... Allow them to become heavier and heavier...the arm and the hand begin to drift down...just watching and observing them... they become heavy.

EYE CLOSURE

As the arm drifts down...to a comfortable resting position...allow your eyelids to close...a sign of your readiness to experience a deeply relaxed state and to experience compassion and loving-kindness...as your eyelids remain closed ...feeling more calm...more relaxed.

FOCUS ON BREATHING

Noticing now...your breathing...the sensations of breathing in...and breathing out...each breath of air...taking you to a deeper hypnotic state...more aware of these sensations of breathing...your own personal feelings...of breathing in...and breathing out.

Notice that it is possible to become more relaxed...notice that you may have already allowed your arms to relax...you may notice images...light... calmness...relaxing...and more aware of your own internal experience.

Each breath of air can seem to take you to a calmer and a more peaceful feeling....As you breathe in...the word "calm" may come to you...and as you breathe out...the word "relaxed" may come to you...it results in a calm, relaxed state.

SUGGESTIONS FOR RELAXATION

And as you become...more relaxed...the body and the mind work together... and positive changes begin to occur...blood pressure decreases...heart rate becomes slower...muscles relax...tension begins to drift away.

Noticing the relaxation...is a process of letting go...letting go of any worries...letting go of any tension...so you are more aware just of the present moment...aware of the breathing...becoming more and more relaxed.

For this time there is no need for any tension or tightness...it is possible to let go...and drift more and more relaxed...and drift into a deeper hypnotic state.

DEEPENING SUGGESTIONS

If it is all right with you, you may drift into a deeper hypnotic state as I begin to count from 10 to 1...with each number...drifting...deeper and deeper relaxed...drifting into a deeper state of hypnotic relaxation...as if you were near a beautiful beach...just walking along the beach...near the ocean...or perhaps another place in nature where you feel calm...whatever is best for you...and just observing what is there...observing the sky...the blue sky...or other things in nature.

Step number ten...allow your forehead to relax ... your jaw to go slack... muscles of your face to smooth out.

Step number nine...shoulders slump...tension drifts away...as if a weight were being lifted from your shoulders.

Step number eight...deeper relaxed now...and notice your breathing... breathing in and out...watching the waves come in and go back out.

Step number seven...allowing all tension to be released from your back and shoulders...they relax...deeply relaxed.

Step number six...more relaxed...stomach relaxes...breathing becomes easier...shoulders may relax and slump even more.

Step number five...all the tension drifts away from your head...neck... shoulders...arms...back...stomach and chest...your neck can go limp.

Step number four...legs begin to relax...deeply relaxed.

Step number three...legs and feet...relax...they become limp...they become more calm...they can relax...your right leg and your left leg...relaxed... your right foot and your left foot relaxed.

Step number two...and the matter of internal, mental, and emotional calmness and relaxation...begins to occur...and a deep hypnotic state.

Step number one...letting go all the way now...with each deep breath...leading to a deeper hypnotic state...and a greater awareness of each experience as it arises.

MENTAL IMAGERY

So that now you have come to a very beautiful place such as along a beach...or another place where you can rest...and consider many things...sitting... under a large umbrella...it is cooler here...and it is a calm place...it is quiet...[pause]....

Here you can consider many things...Consider the ocean...and how the waves...come in...and go back out on an ocean...as they have always done...for centuries... Consider the grains of sand...each grain so small...but yet...together...the tiny grains make up an immense beach...that stretches out for miles...and miles...across the earth...across the seas...across continents...to lands...and people around the earth...Consider the sky... that surrounds the earth...and reaches out to the universe...the beauty that surrounds us all...there...to be observed and noticed.

ACCESSING COMPASSION FOR SELF AND OTHERS (LOVING-KINDNESS)

Awareness of your breathing...peaceful...and perhaps there is someone...some time in your life...when you were treated with compassion...if only for a moment...someone who is easy to feel kind feelings toward...and as this person comes to mind, your feeling of compassion grows...feeling positive feelings toward this person...who was kind to you...someone you love...or have loved... perhaps someone who makes you smile when you think of them... notice how easy it is to feel kindness toward this person.

But notice now how the feeling is growing...and as it grows. it is possible to feel these same feelings toward yourself...realizing that you, too, deserve kindness ...and love...understanding...and compassion...The same feelings you have toward this kind person...now felt toward yourself, as your feelings of compassion grow and grow...wishing yourself well...good health...kindness...goodness...peace...well-being...You may notice that your feelings of love, kindness, and compassion are quite strong now...and they will continue to grow...

...To the point that now...that those feelings begin to extend further... bringing to mind someone you have positive feelings toward...identify a specific person...feeling compassion for that person now...compassion...loving-kindness...to open your heart toward them...with appreciation... love for someone who has been kind to you...yourself...and now extending it outward to another...wishing them goodwill, kindness, love, safety, health, ease of body and mind, peace and calmness...as your compassion grows further, feeling a boundless ease and joy within you.

Now...it is possible to extend those feelings even further outward...even to someone who is more difficult to feel goodwill toward...a difficult coworker, or someone who is stressful to deal with in your personal life...the person who comes to mind is up to you...With this great compassion that has grown within you...you may find it acceptable...to wish even this difficult person well...to wish them safety...health...ease of body and mind...peace and calmness...to extend compassion and loving-kindness...mercy... forgiveness...when it is appropriate for you.

And so...now...considering the world...and sending out from your heart...a sense of compassion and loving-kindness...to the world at large...to wish... everyone...in the world...to be saf...healthy...well-being...peace...of mind...body...and spirit...feeling loving-kindness within and for yourself... so that you can then extend it out to others...in the world.

SUGGESTIONS FOR AWARENESS OF COMPASSION AND LOVING-KINDNESS

And as you experience compassion and loving-kindness...filled...more and more...with feelings of happiness...feeling more connected with the world... with nature...with all things in the universe...as sense of connection...happiness and joy...within yourself...acceptance... more at peace within yourself...and with everything...with everyone...around you...and as you do...a sense of caring...and a sense of balance...an awareness of things that matter most: love...kindness...consideration...happiness.

POSTHYPNOTIC SUGGESTION

More and more...everyday...you will find it is possible to be more aware... aware of loving feelings toward yourself...compassion...so that it becomes more automatic...a part of you...that occurs naturally...almost effortlessly... and feeling...more and more...every day...more connected with the world around you...more loving-kindness toward yourself and others...more at peace within yourself...a sense of balance in all...things.

AWARENESS OF BREATHING

These things can occur just as naturally as breathing...so bring your attention again to your breathing...relax deeply...feelings of compassion and loving-kindness...that grow as you are aware of breathing in...and breathing out...notice your chest and stomach...they move...naturally...automatically...as you are aware...of breathing in...and breathing...out...each breath of air bringing good oxygen...to all the vital organs of your body...and each breath out...releasing carbon dioxide...letting go of any negative...feeling or concern.

CALMNESS AND CONNECTION

In a few moments I will give you suggestions to begin to return to conscious alertness...with a feeling of connection and feelings of calmness...a greater degree of inner peace that will remain with you...feeling safe...taking care of your health...treating yourself...and others with kindness...more at ease ... every day...in mind and body.

ALERTING

All right...beginning to return to conscious alertness...now...as I count the numbers from 1 to 4...returning to conscious alertness.

One...soon your eyelids can begin to open...more aware of this room... this time and place...returning to conscious alertness.

Two...more alert now...eyelids opening...returning to full conscious alertness...normal sensations returning...in every way.

Three...eyes open...alert...refreshed...relaxed.

Four...fully alert...relaxed...at peace...calm...and fully conscious and alert in every way.

Posthypnotic Inquiry, Assigning Homework, and Closing the Session

As usual, a conversation that takes place after the hypnotic induction and re-alerting will be helpful in discovering what your client experienced. This can help you to personalize the next sessions, and it also allows the client to reflect on how he or she would like to use the home-practice audio and self-hypnosis during the week to accomplish his or her goals. Also, after the hypnotic induction is completed, it is helpful to ask the client to again rate the level of stress on the 0 to 10 scale.

As a final note regarding practice, encourage your clients to reflect upon the meaning of compassion and self-compassion regularly during the week. This can be a part of their informal mindfulness practice; just as they are (you hope) noticing their present-moment thoughts and physical sensations during the day, clients can also check in with themselves by asking, "If I deeply and truly loved myself in this moment, what gift would I give myself?" The gift of self-compassion should be within their power to give, and should help them to find greater mental, emotional, and physical wellness in life.

The session can conclude with the homework assignment and a reminder to continue to record the practice using the Mindful Self-Hypnosis Daily Practice Log (Appendix B). Also, the client should be provided with an audio recording of the hypnotic induction for compassion and asked to practice with the recording at least once per day.

Summary and Closing Thoughts for Session 5

Session 5 falls just past the middle point of MH and occupies an important place in the overall intervention. If the prior sessions of MH were intended to introduce new concepts and build a foundation of understanding, then session 5 is where that understanding can become much deeper and more meaningful. Think of session 5 as a kind of "fulcrum" for MH. It is an opportunity to leverage clients' burgeoning understanding of mindfulness to approach some very difficult emotional content and make a profound change in their attitudes toward themselves and the world. If the same material were presented in session 1, it is unlikely that it would have the same impact.

It is up to you as a clinician to recognize when a client is gaining a greater mental and attitudinal flexibility through MH practice. When opportunities arise during the session, you can collaboratively explore how this new flexibility can be put to use in transforming the client's sense of compassion. By doing so, you can help a client cultivate a kinder, gentler mental landscape that aligns more fully with his or her intentions and goals. This will set the stage for getting the most out of session 6 (Chapter 13).

CHAPTER 13

Session 6

MINDFUL HYPNOTHERAPY FOR AWARENESS OF VALUES

Man is not fully conditioned and determined but rather determines himself whether he gives in to conditions or stands up to them. In other words, man is ultimately self-determining. Man does not simply exist but always decides what his existence will be, what he will become in the next moment.

—*Viktor Frankl (1946/1959)*

Introduction

A central goal of mindful hypnotherapy (MH) is to facilitate a deep and meaningful change. To this end, MH goes beyond symptom reduction. The goals of session 6 includes helping clients explore their values, meaning, and purpose. This aspect of MH is based on the belief that clients who are aware of their sense of meaning and purpose in life will guide themselves toward greater wellness. Clients' awareness of the things that make their life meaningful and the values that are important to them can help them seek out personal connections, healthy activities, and other things that help to build resilience.

Strategic Themes of Session 6: Mindful Awareness of Values

In session 6, your primary goals as a clinician will be to help clients to discover their own sense of meaning and fulfillment in life and to explore the values that they would like to guide their actions.

Furthermore, you will be inviting clients to live with greater authenticity with these values. In this respect, session 6 is a natural extension of session 5. Over the course of the previous week, clients have begun to explore what they need in the present moment to be well and care for themselves. This principle of compassion can be expanded to encompass their greater life goals and embrace a greater sense of congruence with their values. Naturally, some clients will already be aware of many of the themes that are discussed in session 6. For clients who have a clear understanding of their values and sense of purpose in life, session 6 can be an opportunity to reflect on these themes and rededicate themselves to those activities and perspectives that feed their sense of meaning.

Review Home Practice

Review of the Mindful Self-Hypnosis Daily Practice Log can give good insight into a client's progress and consistency in home practice at this stage of the MH process. In most cases, clients tend to adhere rather well to MH home practice with the audio.[1] Whenever adherence to home practice is good, the beginning of session 6 can be spent discussing the *impact* that MH is having on a client's life. For example, you can discuss new perspectives and observations that are beginning to emerge, and new questions that a client may have about mindfulness. As in previous sessions, it is advantageous to help clients feel more confident of the material they have already covered before moving into the new content for session 6. This will help them to feel a greater sense of self-efficacy and mastery. In contrast, if clients are already feeling lost and you continue to pile on more information, they are likely to become even more confused.

In addition, it is important to keep treatment goals at the forefront of your clinical work by referring back to the client's original treatment goals. Doing so can facilitate new connections and understanding for a client by priming them to think about how mindfulness and self-hypnosis can be brought to bear on stress and anxiety in their lives. For example, during session 6, the conversation might include a discussion of how stress and anxiety can be a side effect of living in conflict with their own values. Clients can also consider how intentionally seeking out fulfilling activities might act as a buffer for stress.

---

[1] If this is not the case with a client, the beginning of this session can be spent discussing obstacles to home practice and workshopping possible solutions.

Exploration of Meaning and Values

The topic of meaning and values can be difficult to broach because these issues are often discussed in abstract terms, if they are even discussed at all. Therefore, the primary challenge of the session is to make connections to a client's concrete, felt sense of meaning in life. For some people, this might involve spending quality time with their family or close friends. Others may experience a deep sense of fulfillment when they spend time alone in nature. Once a client grasps the concept of what you are trying to convey and brings his or her own experiences of meaning to mind, the remainder of the session often flows smoothly.

Once clients have identified one or more meaningful experiences in life, therapists can then help them identify the central aspects of those experiences that seemed meaningful. For example, consider a few of the following instances of meaning and fulfillment that clients may report:

> Client 1: "Well, now that you mention it, last summer I took a vacation to Barbados. It was the first real vacation I'd taken in over a year, and as I sat on that beach watching the sunset, I thought to myself: this is it ... this is what I work so hard for. I remember how much my parents struggled to make ends meet when I was a kid and I've made a commitment to build on what they gave me, work hard, and make sure I'm never in that position again."

> Client 2: "Yeah, I think I know what you mean. For me, that moment [of fulfillment] is when I'm with friends; on the back porch, talking until 2 in the morning. It doesn't even matter what we're talking about, and half the time it's stupid stuff. I don't know—I just feel alive in that moment, you know?"

For client 1, further examination of the situation may reveal that achievement and financial security are important values that evoke a sense of meaning and fulfillment when they come to the forefront. For client 2, it may be that the person finds fulfillment amidst a sense of belonging and connection. If you are able to find a small handful of meaningful memories for a client, this can help you to collaboratively explore the common themes with your client and draw out the values that are most important to him or her.

Once you have discovered (or reviewed) the kinds of things that make a client's life more meaningful and explored the kinds of activities that tend to evoke this sense of meaning, this may be an opportune time to discuss how these activities can be integrated more purposefully into a client's life. If your client has not been doing the activities that bring them meaning in life very often, why might this be? Perhaps clients can spend 5 minutes at the beginning of each day drinking a cup of coffee and reflecting on *why* they are going to be working hard at the office that day. If clients have the financial means, they might make a point to buy a small treat for themselves each month as a reminder of what they are working so hard for.

CLINICIAN NOTE

Internal and External Barriers

Sometimes, clients may feel as though external circumstances hold them back. For example, client 1 can't be expected to spend every other weekend on vacation in Barbados! However, there may be other activities that evoke core aspects of the experience they described.

For some clients, external circumstances have something to do with why they aren't integrating meaningful activities into their lives, but their real reasons have more to do with having fallen into a comfortable routine. If this seems to be the case for your clients, you might invite them to consider how their experiences in MH thus far may help them to effect change. For example, session 1 can help them to *notice* when they are on autopilot, sessions 2 to 3 can help them to be less controlled by their physical or emotional discomfort, and session 5 can help them get in touch with their needs and decide whether a life change would be beneficial.

If you are struggling to help clients find their sense of fulfillment in life or what is most important to them, consider the following activities:

- **Process of Elimination:** Have clients make a list of the qualities that make them who they are. Encourage them to include a variety of qualities; they can range from physical characteristics (e.g., hair color, race, height) to cultural ones (e.g., native language, ability/disability status, place within the family) to personality and beyond (e.g., pragmatic, idealistic, friendly, gruff, intelligent). Once clients have a list of about 10 things, have them close their eyes and imagine that one of the items on the list changes or is no longer a part of them. Then, have them mentally ask themselves: Am I still essentially *me*, even if this thing is not in my life? Continue progressively through the list until the client discovers which elements of their being are most essential and which ones are most incidental. At the end of the exercise, it can be useful to have a follow-up discussion about what the experience felt like, and explore whether it provoked any new thoughts about what is most meaningful in the client's life.

- **Existential Bravery:** Ask your clients what they would do if they were not afraid of failure. What would they aspire to in life? Which interpersonal risks might they take with others (in terms of being more vulnerable, or perhaps exploring what it would be like to be more assertive or more flexible)? This discussion can illuminate both clients' aspirations toward personal growth and what might be holding them back from pursuing these goals.

Hypnotic Induction for Awareness of Values

Asking the client to rate his or her level of stress on the 0 to 10 scale before the hypnotic induction for awareness of values is recommended. In the second portion of the session, the hypnotic induction is meant to evoke a greater sense of meaning in life. In personalizing the hypnotic induction, you may consider including imagery and suggestions based on information gained earlier in the session. For example, for client 2 in the previous example, you might specifically mention the person's friends and a mutual sense of love and belonging. This sense of belonging can be anchored in those times when the client is physically with them, but the sense of fulfillment can linger throughout the day. During the following posthypnotic inquiry, it can be helpful to ask a client about the aspects of the induction that were more or less helpful, and ask about the degree to which hypnosis was helpful in drawing out a greater sense of meaning and connection to life.

INTRODUCTION

This session of MH is directed toward pursuing and living a life that you find personally meaningful. This may be an opportunity to discover or reflect upon what drives, you... what gives life meaning. It may be a time to bring to mind what is most important in your personal life, or if you have spiritual or religious beliefs, it may be an opportunity to reconnect with an aspect of experience that you consider divine or transcendent. How you use this time is up to you, because each individual is unique. The important thing is to discover and pursue what is truly meaningful in your life. If you already have a strong sense of meaning in your life and don't feel as though anything is holding you back, you might use this time to reflect on this meaning and rededicate yourself to whatever is personally meaningful in your life.

During this session, you will be given suggestions for relaxation and mindfulness. You will then notice a sense of meaning growing from within this experience of mindfulness, where you will become more aware of what is personally meaningful to you. During this exercise, you may also become aware of any obstacles that have been holding you back from pursuing what is personally meaningful in your life. Your integration of mindfulness into your daily life can allow you to overcome these obstacles: Difficult emotions can be faced and accepted; physical discomfort can be viewed mindfully as well. Forgiveness for yourself and others may set you free to pursue what is truly meaningful in your life.

EYE CLOSURE

Now setting aside any distractions so that you can become fully present...relaxing as you set aside your cares and worries for a time and become very relaxed...and it may be helpful to take a deep breath now...and hold...and when you exhale...allow your eyelids to close, and feel your muscles unwind...as you allow your eyelids to become heavy and drift closed...a sign of your readiness to experience a deeply relaxed state and to experience compassion and loving kindness...feeling more calm...more relaxed.

AUDITORY FOCUS AND NARROWING OF ATTENTION

In a moment, you will hear a tone...and this tone will at first be clear and eventually become softer until it disappears. When the tone sounds...you will focus on it so intently...that everything else begins to...fade...into the background...easily focusing on how the tone changes from moment to moment...attending closely to each nuance of the sound...and allowing each of these things that you notice to pass easily from your awareness as you attend to what is happening now with the sound...focusing more and more on the present moment. When the sound starts to fade, you will find your mind becoming more and more focused on the fading sound...as the sound becomes fainter and fainter, you will pay closer and closer attention...more and more focused...and when the tone can no longer be heard, your mind will be as focused as it is capable of being...as focused as you allow it to be. I will stop talking while this tone sounds, so that you can focus fully on the sound...and when I speak again, your mind will be in a deep state of focus...able to easily respond to each suggestion that I give. And here is the tone now...[Wait 5 seconds; then ring the bowl, chime, or bell.]

INTEGRATED MINDFULNESS SUGGESTIONS

And now that your attention has become very focused...soon you will notice yourself becoming more mindful...by now it is a familiar feeling for you...attention focused on your experiences in this present moment...letting them come and go with acceptance...not clinging to any experience or moment but letting them come and go as they are...becoming more and more centered... and feeling a sense of peace settle into your being as you let concerns about the past and the future go.

This feeling begins to occur now...perhaps beginning the process with an awareness of breathing...feeling your mind let go of concerns and worries as you focus more and more on your breath...becoming more centered and aware ...the sensations of breathing in...and breathing out...each breath of air... taking you to a deeper hypnotic state...more aware of the unique sensations at each stage of your breath...attending only to the sensations unfolding in this very instant.

And as you allow yourself to become more peaceful...more centered, focused, and relaxed...you might notice a feeling of gentleness...a loving kindness for yourself and others as you focus easily on the present-moment sensations of breathing...and as this feeling grows...you may notice that it brings a feeling of lightness and joy to the experience of mindfulness...and just allow this to happen so that now you are experiencing a relaxed, centered attention... focused on the sensations of breathing in this moment...accepting your experiences as they come and go...a sense of ease as you are filled with a sense of compassion for yourself and others.

SUGGESTIONS FOR RELAXATION

And as you become more relaxed...the body and the mind work together... and positive changes begin to occur...blood pressure decreases...heart rate becomes slower...muscles relax...tension begins to drift away.

Allowing a wave of relaxation to soon spread through your body from head to toe...starting with your head and spreading down now...through your face and neck...muscles unwinding...becoming loose and relaxed...the wave of relaxation...spreading down through the shoulders...the arms...allowing yourself to settle more deeply...you may feel a sense of heaviness as your chest and stomach become more relaxed...the wave spreading through your body...spreading throughout your back...upper and lower back as you become more relaxed...perhaps feeling warmth or a tingling sensation as this wave soon spreads down...through your legs...and eventually into your feet...so that...now...your entire body is feeling deeply relaxed...the tension is gone now and you rest easily...your body supported completely as you rest.

Noticing that relaxation...is a process of letting go...letting go of any worries ...letting go of any tension...so that you are more aware just of the present moment...aware of the breathing...becoming more and more relaxed.

For this time there is no need for any tension or tightness...it is possible to let go...and drift more and more relaxed.

DEEPENING SUGGESTIONS

And soon allowing yourself to sink deeper into hypnosis...journeying inward ...toward a place of complete and utter serenity...a place of calmness and relaxation...where your mind is at ease, and nothing troubles you...where your thoughts are clear like a cool mountain lake...still, and serene...not burdened by the slightest care...this may be a familiar place...and you may find it pleasant to journey inward toward that place within you now...and as you hear my voice count from 10 to 1, with each number finding yourself settling into an even deeper level of hypnosis...deeper toward that place of complete mental and physical relaxation within you.

[Count each number as the patient exhales.]

Ten...Setting your cares aside now as you embark on this inner journey...you needn't worry about losing track of them...they will be safe, and right where you left them if or when you choose to pick them up again.

Nine...feeling a sense of relief...relaxing...your body leading the way on this journey by becoming very relaxed...muscles unwinding...tension that you didn't even know you were carrying is now drifting away...bringing a sense of deep relief.

Eight...deeply calm...number eight and already so deeply relaxed...and you may begin to notice a warmth or tingling sensation in your body, as it relaxes even further.

Seven... and now a sense of profound calmness begins to blossom...unfolding...effortless, like a flower to the sun...and as you feel this, you might realize that mental and physical relaxation is not something that you do...it is a process of letting go...of not doing...even if just for this short while...like holding a ball in your hand...if you want to send the ball toward the ground...you needn't throw it, or exert effort or do anything...just the opposite, in fact...the only thing you need to do is let it go.

Six...halfway there, and already so profoundly relaxed ...letting go of struggles and cares...letting go of any tension...letting go and simply being...in the present moment.

Five...perhaps at one time it took effort to calm your mind and body from its busyness...but now you are effortlessly still and serene...settled so deeply into the present moment...that to direct your mind to the past or the future or other things would require effort, and you would prefer not to try.

Four...allowing your mind to settle...become still and calm...profoundly peaceful.

Three...deeper and more calm...no worries in this special moment.

Two...almost there...deeply relaxed, nothing bothers and nothing concerns... and perhaps it would be OK, with the final number I count...to let go of even the smallest vestige of tension or worry...to settle into complete and utter stillness and serenity...peaceful and content...or perhaps you will prefer to be very calm but not take that last step...trusting now that whichever your mind chooses is the right choice for you in this moment...what you truly need.

One...at the final step of your own inner journey...comfortably and deeply hypnotized...resting in the present moment...your thoughts uncluttered...still... and calm.

AWARENESS OF MEANING AND VALUES

And being in this place of peace...the clarity of your thoughts...the simplicity of the present moment...it will allow you to become aware of what is truly meaningful in your life. And in a moment, that feeling of meaning and fulfillment in your life will grow...and you will become aware of what is meaningful.

This may involve becoming aware of something that is already present in your life...or perhaps something that you would like to be working toward...It may be an image...a feeling of connection or transcendence...you may find yourself in a different place, doing something that you find deeply fulfilling.

Whatever it is, there is no need to search for this sense of meaning...it is within you...and in this moment of stillness and inner peace...this feeling or image begins to grow now...it may be subtle at first, but even now it is growing more clear...more vivid...aware of this deep sense of meaning...aware of the preciousness and beauty of life...and aware of what you find meaningful and deeply fulfilling.

Your experience is unique...and as this experience of meaning and fulfillment grows and grows...you may experience a greater sense of self...getting in touch with who you really are...or it may be that your sense of self fades away for a time...as you become more connected with and absorbed in this feeling of meaning or transcendence...whatever you experience is just fine as these positive feelings grow.

COMMITTING TO VALUED ACTION

As this image, scene, or feeling becomes more and more vivid...a sense of meaning in your life growing from within you and enveloping you...You might find yourself wondering...what has held you back from experiencing this sense of meaning more fully or more frequently in your life.

Perhaps it is fear or doubt that has held you back...or being "too busy"...or something else...Whatever it is...maybe you don't have to wait until this thing disappears from your life...before pursuing a life that you find meaningful and fulfilling.

The essence of mindfulness is to become aware of your experiences in the present moment...accepting them without letting them rule you...freeing you to pursue a life that you find most meaningful and fulfilling.

Over the past weeks, mindfulness has become part of you...allowing you to experience the world and yourself in new ways...and this will enable you to enter a new chapter in your life.

If you choose to, and if you allow this change to occur...you may use this opportunity, right now, to commit yourself or recommit yourself to living a life that you find personally meaningful and fulfilling.

Reinforcement of Response. You are worthy of love and compassion...and when you are connected with a sense of meaning and fulfillment in your life...other things in your life become easier...You will feel a sense of meaning and fulfillment pervading your life...and as this occurs, you may find that you have more energy in your daily life...and that other positive changes occur...you may feel more at ease...more engaged with your daily activities.

Personalization

You may also find that...

[Personalized description of the client's sense of meaning]

____

____

____

____

POSTHYPNOTIC SUGGESTION

These changes will be reinforced by a daily experience of mindfulness...you will be mindfully aware and present with your experiences during the course of the day...mindfully aware of experiences as they unfold in the present moment ...able to accept these experiences just as they are...Even if you decide to change your circumstances to enable you to thrive and grow...you will accept your internal experiences for as long as they last...and gently let them go if or when they fade or change.

The presence or absence of pleasant or unpleasant experiences will not hold you back in your daily life...Your sense of meaning and fulfillment in life will ground you and empower you...Your pervasive attitude of mindfulness will allow you to thrive regardless of internal and external circumstances...Your practice of MH will enable you to feel a deep sense of compassion for yourself and others.

Day by day your stress will become less and less...and positive feelings will grow...enabling you to live a rich and fulfilled life.

ALERTING

> All right...beginning to return to conscious alertness...now...as I count the numbers from 1 to 4...returning to conscious alertness.
>
> One...soon your eyelids can begin to open...more aware of this room...this time and place...returning to conscious alertness.
>
> Two...more alert now...eyelids opening...returning to full conscious alertness... normal sensations returning...in every way.
>
> Three...eyes open...alert...refreshed...relaxed.
>
> Four...fully alert...relaxed...at peace...calm...and fully conscious and alert in every way.

Posthypnotic Inquiry, Assigning Homework, and Closing the Session

As you close the session, it can be helpful to invite a client to create his or her own homework for the next week. Also, after the hypnotic induction is completed, it is helpful to ask the client to again rate the level of stress on the 0 to 10 scale. In addition to the daily practice with the audio and self-hypnosis, you may consider asking your client if there are any changes that he or she would like to make in life to create a greater sense of meaning, fulfillment, and authenticity. If a client identifies specific behavioral changes he or she would like to make in life, it may help the client to follow through with this commitment if you check in about this progress at the beginning of session 7. This can also identify hidden barriers to behavioral change if a client has not followed through with the self-directed homework for session 6. It is very important to also provide the Mindful Self-Hypnosis Daily Practice Log for recording practice between sessions.

Summary and Closing Thoughts for Session 6

Once clients have a firm sense of what makes life meaningful for them and they have considered some of the ways that they can live congruently with their own values, they have the lion's share of what they need to succeed. Previous sessions have provided the means to ameliorate and overcome internal barriers, as well as creating a compassionate orientation toward themselves and the world. Session 6 adds a greater sense of meaning and an awareness of the values that can steer a person toward greater wellness.

Session 6 is most effective when it doesn't feel forced and when a client is able to discover his or her own sense of value and meaning in life. MH aims to facilitate significant life changes and a new outlook for life. Your ability to facilitate deeper changes for your client will rely heavily on your ability to be empathically attuned to your client's goals and needs. If you find yourself straying into suggestions and interpretations that are distorted too heavily by your own perspective, this is very likely to provoke a client's resistance to change. Therefore, your own work in becoming a mindful hypnotherapist will be important so that you can bring compassionate, nonjudgmental awareness to what a client is saying in various ways, including verbally, with body language, and with tone of voice.

REFERENCE

Frankl, V. (1959). *Man's search for meaning*. Boston, MA: Beacon Press. (Original work published 1946)

CHAPTER 14

Session 7

DEEPENING AND INTEGRATING MINDFUL HYPNOSIS

If you hope to mobilize your inner capacities for growth and for healing and to take charge of your life on a new level, a certain kind of energy on your part will be required.

—*Jon Kabat-Zinn (2013, p. xlix)*

Introduction

The intention behind mindful hypnotherapy (MH) was to create an intervention that provides some core structure but remains flexible to differing client needs and diverse clinical orientations. If the session outlines are followed closely, therapists will have a powerful instrument of change at their disposal. If a therapist intends to diverge from a strict adherence to the manual, it is our hope that this book provides a robust core intervention from which to draw inspiration and customize as needed. Although each session of MH leaves space for flexibility when working with a client, session 7 has the most built-in flexibility for deepening the client's experience. It was designed with the intention to empower a therapist to use it in the way deemed most beneficial for the client.

Over the course of the past seven weeks, the MH intervention has been gradually building the client's understanding of mindfulness and hypnotherapy piece by piece. MH's focus on one aspect of mindfulness in the first six sessions helps to make mindfulness and hypnotherapy more accessible, so that by session 7, clients have an excellent foundation. Furthermore, most clients should also have concrete experiences with applying the content from each of the sessions to their lives and their presenting concerns.

For clients who are still struggling with their particular presenting concern, this session is an opportunity to bring these concrete applications of mindfulness to the forefront. For clients who have demonstrated good understanding of how to apply mindfulness throughout the intervention, this session might focus on integrating mindfulness concepts more fully (a topic that is otherwise covered in session 8). If your clients are in need of specific skills and knowledge to overcome some obstacle in their life (such as assertiveness training, sleep hygiene, or psychoeducation for relapse prevention for addiction), session 7 can be an excellent opportunity to blend other interventions and skill sets into the structure of MH. Oftentimes, the strong foundation of mindfulness that MH provides enables clients to use these skills more consistently and in different ways than they otherwise would.

Strategic Themes of Session 7: Deepening and Integrating Mindful Hypnosis

Two important strategic themes for session 7 are to deepen a client's understanding of mindful hypnotherapy and to make sure that the client is progressing well toward addressing his or her individual concerns. This session provides a context for reviewing and fine-tuning specific mindful hypnotic suggestions as well as identifying ways that the client can best integrate mindful hypnosis into everyday life. A discussion of the client's goals and progress can be a basis for refining the intervention so that what the client gets out of MH is consistent with his or her unique circumstances. Session 7 is an opportunity to make sure that MH is helping the client to address the presenting concern. Some clients may still be struggling with some obstacle in their lives, and they may be feeling unsure of how to apply what they know to overcome it. Session 7 can be used to collaborate with clients to generate some ideas about how to overcome or circumvent these barriers to change. In addressing specific problems, you can bring in the myriad components of MH practice and provide a model for how a client can bring MH to bear on future problems once treatment ends.

CLINICIAN NOTE

Reinforcing Understanding

In session 7, pay close attention to whether your client understands the core concepts of mindfulness clearly. Over the course of the session, you should reinforce the things that the client is doing well and help to shape the client's understanding if there is an aspect of mindfulness that is being distorted or misunderstood.

By this point in the intervention, many clients have undergone significant shifts in their perspective toward their experiences and have begun to see symptomatic changes. However, it may become apparent as you are reviewing the previous sessions that some concepts have resonated with clients, while they continue to struggle to understand and apply other topics in their lives. Session 7 is an excellent opportunity for a client either to "catch up" or to deepen the understanding of mindfulness beyond the surface-level applications.

Just as in previous chapters, you should look for opportunities to make connections with previous material and the material from the next session. Session 7 often focuses on solidifying a client's knowledge of previous sessions and applying that knowledge to specific problems. However, over the course of session 7, there may be small opportunities to begin *integrating* a client's understanding of the mindfulness concepts and to help a client gain a greater sense of self-efficacy with being able to do this on his or her own when treatment comes to an end. If these opportunities arise, taking advantage of them now may allow for a smoother transition into session 8 and termination.

Review of Home Practice, Discussing Specific Stressors, and Integrating Mindfulness

In this session, your review of home practice, the Mindful Self-Hypnosis Daily Practice Log, and specific stressors will often provide the basis for the content in the first half of the session. If a client has been exhibiting good comprehension of mindfulness topics throughout the intervention, this may be an opportunity to allow the client's understanding to develop more deeply through reviewing mindfulness concepts with a greater degree of subtlety or to help the client understand how different facets of mindfulness can interact with one another to produce a greater impact than they could alone. Chapter 7 of this book discusses many of these themes and issues and can provide a helpful basis for this type of conversation.

For other clients, there may be value in using most (or even all) of the first half of the session to discuss a previous topic of MH in more detail. For example, some clients have particular difficulty being mindful with thoughts or emotions, while others may struggle with intense chronic pain that overwhelms their attempts at nonjudgmental awareness. The best use of time will vary from client to client, but generally it is best to use the session to build a client's understanding and help the client to integrate the content from multiple sessions. Furthermore, reflecting on how this integrated perspective can be brought to bear on particular, real-life stressors can help a client to make strides toward the treatment goals and provide a model for overcoming future obstacles.

VIGNETTE 1: ADAPTATION TO DAILY LIFE

Client: *You know, the hypnosis is great and all, but it's just 20 minutes or so out of my day. I've gotten in the habit of waking up early to practice with the [home practice] recordings, but once I get to work, it's "Go-Go-Go!" and there really isn't time to take a break. As a nurse, I sometimes work 16-hour shifts, and from the moment I walk in the door I'm already behind on what I need to do. The mindfulness stuff works great when I have time to use it, but if I took even 5 minutes to myself...well, who knows what would happen!*

Therapist: *I hear you, Cindy. It really sounds like you've got a high-pressure job. Not only are you incredibly busy from the moment you walk in the door, but I remember how a few weeks ago you were mentioning how lives are on the line if you make a mistake and that weighs on you, too.*

Client: *Yeah, exactly. So what can I do? I mean, over the past few weeks I've really started to notice how much stress I've been under, but now it seems like I'm just not in a position to do anything about it.*

Therapist: *Well, let's put our heads together on this one. I'm glad you've been using the formal practice at home.*

Client: *[interjecting] Mmhmm, it actually has helped in keeping me sane. It's nice to have a calm start to the day at least. I used to feel stressed just thinking about work on the bus ride in, but now at least I've got a calm start to the day.*

Therapist: *Right! So I'm thinking that one way to add to that and keep that sense of groundedness going is to integrate a bit more of the informal mindfulness practices into your day. In nonemergencies, maybe you can afford to take a single, mindful breath when your hand touches the door* *handle of each patient's door as you're making your morning rounds. You mentioned before that sometimes you need to make mental lists or do some planning as you walk. When you don't need your mind for those things, maybe you can pay attention to the sensations in the soles of your feet as you walk. When something hits you hard emotionally in the course of your day, maybe you can't unpack that right in the moment, but as you're walking out of the room or take a break for lunch, maybe it would be OK to at least acknowledge the feelings that are there underneath the surface? Does any of that sound like it might be possible to integrate during your day?*

Client: *Well. . .yeah, maybe. Now that you mention it, I have to wash my hands like 50 times a day, so maybe I could use that time to pay attention to the sensations of the water?*

In Vignette 1, the client is already using the mindfulness well as a way to decompress before work and get back in tune with her experiences, and she is also using self-hypnosis regularly. Since this is the case, the therapist decides to focus on helping her generate some creative ideas to integrate informal mindfulness practice throughout her day in a way that is realistic. It might also be helpful to review the importance of maintaining a mindful awareness as often as possible throughout the day, and to emphasize that mindfulness isn't something that happens only during formal practice. Posthypnotic suggestions may be helpful to Cindy in linking common cues (like washing her hands) to bring more mindful awareness to her daily life. These posthypnotic suggestions could be discussed during the session and provided by the therapist later in the session, or Cindy can integrate the suggestions into her regular self-hypnosis practice.

VIGNETTE 2: REVIEWING AND FINE-TUNING

Therapist: *So today is an opportunity to kind of "bring things together" in terms of the topics we've been talking about over the past several weeks we've been working together. It's also a good time to revisit some of the earlier topics we talked about if there's something that you feel we rushed through or you're still struggling with. Any thoughts on where you'd like to dive in, or would you like me to start with a general review?*

Client: *Actually, could we talk about being mindful with emotions again? I know we talked about it like a month ago, but I'm still having a hard time with that one.*

Therapist: *Well, sure. Tell me more about what's going on.*

Client: *Huh. Well, I know you said to be mindful with my anxiety, or whatever, but when I pay attention to it, I'm curious, I'm open, I notice how I'm* *feeling...but the feelings are still there. It seems like it was working better a few weeks ago. I can still use mindfulness with the physical stuff, but with emotions at least the mindfulness isn't working as well as it used to.*

Therapist: *I think I know what you mean...it kind of feels like the emotions are sticky, and they hang around longer than you want them to. Maybe even get worse sometimes when you pay attention to them?*

Client: *Well, maybe sometimes, but pretty much it's just that they don't get better.*

Therapist: *OK, thanks for the clarification on that. If I could ask another follow-up question, though: What do you mean when you say mindfulness isn't working as well as it used to?*

Client: *Well, mostly it's like I'm there, I'm being mindful, but nothing is different, you know? I'm still anxious.*

Therapist: *I wonder whether, deep down, your attempt to get rid of your anxiety might be working against you. If you're being "mindful" toward your anxiety only to make it go away, are you really open to it? Granted, mindfully "being with" your emotions is easier said than done. Even people who have been doing mindfulness for years sometimes find themselves shutting down and trying to push away things that are unpleasant. It's a deeply ingrained instinct, but there aren't really any shortcuts or tricks here to making the anxiety go away. It's a matter of truly doing something counterintuitive and accepting your anxiety as it is. Noticing how it feels while it's there inside of you; physically, what it makes you want to do ... all of it. If you can bring that mindful attention and compassion to your anxiety, sometimes it goes away and sometimes it doesn't.*

Client: *Well, then, what's the point?*

Therapist: *That's a good question! I invite you to explore the answer for yourself between this session and next session and beyond. A lot of people find that when they're able to develop a different perspective on their anxiety, it's still there, but it doesn't suck them under like it used to. You might find that if you can take the leap of faith and genuinely accept your anxiety, turn toward it, examine it with compassion and curiosity...those things might help you to feel more grounded and OK regardless of whether you're anxious. I'm curious to see what you find, though, if you're willing to see what that's like.*

In this exchange, the client's lingering difficulties with mindfulness reveal a persistent reactivity/aversion toward unpleasant emotions. The therapist takes the time to understand the client's difficulties and what may be causing them. The client's description of mindfulness as "working well at first" may be a clue that the client regarded the emotions mindfully in the first weeks of treatment, but that the goal (relieving anxiety and distress) gradually became more important than the process of actually getting to that goal (through *genuinely* changing the relationship with anxiety). In this vignette, the therapist avoids getting defensive about mindfulness, but instead invites the client to consider a different perspective and investigate the experiences further. By doing so, the therapist helps the client to embrace curiosity and pay close attention to what is actually being experienced. These behaviors and attitudes may help the client to experience a deeper sense of well-being and groundedness even if anxiety and stress linger, and give the client a greater chance of reducing stress through greater mindfulness.

VIGNETTE 3: WHERE ACCEPTANCE AND CHANGE MEET

Therapist: *You mentioned a few weeks ago that your brother-in-law lost his job and came to live with you and your wife. It seemed like last week that was causing you some stress, so I wanted to check in and see how you're doing.*

Client: *I've really noticed a big change with my ability to roll with my emotions when my brother-in-law's around, but I've got a ways to go, too. Sometimes it really gets to me when I come home after a long day of work, then have to cook dinner and clean up after him. Yesterday I found out he's applied to only one or two jobs since living with us, but I just took a minute to myself and noticed the emotions that were stirring around inside of me, and I felt much better even in spite of everything.*

Therapist: *It sounds like you're really starting to turn the corner with your understanding of mindfulness, and it's starting to "click" for you!*

Client: *It is; I think I finally get it now. I mean, like I said, I've got a ways to go but it's getting better.*

Therapist: *I wonder whether it might be worth taking a look at the situation itself, though, and whether something needs to change for you and your brother-in-law's sake. Mindfully acknowledging your emotions in the moment is great, but remember that it doesn't need to mean that you can't change the situation if it isn't healthy. That doesn't sound very compassionate or fair toward you. I hope you don't mind me saying so, but the way you've been describing your interactions with your brother-in-law, it sounds like in some ways he's been taking you for granted and isn't doing much to either help out around the house or change his situation...So what do you think?*

Client: *I think you are right. I have been avoiding dealing with the situation in a healthy way. I guess I was afraid of confrontation.*

Therapist: *Mmhmm. Now that you understand a bit more about how to assert yourself, is there anything from what we've been practicing in here that might help you overcome that fear and notice when you're falling back into old habits of letting people walk all over you?*

Client: *[sigh] Yeah, I see what you mean. I guess I could try to be mindful toward my anxiety about being assertive with him.*

Regarding the Vignette 3, it is essential to remember that no treatment is a panacea. Mindfulness, hypnotherapy, and MH are no different. In this situation, the therapist has decided that some brief assertiveness training would be useful in helping the client find a healthier pattern of interaction with the brother-in-law. Accordingly, the therapist weaves this information into the session. Later, the therapist integrates the new information with mindfulness to help overcome the barriers that the client may have in actually implementing the new information that he or she has been given.

Another thing to notice about Vignette 3 is that the client is paying attention to a particular aspect of mindfulness (mindfulness of emotion) without considering how another aspect (compassion for self and others) factors in. The client has begun to increase the level of distress tolerance when emotions arise, but could use a gentle reminder that mindfulness often involves a dichotomous relationship between (a) acknowledging and accepting experiences as they are in the present moment and (b) acting to change the situation if it is harmful and something can be done to change the situation.

Hypnotic Induction for Deepening and Integrating Mindful Hypnosis

The hypnotic induction for this session is an opportunity to develop the client's lived experience of the things that you have been discussing during the session. The standardized hypnosis script created for this session includes blended suggestions for mindfulness, but the brevity of the script provides ample opportunities to add suggestions specific to the client's individual needs. If you have been focusing on a particular aspect of mindfulness to solidify a client's understanding, consider using the script for that particular session as a basis for your hypnotic induction. You can modify the basic script to emphasize the particular things you were clarifying with your client during session 7. As with prior sessions, asking the client to rate the level of stress on the 0 to 10 scale before the hypnotic induction for this session is recommended.

INTRODUCTION AND SETTING EXPECTANCY

In this session, you will have the opportunity to deepen your experience of MH in a way that is most helpful to you. The aspect of mindfulness that you choose to focus on is up to you. You might choose to focus on an aspect of mindfulness that you would like to explore or experience more deeply in your life, or an aspect of mindfulness that will be particularly restorative or helpful at this particular junction of your life. Alternatively, you might choose to experience an integrated session of mindfulness. Examples could include greater awareness of your breathing and the present moment, noticing and nonjudgmentally allowing thoughts and feelings to pass by, compassion for yourself and others, awareness of loving-kindness, or connection with the universe in whatever way you conceive it to be, or whatever you may wish to acknowledge that gives meaning to your life. Whatever you choose, this session can enable you to relax more deeply, rediscover a sense of steadiness in the midst of adversity, and increase your quality of life, enabling you to thrive.

FOCUS OF ATTENTION

During this session, I would like you to begin by choosing an experience or an object to focus your attention. This may be a consistent sound (such as a singing bowl), a sensation (such as the sensation of your breathing), or perhaps a spot on the ceiling (or another object of your choosing in the room). Whatever it is that you choose to focus on is fine as long as it is acceptable to you...just allow your entire attention to become absorbed in focusing on this thing...still aware of my voice as I am speaking but allowing yourself to become absorbed by what is happening from moment to moment in your object of focus... focusing more and more intently.

EYE CLOSURE

As your focus becomes more complete, you may notice that your eyes begin to get heavy...perhaps they are already closing...drooping, and finally...closing ...whenever it feels most natural to you...As this occurs, you will find yourself sinking more deeply into a hypnotic state of deep relaxation.

FOCUS ON BREATHING

Now that your eyes have closed...now noticing your breathing...the sensations of breathing in...and breathing out... each breath of air...taking you to a deeper hypnotic state...more aware of these sensations of breathing ...your own personal feelings...of breathing in...and breathing out.

Notice that it is possible to become more deeply relaxed...as you drift into a state of hypnotic relaxation...notice that you may have already allowed your arms to relax...you may notice images...light...calmness...relaxing...and more aware of your own internal experience.

Each breath of air can seem to take you to a calmer and a more peaceful feeling...As you breathe in...the word "calm" may come to you...and as you breathe out...the word "relaxed" may come to you...it results in a calm, relaxed state.

SUGGESTIONS FOR RELAXATION

And as you become...more relaxed...the body and the mind work together...and positive changes begin to occur...blood pressure becomes less...heart rate becomes slower...muscles relax...tension begins to drift away...noticing that relaxation...is a process of letting go...letting go of any worries...letting go of any tension...so you are more aware just of the present moment...aware of the breathing...becoming more and more relaxed...for this time there is no need for any tension or tightness...it is possible to let go...and drift, more and more relaxed...and drift into a deeper hypnotic state.

DEEPENING SUGGESTIONS

If it is all right with you, you may drift into a deeper hypnotic state as I begin to count from 5 to 1...with each number...drifting...deeper and deeper relaxed...drifting into a deeper state of hypnotic relaxation...as if you were in a peaceful place...perhaps someplace in nature where you feel calm... whatever is best for you...and soon noticing the sights, sounds, smells, and feelings...as you relax more deeply into this hypnotic state.

Five...relaxing deeply...noticing any residual tension...and then letting go...and as you become...so relaxed...letting go of your awareness of this place as you soon...become aware of a peaceful place.

Four...so deeply hypnotized...that you may begin to feel a drifting, or floating sensation...or perhaps a sensation of warmth or tingling...as you begin to enter this peaceful place...I wonder what you might notice first about this place?...Perhaps a distinct color...or even just the feeling of peacefulness.

Three...this place is becoming more vivid now...you might begin to notice the feeling of the air on your skin...or the feeling of walking, sitting down, or lying down...it may be that distinctive sounds can be heard soon...as you relax so deeply...drifting into a deeper hypnotic state.

Two...almost there...experiencing each sight...sound...smell...and sensation of this peaceful place...sinking more deeply relaxed...more deeply peaceful...in this place of absolute comfort and safety.

One...fully there now...feeling comfortable and calm...fully relaxed...able to experience each suggestion easily during hypnosis...as you allow the details of this peaceful place to sink in.

SUGGESTIONS FOR BREATHING, ACCEPTANCE, AND AWARENESS OF THE PRESENT MOMENT

And in this place...you will find that your experience of mindfulness will soon begin to deepen. . .aware of the breath...focusing on the sensations of breathing in...and breathing out...focusing on the nuances of the sensations ...letting go of expectations of what this experience will be like...letting go of what it was like in this past moment...letting go of thinking about the feelings...just noticing what it is unfolding now...as your experiences flow past you...like a rock in the midst of a gentle stream...you will begin to feel a growing sense of peace...calmness...[Wait 5 seconds.]

As you do this...serenity...peace...calmness arise...focused and relaxed ... [Wait 5 seconds.]

INTEGRATED SUGGESTIONS FOR MINDFULNESS

If you choose to, you may continue to pay attention to this consistent experience...noticing small changes from moment to moment...becoming more and more relaxed...more and more focused...until you awaken feeling relaxed, refreshed, and clear-headed...If you choose to do this, my voice and what it is saying will remain perceptible...but in the background of your awareness ... until I begin to give you instructions for awakening.

Soon you may choose to allow your awareness to drift toward a particular aspect of your mindfulness experience...toward a greater focus on the present moment...perhaps being present with the experiences unfolding in one or more of your five senses...or being mindful of the thoughts and feelings that you are experiencing...you might find yourself focusing on a felt sense of compassion for yourself or others...and allowing that compassion to grow and grow...or you may feel a sense of meaning and fulfillment grow within you.

As your mind chooses what it would like to focus on today...whatever it is that you experience...now allowing your awareness of this experience to grow... being present with this unfolding experience...accepting it as it is...as your awareness of the experience grows...neither mentally clinging to it nor trying to push it away...just noticing and accepting without judgment...allowing your mindful attentiveness to this experience to...relax you, further and further... without any need for willful effort on your part.

Aware of an aspect of mindfulness that you would like to explore or experience more deeply in your life...or an aspect of mindfulness that will be particularly restorative or helpful for you...or possibly experiencing an integrated session of mindfulness...whatever you choose, can enable you to relax more deeply, rediscover a sense of steadiness in the midst of adversity, and increase your quality of life, enabling you to thrive.

And in a moment...I will be silent to allow you to mindfully observe this experience...that is growing within you. When I speak to you again...you will remain...in a deep state of hypnosis and mindfulness...able to easily respond to each suggestion that I give.

[Pause for 90 seconds.]

POSTHYPNOTIC SUGGESTION

Very good...and this experience of mindfulness...is now becoming more a part of you...and more and more, every day...you will find that...mindfulness has become a part of your everyday experiences...nonjudgmental awareness of the present moment...whenever your mind is not needed to plan or reflect.

Compassion for yourself and for others...will come easily and automatically... and your practice of mindfulness will allow you to pursue a life that you find truly meaningful and fulfilling.

ALERTING

In a few moments, I will give you suggestions to begin to return to conscious alertness...and you will do so comfortably...in a way that feels just about right for you today...bringing the benefit and good feelings from today's mindfulness-based hypnosis session with you...Now as I count the numbers from 1 to 4...gradually returning to conscious alertness...

All right, now beginning to awaken with...

One...soon your eyelids can begin to open...more aware of this room...this time and place...returning to conscious alertness.

Two...more alert now...eyelids opening...returning to full conscious alertness ...normal sensations returning...in every way.

Three...eyes open...alert...refreshed...relaxed.

Four...fully alert...relaxed...at peace...calm...and fully conscious and alert in every way.

Posthypnotic Inquiry, Assigning Homework, and Closing the Session

After the hypnotic induction is completed, it is helpful to ask the client to again rate the level of stress on the 0 to 10 scale. It may be useful to encourage self-efficacy by asking the client to set his or her own homework for the next week in light of the things you have discussed during session 7. If you discuss homework prior to the hypnotic induction, posthypnotic suggestions for following through on the homework can be integrated into the script.

After the hypnotic induction is complete, it may also be helpful to remind clients that they will soon be guiding their own MH practice. At your discretion, you might ask clients to begin considering what their next goals are for themselves, and which habits, resources, and further development in MH may help them to accomplish these goals.

Close the session by providing the client with the Mindful Self-Hypnosis Daily Practice Log and an audio recording of the hypnotic induction for this session and encouraging the client to practice with it every day during the week. At the client's discretion, he or she may also feel free to practice with any of the audio from previous weeks' sessions.

Summary and Closing Thoughts for Session 7

Session 7 is meant to put a great deal of discretion in your hands as a clinician. The chapter has provided some thoughts and direction for how you might use this session, but it is our hope that you consider these as only suggestions, not as necessities. Most clients will be experiencing the world more mindfully by this point in treatment. This mindful change can be an opportunity to delve deeper into the subtlety and nuance of mindfulness or can help clients see how mindfulness can help them feel less distressed in the face of their presenting concerns. MH can also be integrated with traditional interventions and psychoeducation if needed. The foundation of MH often helps clients to overcome the resistance that can interfere with implementing these changes.

REFERENCE

Kabat-Zinn, J. (2013). *Full catastrophe living: Using the wisdom of your body and mind to face stress, pain, and illness.* New York, NY: Bantam Books.

CHAPTER 15

Session 8

TRANSITION TO LONG-TERM PRACTICE OF MINDFUL HYPNOSIS

I hear and I forget, I see and I remember, I do and I understand.
—Confucius

There are only two mistakes one can make along the road to truth: not going all the way, and not starting.
—Unknown

Introduction

Session 8 is intended to make the transition to self-guided practice after the last formal mindful hypnotherapy (MH) session. The two quotes capture the essence of session 8. First, "I hear and I forget, I see and I remember, I do and I understand" means that practice leads to experience, and experience leads to understanding. It is only through repeated practice of mindful self-hypnosis that deep understanding and lasting therapeutic change occur. Each session of MH includes instructions and support for home practice of mindful self-hypnosis, both with and without audio recordings of guided practice. This is essential; it is necessary. The second quote, "There are only two mistakes one can make along the road to truth: not going all the way, and not starting," means that continued experience of mindful self-hypnosis and integration into daily life *are good* and to be encouraged. In engaging in MH, the client and the therapist have started the process; all that is left is "going all the way," with the client transitioning to long-term practice after all MH sessions have ended. One of the more important things to keep in mind about session 8 is that it is not the end of MH, but merely a transition from clinician-guided practice to client-guided practice.

In maintaining a mindful approach to life and the stresses associated with living, we are all tethered to the necessity of ongoing mindful practice. It is important that a client understands the importance of continued practice of mindful self-hypnosis. The recommended structure and themes for session 8 are as follows:

1. Review treatment gains and the practices/perspectives that enabled them
2. Discuss the client's future plans and goals for continued progress
3. Make a plan for how the client can accomplish these goals
4. Bring closure to your therapeutic relationship

While session 8 does not necessarily introduce new mindfulness concepts, it *is* an opportunity to help clients to integrate what they have already learned so that they can implement mindful self-hypnosis flexibly and effectively to overcome or circumvent future difficulties and continue practice. It is important that clients continue practice of mindful self-hypnosis after therapy sessions end to maintain the benefits and personal growth. Therefore, session 8 builds upon the previous sessions to support integration, relapse prevention, and transition to long-term practice.

Strategic Themes of Session 8: Transition to Long-Term Practice of Mindful Hypnosis

The strategic themes of session 8 include reviewing and reinforcing what clients have learned over the course of the intervention, as well as helping them maintain their therapeutic gains and transition to long-term practice. In most cases, the therapist will also discuss termination issues, as this will be the last session and, therefore, the end of the therapeutic relationship of the past 8 to 10 weeks. This can bring up feelings for both parties since collaborating to bring about meaningful life changes usually creates a special kind of bond between people. It is important to pay attention to the feelings that arise during termination and give these feelings space to be processed in session.

CLINICIAN NOTE

Key Topics

In session 8, it is important to review positive changes that have occurred, plans for continued mindful self-hypnosis practice, and personal goals.

One strategy to keep in mind for MH is bringing attention to any positive changes the client has noticed in his or her life. Taking time to notice and celebrate positive changes are often important activities in their own right, but it is also important to review how the client made these changes. The process by which changes were made, through MH practice, is the same process by which they will be maintained and continue to make a difference in a client's life.

Session 8 is also an opportunity to integrate clients' understanding of each of the previous sessions into a single, unified concept. When clients begin to understand how differing aspects of mindfulness act synergistically, their knowledge of mindfulness can continue to deepen even without therapist input. Clients can continue to develop insights through their own direct experiences of mindfulness in their lives. Furthermore, clients who are gaining a greater facility with self-hypnosis can use this skill to explore and understand their experiences within a trance state. This kind of practice can result in a kind of self-sustaining positive feedback loop:

1. A deeper insight allows for more wholesome and empowering mindful self-hypnosis practice toward greater mindfulness in daily life and more compassionate, purposeful action.
2. With effective mindful self-hypnosis practice, perceptions become less clouded by preconceptions and bias. Mindful observation of experiences involves paying attention to things as they are, in the present moment. Clear perception allows a person to see subtle aspects of harm in some habitual activities and subtle opportunities for compassion in otherwise difficult actions.
3. Clearer perceptions enable wiser self-suggestions during self-hypnosis and guide future explorations of mindful awareness and action.

In this session, the therapist will have the opportunity to help the client to see an integrated picture of what mindfulness and hypnotherapy

CLINICIAN NOTE

Continuing Practice

When treatment ends, there can be a temptation to "ease up" on practice and eventually discontinue practice entirely. It is important to discuss these issues and plan for any obstacles.

can do together. Once a client grasps the way that different pieces of mindfulness fit together and how hypnosis can be used to reinforce the understanding of those elements, the client can use MH flexibly to address his or her goals. In the penultimate session, one of the important strategic themes will involve preparing the client to be able to maintain therapeutic gains and continue the journey independently. As clients, over the course of the intervention, have likely already made some connections between different aspects of mindfulness and hypnosis, session 8 will seem like a natural extension of previous sessions.

Review Progress and Future Goals

Session 8 includes a review of the Mindful Self-Hypnosis Daily Practice Log from the past week, treatment goals, and goals for the session as in prior sessions. However, in this session, there will be a new discussion of the extent to which these goals have been achieved. As the therapist reviews a client's progress over the course of the intervention, changes often start with small and seemingly inconsequential shifts in perception. For example, an anxious client may begin to notice that his or her muscles are often tense during the day, whereas in the past the client felt fatigued and achy at the end of the day without knowing why. A different client may notice a subtle and delightful nuance of flavor in his or her coffee for the first time, even though the client has been drinking the same brand of coffee for years. These small changes often herald larger and more direct therapeutic transformations. For example, that same anxious individual with the tense muscles may begin to notice that anxiety has an ever-diminishing power to destabilize his or her day. Excessive anxiety may arise far less often than it used to, and even when it is present, it may be a mere annoyance.

Identifying a time and place for regular practice of mindful hypnosis can help maintain MH practice and provide added motivation and structure. In addition, discussing some of the ways the client has improved can serve to remind the client of the practices that made therapeutic change possible. Core concepts of present-moment awareness, living in "the now," acceptance of "what is," and the inner calmness and peace that flow from mindfulness are examples of topics for this discussion. Also, to support continuing growth, some clients may consider a mindfulness retreat, taking a yoga class, or further reading on mindfulness and hypnosis. The following vignette illustrates this dialogue:

Therapist: *Let's discuss some of the things that you have noticed about yourself as you have practiced mindfulness and mindful self-hypnosis these past many weeks. Do you feel that you are living more in the present moment instead of being weighed down by the past and future?*

Client: *Yes, I do feel more present-focused most of the time. Sure, I still get caught up in the past and the future sometimes, but it happens a lot less than it used to. I really notice a difference when I skip a day or two of practice, though. I'm beginning to realize that what you've been saying all along is true...it's important for me to listen to the CD at least once a day.*

Therapist: *When do you usually practice with the CD? Which one do you like?*

Client: *I really like the first one and the one on acceptance of thoughts and feelings. I kind of go back and forth between those two the most. Usually, I practice in the evening before bed or in the morning before starting my day.*

Therapist: *Do you find that you are more relaxed and calm during your days?*

Client: *That is one of the best things that I have gotten out of this therapy. I have learned how to relax and stay calm. The relaxation is something that I need and want in my life.*

Therapist: *There is the process of being physically relaxed, and then there is the process of emotional relaxation and nonjudgmental acceptance of self and of others. How do you see yourself in regard to acceptance and nonjudgmental awareness of your thoughts and feelings?*

Client: *I am making progress! I know that I will need to continue to be aware of a mindful attitude and keep practicing self-hypnosis. Also, I am going to start taking a yoga class. I think that will help, too.*

Therapist: *I agree, that sounds great!*

In addition to reviewing the therapeutic goals that were achieved, it is often helpful to explore whether any goals were *not* achieved, the obstacles that interfered with achieving these goals, and any additional goals the client may wish to work toward. This avenue of discussion can provide clients with a concrete idea of what they can be working toward post-termination. It may also provide a safeguard against premature termination if there are symptoms that require professional guidance to resolve. For clients who will be continuing MH on their own, the therapist may wish to explore whether there are any particular aspects of mindfulness that they would like to examine more deeply during the next phase of their practice and provide them with some resources that will help them to continue this exploration on a post-termination basis.

Relational Closure

A shared aspect of MH and other interventions is the importance of relational closure. In ideal circumstances, the therapist's authentic and mindful presence in the therapeutic relationship will evoke a genuine bond between the therapist and the client. Veteran clinicians will already know the importance of this bond: It helps to create the conditions for effective therapy to take place, for *meaningful* therapy to take place. However, a healing and healthy therapeutic relationship is defined as much by its boundaries as it is by its warmth. For some clients, therapy may be a unique experience of closeness and safety that they do not often encounter in their personal lives. Other clients may experience such closeness in abundance. In either case, it behooves you to give some consideration to how to bring your therapeutic relationship to a close when your intervention ends.

■ CLINICIAN NOTE

Authenticity

Relational closure involves processing issues associated with the termination of therapy sessions, and the unique experience of MH. The therapist should acknowledge his or her own feelings as well as those of the client. Discussing the client's distinctive journey through change can help the client to become more acutely aware of the changes he or she has made.

An important question for therapists to ask themselves during the termination session is "How will you and your client decide to say goodbye, and what would bring a good sense of closure for your work together?" If the therapist's clinical orientation allows for appropriate therapist self-disclosure, closure often involves simply acknowledging the emotional importance of the work that has been done together, and perhaps the therapist's hopes for the client's continued progress. However, in keeping with the theme of furthering a client's autonomy, it may be helpful to adopt an egalitarian and transparent approach by including the client in deciding how to end the therapeutic relationship (of course, within the bounds of ethical and professional practice). It may also be worth discussing and processing any feelings of reticence or anxiety a client has about continuing the work on his or her own.

Therapist: *So, Sam, I'm aware of the fact that this is our last session. I know that sometimes it can feel like kind of a sudden transition to be meeting every week and then not meet at all. I'm also aware that normally in our society we don't often have a chance to say goodbye. We tend to beat around the bush and say "see you later" or simply drift apart or not acknowledge the ending of a relationship.*

Client: *Mm-hmm.*

Therapist: *So I just wanted to make a bit of space in our session today to consider these things, and check in with you to see what your thoughts are on therapy coming to an end, to see if there's anything that would be important to you in terms of bringing things to a close.*

Client: *OK. Well, yeah, it's going to feel a little different on Tuesday afternoons when we normally meet. I've kind of gotten used to coming here, and I look forward to it. I'm glad for the things I learned though. Things were pretty different when I came in a couple of months ago, that's for sure.*

Therapist: *I remember well. You've put in a lot of really hard work over the past weeks and months and have really turned things around. You mentioned that you look forward to our meetings, and I just want to say that it's felt like we've done some really meaningful work together. I feel grateful for the time that we've been able to come together on this, and I just want to say what an honor it's been to work with you and see you transform.*

Client: *Well, thanks! It's been a pleasure to work with you, too.*

Transition to Long-Term Practice and Integration

As far as mindfulness or hypnotherapy is concerned, the final session does not add any new content to a client's knowledge base per se. Instead, this session of MH is an opportunity to solidify a client's understanding of how the parts fit together into a seamless whole that the client can continue to use MH after termination of the therapy. Integration of the facets of mindfulness and hypnotherapy is important because the whole is certainly greater than the sum of the parts. Mindfulness alone is known for being a practice that can continue to offer new insights after years or even decades of practice. By integrating hypnosis with mindfulness, the possibilities for deepening mindfulness practice certainly don't diminish, and novel opportunities may arise through the unique combination. Also, as noted previously, clients can be encouraged to engage in other mindfulness practices with and without hypnosis. This can include classes on mindfulness as well as other experiences or learning opportunities. Some resources are included in the appendices of this book.

The therapist cannot address all of the multifarious possibilities for continuing and deepening practice—that is beyond what a clinician *could* offer. Instead, the task as a therapist will be to open clients' eyes to the beginning of that path that lies before them, allowing the final session of MH to be a new beginning rather than an ending. At the therapist's discretion, integrating the various facets of mindfulness and hypnotherapy may be part of the overall review of treatment gains and exploring future directions. It is helpful to review the themes discussed in Chapter 8 in addition to drawing upon your own firsthand knowledge of mindfulness and hypnotherapy. The following vignette illustrates this discussion.

Therapist: *You know, Chantal, I'm aware of how well you seemed to connect to the idea of nonjudgmental awareness of emotions. It seemed like at first that was kind of hard to be mindfully aware of the frustration and anxiety you feel at work, but once the content from that session "clicked," you noticed a real change.*

Client: *You've got that right. I feel much lighter at work, if you know what I mean. I mean, don't get me wrong—it's still stressful at times and I still think that I'm sometimes treated with disrespect, but I don't carry so much of that burden home with me anymore.*

Therapist: *Exactly, and I'm so happy to hear that! I wonder if you've given any thought to how that mindfulness of emotion might connect to what you were talking about a couple of weeks ago? You were mentioning how important your activism is to your sense of meaning…I wonder if you can unite that sense of lightness and energy that you feel to gain a greater sense of resilience in the activism work that you do.*

In addition to the discussion of relevant issues, the session includes a hypnotic induction for transition to long-term practice and integration. The session concludes with posthypnotic inquiry, providing an audio recording, processing experience, and closure.

Hypnotic Induction for Transition to Long-Term Practice and Integration

Note: A singing bowl, chime, or bell is required to complete this script as written. An instrument of this sort can be useful as an auditory focus of attention, and the hypnotherapist may supplement it with another sound or use an alternative means of focusing attention mindfully. If you choose to use a singing bowl, chime, or bell, have this tool at hand and ready to use. As with prior sessions, asking the client to rate the level of stress on the 0 to 10 scale before the hypnotic induction for this session is recommended.

INTRODUCTION AND SETTING EXPECTANCY

In this experience of mindfulness-based hypnotherapy, you can expect to feel a deep sense of relaxation, well-being, steadiness, and focus that comes from mindfulness practice. Remember that mindfulness involves an awareness of your experiences in the present moment, an awareness of experiences without the need to control them or judge them. When you accept your experiences just as they are, you will notice that you have a greater sense of steadiness and equanimity even when experiencing stressful events. When this attitude toward your experiences is practiced with an abiding attitude of openness and compassion for yourself and others, this experience can have a profoundly transformative effect on your life.

This hypnosis session will guide you toward an integrated experience of mindfulness, with suggestions for continuing to practice mindfulness-based hypnotherapy on a regular basis. This will enable you to relax more deeply, rediscover a sense of steadiness in the midst of adversity, and increase your quality of life, enabling you to thrive. Each time you practice with self-hypnosis or one of the audio recordings, you will also reinforce your tendency to experience mindfulness and all of its benefits as a default state of mind in your daily life.

HYPNOTIC INDUCTION WITH SUGGESTIONS FOR RELAXATION AND EYE CLOSURE

You may begin by allowing your body to relax, discovering a sense of ease, and clearing your mind...you might begin this process by taking a series of three deep breaths...and you may find that as you relax...so deeply...your eyes may begin to get heavy...and you may allow your eyes to close whenever it feels most natural to you...Now taking a deep breath, and holding it for a moment...hold...and as you exhale, allow all of your muscles to relax...unwinding...tension draining from your body...And when you're ready, take another deep, deep breath...and hold...and now exhaling all of your cares and worries...perhaps feeling lighter as your burdens pass from you...a sense of ease settling deeply into your being...and in a moment...your final deep, deep breath will carry you into the present moment...becoming deeply mindful and present even more easily than you have in the past...effortlessly. Breathing in now for the third time...and hold...and as you breath out, entering the present moment...leaving concerns of the past and the future behind.

AUDITORY FOCUS AND NARROWING OF ATTENTION

In a moment, you will hear a tone...and this tone will at first be clear and eventually become softer until it disappears. When the tone sounds...you will focus on it so intently...that everything else begins to...fade...into the background...easily focusing on how the tone changes from moment to moment...attending closely to each nuance of the sound...and allowing each of these things that you notice to pass easily from your awareness as you attend to what is happening now with the next sound...focusing more and more on the present moment. When the sound starts to fade, you will find your mind becoming more and more focused on the fading sound...As the sound becomes fainter and fainter, you will pay closer and closer attention...more and more focused...and when the tone can no longer be heard, your mind will be as focused as it is capable of being...as focused as you allow it to be. I will stop talking while this tone sounds, so that you can focus fully on the sound as it rings...and when I speak again, your mind will be in a deep state of focus... able to easily respond to each suggestion that I give.

[Wait 5 seconds, then ring the bowl, chime, or bell.]

Allow the sound to ring and fade [you may gradually muffle the sound if it rings longer than 45 seconds to 1 minute].

[Wait 5 seconds after the sound is no longer perceptible, then continue with the script.]

DEEPENING SUGGESTIONS

And soon allowing yourself to sink deeper into hypnosis...journeying inward... toward a place of complete and utter serenity...a place of calmness and relaxation...where your mind is at ease, and nothing troubles you...where your thoughts are clear like a cool mountain lake...still, and serene...not burdened by the slightest care...this may be a familiar place...and you may find it pleasant to journey inward toward that place within you now...and as you hear my voice count from 10 to 1, with each number finding yourself settling into an even deeper level of hypnosis...deeper toward that place of complete mental and physical relaxation within you...[Count each number as the client exhales]

Ten...setting your cares aside now as you embark on this inner journey...you needn't worry about losing track of them...they will be safe, and right where you left them if or when you choose to pick them up again.

Nine...feeling a sense of relief...relaxing...your body leading the way on this journey by becoming very relaxed...muscles unwinding...tension that you didn't even know you were carrying is now drifting away...bringing a sense of deep relief.

Eight...deeply calm...number eight and *already* so deeply relaxed...and you may begin to notice a warmth or tingling sensation in your body, as it relaxes even further.

Seven...and now a sense of profound calmness begins to blossom...unfolding ...effortless, like a flower to the sun...and as you feel this, you might realize that mental and physical relaxation is not something that you do...it is a process of letting go...of *not* doing...even if just for this short while...like holding a ball in your hand...if you want to send the ball toward the ground...you needn't throw it, or exert effort or *do* anything...just the opposite, in fact...the only thing you need to do is let it go.

Six...halfway there, and already so profoundly relaxed...letting go of struggles and cares...letting go of any tension...letting go and simply *being*...in the present moment.

Five...perhaps at one time it took effort to calm your mind and body from its busyness...but now you are effortlessly still and serene...settled so deeply into the present moment...that to direct your mind to the past or the future or other things would require effort, and you would prefer not to try.

Four...allowing your mind to settle...become still and calm...profoundly peaceful.

Three...deeper and more calm...no worries in this special moment.

Two...almost there...deeply relaxed, nothing bothers and nothing concerns...and perhaps it would be OK, with the final number I count...to let go of even the smallest vestige of tension or worry...to settle into complete and utter stillness and serenity...peaceful and content...or perhaps you will prefer to be very calm but not take that last step...trusting now that whichever your mind chooses is the right choice for you in this moment...what you truly need.

One...at the final step of your own inner journey...comfortably and deeply hypnotized...resting in the present moment...your thoughts uncluttered...still ...and calm.

SUGGESTIONS FOR BREATHING, ACCEPTANCE, AND AWARENESS OF THE PRESENT MOMENT

And in this place...you will find that your experience of mindfulness will soon begin to deepen...aware of the breath...focusing on the sensations of breathing in...and breathing out...focusing on the nuances of the sensations...letting go of expectations of what this experience *will* be like...letting go of what it *was* like in this past moment...letting go of thinking *about* the breathing ... just noticing what it is unfolding *now*...abiding in this beautiful present moment as your experiences flow past you...like a rock in the midst of a gentle stream...you will begin to feel a growing sense of peace...calmness.

[Wait 5 seconds.]

As you do this...serenity...comfort...focused and relaxed.

[Wait 5 seconds.]

And as you feel these things, just nodding your head yes.

[Wait for confirmation before proceeding. If no confirmation is given, check to see what the client is experiencing and work hypnotically with that experience.]

Good, being present with your experiences...accepting them as they flow past you...sensations, sounds, thoughts, feelings...accepting them without judgment...in the simplicity of nonjudgmental awareness...in this present moment...the mind becomes relaxed, clear, and focused...noticing thoughts and feelings as these arise, and returning your attention to the breath if or when they pass.

And it is possible for a sense of compassion to arise within this experience...in the background...feeling it like you might feel sunshine on your shoulder... warm...a deep love and openness as you continue to be aware of what is happening right now with your breathing.

That sense of deep love and compassion begins now...a sense of gentleness toward yourself...and openness...aware of the experiences of breathing.

[Pause 5 seconds.]

Love and compassion...aware of the present moment...accepting your experiences without trying to push them away or cling to them...a rock in a gentle stream...and in a moment...I will be silent to allow you to mindfully observe this experience...that is growing within you. When I speak to you again ...you will remain...in a deep state of hypnosis and mindfulness...able to easily respond to each suggestion that I give.

[Pause for 90 seconds.]

And soon allowing these experiences to become more a part of you...sinking in...they will allow you to thrive and to pursue what is truly meaningful in your life...and if you would like to experience these things more fully in your life... you might take a deep, life-giving breath...and do so knowing that you can become more mindful in your daily life.

[If deep breath in...] Good!

POSTHYPNOTIC SUGGESTION

Very good...and this experience of mindfulness...is now becoming more a part of you...and more and more, everyday...you will find that... mindfulness has become a part of the way you perceive and experience the world...nonjudgmental awareness of the present moment...*whenever* your mind is not needed to plan or reflect...able to experience things from your five senses with equanimity and peacefulness...able to experience thoughts and feelings and remain grounded, steady, and calm...compassion for yourself and for others...will come easily and automatically...and your practice of mindfulness will allow you to pursue a life that you find truly meaningful and fulfilling.

And each time you practice, it becomes easier and easier...to maintain a daily practice of mindfulness...effortlessly meeting your own goals for practice... now and in the future...day by day becoming more mindful...deepening your experience of mindfulness each time you practice mindful hypnosis.

ALERTING

In a few moments, it is possible to begin returning to conscious alertness. Returning to conscious alertness in your own time and your own pace, in a way that just feels about right for you today...feeling very good, normal, with good sensations in every way as you return to full conscious alertness...soon you will hear a tone that will signal for you to return to conscious alertness. When that tone sounds, you will begin to gently return to alertness...gradually opening your eyes as the sounds fades...and when the sound can no longer be heard, your eyes will be open. You will be fully awake and alert, in your normal state of wakefulness. Ready now? Returning to alertness with the sound of the tone.

[Wait 5 seconds, then ring the bowl, chime, or bell. Allow the sound to ring and fade (you may gradually muffle the sound if it rings longer than 45 seconds to 1 minute). Wait 5 seconds after the sound is no longer perceptible; then continue with the script.]

Posthypnotic Inquiry, Assigning Homework, and Closing the Session

After the hypnotic induction is completed, it is helpful to ask the client to again rate the level of stress on the 0 to 10 scale. The final hypnosis script emphasizes an integration of mindfulness concepts discussed in the previous seven sessions. If you decide to personalize this script, you might consider discussing the inclusion of posthypnotic suggestions that respond to a client's stated goals for continued practice and working toward the post-termination goals. After the hypnotic induction, the posthypnotic inquiry can be a final opportunity to explicitly reflect with a client on the kinds of things that the client responds most strongly to so that he or she can include these elements of MH in self-hypnosis.

Close the session by providing the client with an audio recording of the hypnotic induction for this session and encouraging the client to practice with it, as the client may find it most helpful, as well as to continue to use the Mindful Self-Hypnosis Daily Practice Log in whatever way the client finds personally helpful. It is likely that, at this stage, many clients will find that they are sufficiently self-aware and reflective that they do not need to use the written log except on some occasions to help maintain consistency in practice. Clients may also be encouraged to practice with any of the audio from previous weeks' sessions in their long-term use and practice of mindful hypnosis.

Finally, bring an end to the session in whichever way seems appropriate and in line with the considerations listed earlier in the chapter.

Summary and Closing Thoughts for Session 8

Session 8 can be thought of as a crossroads between (a) the hard work the therapist and the client have done over the course of the MH, including all of the benefits that work has wrought, and (b) an orientation toward the future and the client's continued practice. MH can be a brief intervention, but the foremost goal is to have a lifelong impact on well-being. For the intervention to achieve this goal, it is imperative that clients continue to maintain the gains they have made and continue to improve themselves through home practice. A skillful termination helps clients to accomplish these aims by summarizing treatment, identifying future goals, and identifying any other sources for continued growth in mindfulness.

SECTION III

CONCLUSION

CHAPTER 16

BECOMING A MINDFUL HYPNOTHERAPIST

Pursue some path, however narrow and crooked, in which you can walk with love and reverence.

—Henry David Thoreau

Introduction

Throughout this book, we have noted that mindful hypnotherapy (MH) integrates mindfulness concepts and practice with hypnotherapy. It is acknowledged that mindfulness and hypnosis have evolved in ways that have led them to become largely independent from each other. However, in recent years an increasing number of practitioners and researchers have noted that mindfulness practice and hypnosis are complementary techniques that could benefit from integration (Lifshitz, Cusumano, & Raz, 2014; Lifshitz & Raz, 2012; Lynn, Malaktaris, Maxwell, Mellinger, & van der Kloet, 2012; Lynn, Surya Das, Hallquist, & Williams, 2006; Olendzki & Elkins, 2017; Raz & Lifshitz, 2016). Further, a flexible and integrative approach to utilizing mindfulness and hypnotherapy for well-being, stress reduction, and treatment has been advocated in a number of publications (Alladin, 2014; Olendzki & Elkins, 2017; Otani, 2016; Yapko, 2011). As the feasibility of integration has already been established, we expect this trend to continue. Practitioners of both mindfulness and hypnosis must "cross over" into the complementary areas of research and clinical methods to gain greater knowledge and skill for the benefit of their clients. In this chapter, we address training considerations regarding clinical hypnosis and mindfulness, standards of training in clinical hypnosis, development as a mindful hypnotherapist, competency, and future research.

Mindful Hypnotherapy: Training Considerations

Training for MH should include a firm understanding of both hypnosis and mindfulness. Workshops in clinical hypnosis and application in practice are essential to deepen understanding. Likewise, workshops, retreats, and personal experiences of mindfulness can be extraordinarily helpful in understanding the phenomenology of mindfulness and can allow a clinician to integrate mindfulness in clinical work more adroitly. Some of these trainings can be garnered by seeking out some of the more traditional vehicles for knowledge, such as maintaining a personal practice or completing workshops or courses. Training considerations regarding hypnotherapy include familiarity with established standards of training in clinical hypnosis and certification. In regard to mindfulness, there are also well-established options for training such as Mindfulness-Based Stress Reduction (MBSR) training programs, mindfulness retreats, and workshops. Also, the firsthand knowledge obtained through experiential-based practice of mindfulness will help a therapist learn these practices more deeply toward integration.

Standards of Training in Clinical Hypnosis

Hypnosis training can include material covered in academic courses, workshops, and continuing education. For clinicians who wish to become proficient in MH, it is vital to understand that technical skill and intellectual comprehension alone will be insufficient. *In addition* to these proficiencies, it is essential that therapists buttress their competence directly through personal practice. Naturally, personal practice will provide numerous benefits in clinicians' personal lives, and it may be advisable for this reason alone. However, personal practice can also have far-reaching consequences for competence and conceptual mastery that simply cannot be conveyed by other means. Therefore, one of the advantages that experienced hypnotherapists have over novice hypnotherapists is that they have seen hypnotic interventions work firsthand.

Standards of training in clinical hypnosis were developed in the 1990s (Elkins & Hammond, 1998; Hammond & Elkins, 1994). The standards (i.e., *Standards of Training in Clinical Hypnosis*, Hammond & Elkins, 1994) outline a core curriculum and learning objectives for "introductory" through "intermediate" workshop material. This material was developed to more clearly define essential knowledge and training and move toward a professional standard. These guidelines have been adopted by leading organizations including the *American Society for Clinical Hypnosis*, the *Society for Clinical and Experimental Hypnosis*, and the *International Society of Hypnosis*, which conduct workshops and scientific meetings for healthcare professionals and researchers.

To be prepared to use hypnotherapy adequately, it is recommended that clinicians should

- Attend an introductory workshop on hypnosis at the Society for Clinical and Experimental Hypnosis (SCEH), American Society for Clinical Hypnosis (ASCH), International Society of Hypnosis (ISH), or a similar organization (i.e., affiliates of ASCH, ISH, or SCEH; Milton H. Erickson Foundation; Society for Psychological Hypnosis; or recognized continuing education providers).
- Experience and practice hypnotic inductions and self-hypnosis themselves.
- Familiarize themselves with the clinical and experimental hypnosis research literature related to the populations and presenting concerns that MH is intended to treat. The *International Journal of Clinical and Experimental Hypnosis* is an excellent resource for contemporary research and empirical studies.

CLINICIAN NOTE

Certification

Consider certification in clinical hypnosis. The SCEH and ASCH offer certification of training programs that follow the established standards of training in clinical hypnosis (Elkins, 2017; Hammond & Elkins, 1994).

In addition, clinicians may want to consider certification in clinical hypnosis. Both the ASCH and the SCEH have established certification of training in clinical hypnosis programs. While there is some variation in requirements, approximately 40 hours of introductory to intermediate workshop training is required, along with additional training (e.g., 20 hours or more of individualized consultation and/or advanced workshops) and ethics education. To be eligible for these certification programs, qualified individuals must demonstrate a minimum of two years of independent clinical practice utilizing hypnotherapy.

The ASCH also offers a second level of certification referred to as an "Approved Consultant in Clinical Hypnosis." Eligibility and licensure requirements must be met and the applicant must have completed 100 hours of post-degree training approved by ASCH and 20 hours of one-to-one or small-group training with an ASCH-approved consultant, in which learning contracts are typically utilized. These certification programs are undergoing revisions as training programs evolve, eligibility requirements change, and learning objectives are updated. There is also the option of board certification for psychologists, physicians, dentists, and social workers (American Board of Psychological Hypnosis, American Board of Medical Hypnosis, American Board of Dental Hypnosis, and American Hypnosis Board for Clinical Social Work, respectively).

In this book we have also discussed the assessment of hypnotizability (i.e., the Elkins Hypnotizability Scale—Clinical Form [EHS-CF]; see Appendix A). We have noted that while the assessment of hypnotizability is an essential skill of the mindful hypnotherapist and is important in clinical research, not all clients will need to complete the EHS-CF. All individuals have a capacity to experience some degree of hypnosis, and it is the clinical judgment of the therapist that determines when and whether to assess hypnotizability. Those in the higher range may benefit more quickly or to a deeper degree.

Training in Mindfulness

Mindfulness is a journey of continually developing expertise. Thus, if therapists were required to *master* mindfulness before implementing MH, the intervention would never be used. A solid intellectual understanding of mindfulness is important for building your expertise and your comfort with delivering an MH intervention. Local, national, and international conferences on mindfulness can be good ways to begin this journey, though it will also be helpful to supplement your education through books and staying abreast of empirical research. Works by well-known authors such as Jon Kabat-Zinn, Jack Kornfield, Chris Germer, and Steven Hayes may be good places to start, though it is advisable to cast a broad net to get a diversity of perspectives.

For those who are ready to take a step beyond self-instruction and single workshops, longer and more in-depth study programs may be available. Although specific programs vary over time, those looking for in-depth information may consider enrolling in a certification program such as those offered through the Center for Mindfulness or the Center for Mindful Self-Compassion (both based in Massachusetts, but providing trainings to teachers worldwide). Although some of the skills taught in these certificate programs may be specific to a particular intervention (e.g., MBSR and Mindful Self-Compassion [MSC] in the previous examples), the core knowledge base will be easily transferrable to MH. Some high-quality training programs exist that are not affiliated with a specific intervention (such as that offered by the Institute for Meditation and Psychotherapy), but it is advisable to look into particular programs in detail to determine whether the education you receive will be of sufficient quality. Since there is no single institution that designates standards for mindfulness education, getting personal recommendations from those who are already knowledgeable in mindfulness may be beneficial.

Although there is no quantifiable threshold of mindfulness training that we would recommend before starting, prospective therapists should be able to do the following:

- Adequately discuss and explain mindfulness to a client, mindfulness-naive colleague, and subject-matter expert such as a meditation teacher, an MBSR teacher, or a colleague who specializes in mindfulness
- Lead a guided meditation (consider practicing with a friend or colleague, for example)
- Experience mindfulness practice themselves
- Familiarize themselves with the empirical mindfulness literature related to the populations and presenting concerns intended to treat with MH

Development as a Mindful Hypnotherapist

Who is a mindful hypnotherapist? Mindful hypnotherapists embody the very traits they are fostering in their clients: presence, empathy, and an open, nonjudgmental curiosity for the experiences that unfold between the client and the therapist. If therapists are able to embody these traits, they may find that treatment is enhanced and their clients are themselves able to adopt mindful traits more readily.

When applied to clinical interactions, "presence" refers to a therapist's capacity to pay attention to what a client is expressing in the current moment without getting overly fixated on what the client will say next or spending too much working memory analyzing what the client has said in the past. This can be easier said than done, since clinical work often involves some degree of planning, analysis, and time management. However, a mindful hypnotherapist allows these considerations to drift to the background of awareness while maintaining the vast majority of his or her attention on the present moment.[1] By adopting an open-minded, present-centered awareness, therapists may find that they are able to notice things that would otherwise escape their attention and connect with their clients more fully.

[1]Of course, this does not preclude treatment planning and analysis once the session is complete. Planning and analysis are important aspects of successful therapy.

In the context of mindfulness, compassion can be thought of as a particular way of paying attention. Focused attentiveness is a useful tool for gathering information on clients, but *compassionate* attention—seeing clients as they are *and* bringing a benevolent warmth to your focus—is a healing force in its own right. Compassion is value common to both traditional mindfulness and traditional psychotherapy. In MH, it can be an important factor in developing therapeutic rapport. Just as importantly, therapists' compassionate attitude toward their clients can act as a subtle form of suggestion over the course of hypnotherapy treatment, a suggestion that reinforces the explicit content of MH that is presented to a particular client.

Similarly, therapists who greet their clients' experiences with an open, nonjudgmental curiosity may find that their clients begin to shift their own attitudes even before this topic is addressed explicitly in MH. Throughout a typical session, there may be many opportunities to evince a nonjudgmental stance toward difficult experiences. For example, clients may disclose something uncomfortable for their therapists to hear (e.g., they may express anger at the therapist or attraction to the therapist, or they may disclose a particularly disturbing traumatic event). If therapists are intolerant, judgmental, and closed toward distressing emotional states, they may find themselves subtly steering the conversation away from the difficult topics or getting defensive and unsettled in response to the disclosures. Nonjudgmental awareness enables therapists to acknowledge and explore the difficult topics with a greater sense of equanimity for the strong emotions this may entail. Just as compassion can be a subtle form of suggestion, a nonjudgmental attitude toward shared experiences can help clients to develop this attitude in themselves.

Therapists who are aware of and develop these characteristics will be better equipped to deliver MH. Therefore, it is important to consider *how* to integrate these factors into treatment. The simple answer is not always the easy answer: Mindful presence is developed through integrity and authenticity to the process. Mindful hypnotherapists will need to genuinely transform themselves so that when they seem like they are mindfully, compassionately attentive, it's because they *are*. If a therapist attempts to fake these qualities in an effort to improve client responsiveness to MH, these attempts will generally fail when the client senses the inauthenticity.

The recommendation that therapists engage in an ongoing mindful self-hypnosis practice is a clear and unapologetic departure from the idea of that clinical work is a technical skill that you *do*, something to be used when needed and set aside when clinical work is done for the day. Instead, mindfulness (and by extension, MH) can become a natural expression of who you *are*. By transforming yourself, you shape the catalyst that enables your client's transformation.

Future Research on Mindful Hypnotherapy

MH builds upon the existing science of both hypnosis and mindfulness research with the goal of flexible integration, individualization of approach, brevity of time for intervention, and optimizing clinical outcomes. Future studies should explore which approaches and elements of intervention, in fact, optimize clinical outcomes and which outcomes are most impacted (e.g., mindfulness, self-compassion, relaxation, self-awareness). Research is also needed to determine those conditions for which MH can be most effective beyond personal growth. Research is needed regarding MH for anxiety disorders, chronic pain, stress reduction, mood disturbance, fibromyalgia, and physical conditions associated with aging. If MH is supported by empirical studies, then options for treatment of these conditions could be markedly improved.

Among the most important next steps is to compare MH to an active control so as to determine its efficacy relative to existing treatments. Conducting a study of MH that compares mindfulness *without* hypnotherapy would be informative, depending on the specific diagnosis and populations of interest. Brief interventions such as MH may be appealing to individuals with chronic health conditions or for economically disadvantaged individuals who may not have the resources or have access to more lengthy mindfulness programs. Consistent with this point, studies are needed to compare different "dosing" effects of MH. It may be that the intervention can be delivered in fewer than eight sessions and may achieve positive results for some conditions or populations.

Additional research is needed to examine the impact of MH delivery in a group format. Group delivery of MH could be beneficial when treatment settings are under-resourced and inundated with clients in great psychological need. Group therapy is an excellent solution to this problem, enabling many individuals to be served at the same time. Both mindfulness and hypnotherapy can be delivered in a group context; in turn, it would seem reasonable to expect that MH can be adapted to group delivery of the intervention.

Neuroscientific data are needed about the particular mechanisms of change when mindfulness and hypnosis are integrated. Both mindfulness and hypnosis have been shown to have neuroplasticity effects (Doidge, 2015; Grant, Courtemanche, Duerden, Duncan, & Rainville, 2010; Lazar et al., 2005). Neuroimaging studies of hypnosis (see Landry, Lifshitz, & Raz [2017] for a comprehensive review) have most consistently identified the anterior cingulate cortex (ACC) as being involved in neutral hypnosis and in pain reduction. A recent study by Jiang, White, Greicius, Waelde, and Spiegel (2016) demonstrated that during a hypnotic state, reduced activity in the dorsal anterior cingulate cortex (dACC) increased the functional connectivity between the dorsolateral prefrontal cortex (DLPFC) and the executive control network (ECN) and the insula in the salience network (SN). The researchers also found reduced connectivity between the ECN (DLPFC) and the default mode network (DMN) activity and posterior cingulate cortex (PCC). This study is particularly enlightening because these areas of neural activity underlie focused attention, enhanced somatic and emotional control, and lack of self-consciousness associated with the hypnotic state. Research is needed to further elucidate the biological mechanisms of MH, as this information may be important in the optimization of the intervention and to advance scientific understanding of both hypnosis and mindfulness.

A theoretical model of mindful hypnosis has been proposed (Elkins, Roberts, & Simicich, 2018) that suggests hypnotic induction may facilitate internal focus, absorption, relaxing imagery, and greater response to suggestion. The model proposes that suggestions for mindfulness can lead to outcomes such as positive feelings, mindful awareness, parasympathetic activation, and mindfulness goals. This model is in general alignment with the prior formulation of mindfulness and hypnosis developed by Yapko (2011). It may be that relaxation is facilitated by both hypnotic imagery and mindful focus of attention. In turn, mindful goals of acceptance and present awareness are affected by hypnotic suggestions.

Also, a biopsychosocial model proposed by Jensen et al. (2015) has asserted that the mechanisms underlying hypnosis may be multifactorial, with biological, psychological, and social factors all being involved. These factors are likely to be a focus of future research in regard to hypnosis, mindfulness, and their integration for the treatment of specific problems and well-being.

Closing Thoughts

This book provides the basics of MH, guidance, and transcripts for use in clinical practice. The development of competency in MH requires learning and practice. A clinical benefit that comes from personal practice is the ineffable sense of confidence, conviction, and empathy that therapists' words will carry when discussing mindfulness phenomena if they have experienced these things for themselves. In this regard, MH requires therapists to be a kind of guide for their clients by "scouting the territory" ahead. Nevertheless, the difficulties you encounter on your own journey through the practice of mindful self-hypnosis can add tremendous richness to your clinical abilities. For example, many people find that it is challenging to establish any regular self-hypnosis or mindfulness practice in the midst of a busy life, and it may be difficult to maintain your practice of mindful self-hypnosis when life is hard and the mind shies away from being "present" with those hardships. If you are able to persevere through these obstacles, your experience will give you new empathy for the difficulties your clients may face in doing the same. It may even provide you with an insight into how to help your clients overcome these common obstacles.

Another benefit from cultivating a personal practice is the transformation that this yields in your clinical presence, as described earlier in the chapter. You may find that this experiential training enables you to be more "present" and empathically attuned with your clients, whether you are using MH or not. When you nurture compassion for yourself and others through mindful self-hypnosis practice, this attitude will be felt by your clients when you interact. When you are able to access genuine openness and curiosity, this attitude will carry over into the way you engage with your clients in small, yet important ways. The changes in your clinical presence that can result from a personal mindful self-hypnosis practice can act as an implicit model for clients who are seen for MH.

As we conclude this book, we encourage therapists to begin to utilize MH as may be appropriate in their clinical practice and mindful self-hypnosis in their personal self-care. Workshops on MH as well as training in the rich foundational knowledge in hypnosis and in mindfulness practices can be an important source of developing competency in these methods. Several resources for books, professional organizations, and workshop providers regarding hypnosis, hypnotherapy, and mindfulness are identified in Appendix C. We hope this book serves to open perspectives on both hypnosis and mindfulness and provide greater understanding of their integration in clinical practice.

REFERENCES

Alladin, A. (2014). Mindfulness-based hypnosis: Blending science, beliefs, and wisdoms to catalyze healing. *American Journal of Clinical Hypnosis, 56*(3), 285–302. doi:10.1080/00029157.2013.857290

Doidge, N. (2015). Hypnosis, neuroplasticity, and the plastic paradox. *American Journal of Clinical Hypnosis, 57*(3), 349–354. doi:10.1080/00029157.2015.985572

Elkins, G. R. (2017). *Handbook of medical and psychological hypnosis: Foundations, applications, and professional issues.* New York, NY: Springer Publishing.

Elkins, G. R., & Hammond, D. C. (1998). Standards of training in clinical hypnosis: Preparing professionals for the 21st century. *American Journal of Clinical Hypnosis, 41*(1), 55–64. doi:10.1080/00029157.1998.10404185

Elkins, G. R., Roberts, L., & Simicich, L. (2018). Mindful self-hypnosis for self-care: An integrative model and case example. *American Journal of Clinical Hypnosis, 61*(1), 45–56. doi: 10.1080/00029157.2018.1456896

Grant, J. A., Courtemanche, J., Duerden, E. G., Duncan, G. H., & Rainville, P. (2010). Cortical thickness and pain sensitivity in Zen meditators. *Emotion, 10*(1), 43–53. doi:10.1037/a0018334

Hammond, D. C., & Elkins, G. R. (1994). *Standards of training in clinical hypnosis*. Des Plaines, IL: American Society of Clinical Hypnosis Press.

Jensen, M. P., Adachi, T., Tomé-Pires, C., Lee, J., Osman, Z. J., & Miró, J. (2015). Mechanisms of hypnosis: Toward the development of a biopsychosocial model. *International Journal of Clinical and Experimental Hypnosis, 63*(1), 34–75. doi:10.1080/00207144.2014.961875

Jiang, H., White, M. P., Greicius, M. D., Waelde, L. C., & Spiegel, D. (2016). Brain activity and functional connectivity associated with hypnosis. *Cerebral Cortex, 27*(8), 4083–4093. doi:10.1093/cercor/bhw220

Landry, M., Lifshitz, M., & Raz, A. (2017). Brain correlates of hypnosis: A systematic review and meta-analytic exploration. *Neuroscience and Biobehavioral Reviews, 81*, 75–98. doi:10.1016/j.neubiorev.2017.02.020

Lazar, S. W., Kerr, C. E., Wasserman, R. H., Gray, J. R., Greve, D. N., Treadway, M. T., … Fischl, B. (2005). Meditation experience is associated with increased cortical thickness. *Neuroreport, 16*(17), 1893–1897. doi:10.1097/01.wnr.0000186598.66243.19

Lifshitz, M., Cusumano, E. P., & Raz, A. (2014). Meditation and hypnosis at the intersection between phenomenology and cognitive science. In S. Schmidt & H. Walach (Eds), *Meditation–Neuroscientific Approaches and Philosophical Implications* (pp. 211–226). Cham, Switzerland: Springer.

Lifshitz, M., & Raz, A. (2012). Hypnosis and meditation: Vehicles of attention and suggestion. *Journal of Mind–Body Regulation, 2*(1), 3–11. Retrieved from https://s3.ca-central-1.amazonaws.com/razlab.org/publications/Hypnosis_and_Meditation_Lifshitz_and_Raz.pdf

Lynn, S. J., Malaktaris, A., Maxwell, R., Mellinger, D. I., & van der Kloet, D. (2012). Do hypnosis and mindfulness practices inhabit a common domain? Implications for research, clinical practice, and forensic science. *Journal of Mind-Body Regulation, 2*, 12–26. Retrieved from https://journalhosting.ucalgary.ca/index.php/mbr/article/download/16000/12655

Lynn, S. J., Surya Das, L., Hallquist, M. N., & Williams, J. C. (2006). Mindfulness, acceptance, and hypnosis: Cognitive and clinical perspectives. *International Journal of Clinical and Experimental Hypnosis, 54*, 143–166. doi:10.1080/00207140500528240

Olendzki, N., & Elkins, G. (2017). Mindfulness and hypnosis. In G. Elkins (Ed.), *Handbook of medical and psychological hypnosis: Foundations, applications, and professional issues* (pp. 579–588). New York, NY: Springer Publishing.

Otani, A. (2016). Hypnosis and mindfulness: The twain finally meet. *American Journal of Clinical Hypnosis, 58*(4), 383–398. doi:10.1080/00029157.2015.1085364

Raz, A., & Lifshitz, M. (2016). *Hypnosis and meditation: Towards an integrative science of conscious planes*. Oxford, UK: Oxford University Press.

Yapko, M. D. (2011). *Mindfulness and hypnosis: The power of suggestion to transform experience*. New York, NY: W. W. Norton.

APPENDIX A

ELKINS HYPNOTIZABILITY SCALE—CLINICAL FORM (EHS-CF)[1]

Protocol for Administration

Introductory Remarks [Note: Ensure that the subject is seated in a comfortable chair with support for the head, neck, and shoulders. A footstool may be provided to allow the subject to elevate the legs; however, if seated in a recliner, the back of the chair should *not* be reclined. See the "General Instructions for Administration and Scoring of the EHS" for further information.]

> This is a scale to measure your ability to experience hypnosis and respond to hypnotic suggestions. It is a standardized scale, so I will be reading from these papers. You may occasionally hear me writing or hear the sound of things outside this room. You can pay as much or as little attention to such sounds as you wish. The best way to determine a person's ability to experience hypnosis is to complete a hypnotic induction. This will involve focusing your attention on a spot on the ceiling and suggestions for calmness. After your eyes close, I will give you some hypnotic suggestions. It is important to *just respond to what you are feeling and experiencing.* There is nothing that you have to try to do; just allow yourself to respond to whatever you experience. Not everyone experiences the same things and not everyone is equally hypnotizable. At times during hypnosis, I will ask you to

[1] Copied with permission from Elkins, G. R. (2014). *Hypnotic relaxation therapy: Principles and applications.* New York, NY: Springer Publishing.

verbally describe what you are feeling or experiencing. You will be able to do so without interrupting your experience of hypnosis. As you listen to my words, just let whatever happens happen so that we can see how you experience hypnosis and how we can learn to make hypnosis work best for you.

[Note: Ask the participant to extend his or her arms and bring them down to a relaxed position on the arms of the chair.]

Hypnotic Induction

Now, please roll your eyes upward and focus on a spot on the ceiling. That's right. Now, *focus on that spot so intently*...that everything else begins to fade into the background...more and more...good. Now take a breath of air and hold it for a moment... hold...and as you exhale, allow your eyelids to close normally and naturally...good...now, allow your body to relax...Notice a wave of relaxation spreading from the top of your head...down to your feet...Letting all the tension go...head, neck, shoulders... relax...arms and legs...relax...as you enter a hypnotic state finding a calm...relaxed feeling. More calm and more at ease...comfortable and calm.

Now, as I count from the number 10 down to 1, with each number that I count...going into *an even deeper state of hypnosis.*

[Note: During the deepening suggestions, numbers are counted on the subject's exhalation.]

Ten...a wave of relaxation spreading across your forehead...neck... and shoulders.

Nine...more relaxed...your jaw goes slack...shoulders slump...and arms become very relaxed.

Eight...that wave of relaxation now spreads across your back...your upper back...and lower back...deeply relaxed.

Seven...a deeper level of hypnosis now as your legs become very relaxed, letting all the tension go...feeling more calm...feeling more peaceful.

Six...entering such a deep level of hypnosis *now*...that you may notice a drifting or floating sensation...just drifting...and floating... deeper and deeper into this hypnotic state.

Five...deeply calm and deeply hypnotized.

Four ...now allowing that calmness to become *even more complete*...and entering *the deepest level of hypnosis*.

Three...so deeply hypnotized that you are able to respond to each suggestion...and experience each thing that I suggest.

Two...calm and peaceful...so deeply relaxed...any tension that has remained is released...*now*...

One...*all the way there*...deeply hypnotized...calm and peaceful.

And it is possible to feel a special sense of calmness...and you will be able to experience and respond to each suggestion during hypnosis today...just listen to my voice and let whatever happens happen so we can see how you experience hypnosis.

Arm Heaviness/Immobilization

Now as you remain deeply calm...you will *soon* become aware of a change in sensation in your *right* arm and hand...soon you will notice that your *right arm* will become *very, very heavy*...just as *heavy as lead*...that heavy feeling begins to occur *now*...that arm becomes *heavier and heavier*...and as this occurs, it can feel as if the arm were becoming *less a part of you...as you allow it to become as heavy as lead*.

[Pause for 5 seconds]

And now that arm will become *even heavier*...so very heavy that you will find that you *cannot lift this right arm*...no matter how hard you *try* to raise it...*it will be too heavy to lift*...and finding that *you just don't want to lift it*, in fact...the harder you *try*, the *heavier* the arm and hand will become...and *now* the arm, the wrist, the hand, *and even the fingers* have become *stuck to the chair...they just won't move*...they are so very heavy.

[Pause for 5 seconds.]

Now...as this hand and arm remain as *heavy as lead* and too heavy to lift, I want you, *in a moment*, to try to lift them, but *they* will not move...the arm, the wrist, the hand, *and even the fingers are stuck to the chair and too heavy to move.* Go ahead and *try* to lift them, genuinely try, but *they* are just stuck to the chair and they are too heavy.

[Pause for 5 seconds.]

Very good. Now allow your arm to relax; this heavy feeling passes and the right hand and arm rest. ...Normal sensation returns...and as *this* occurs going into an *even deeper level of hypnosis.*

Record Observations
1. Did the arm lift?
2. Was there obvious effort to lift the hand and arm?
3. Other observations (finger movements and so on)

Arm Levitation

Now as you go into an *even deeper level of hypnosis*...you will *soon* become aware of a change in sensation in your *left* arm and hand... soon you will notice that your *left* arm and hand will become very, very light...and weightless...*just as light as a feather*...that light feeling begins to occur...*now*...*it* becomes lighter and lighter...and as this occurs it can feel as if the arm were becoming *less a part of you*...as you allow it to become so...*light and weightless.*

[Pause for 5 seconds]

And now...there is a *ribbon* around the left wrist...and at the other end of that ribbon are several *balloons*...red, yellow, green, blue...all different colors....There are quite a few of them...*four or five balloons*...and these balloons are lighter than air and *they begin to float upward*...and as they do...the left hand begins to *float upward*...just notice the balloons are tugging...pulling...lifting the wrist *up...up...up...it just drifts and floats up*...feeling lighter and lighter...floating up *higher and higher*...just allowing the *arm* to float up...*all by itself*...just as high as it wants to go...floating up *now*...higher and higher.

Record Observations
1. Did the hand or arm lift?
2. Was there obvious effort to raise the arm and hand?
3. Did the elbow raise from the arm of the chair?
4. Other observations

[Pause for 5 seconds for the response to occur; wait until levitation stops]

Very good. Now this feeling passes and your hand and arm begin to drift downward to their comfortable resting position...[Wait for the arm to begin to lower; additional suggestions for normal sensations and arm lowering may be given.] The balloons are gone...normal sensation returns to your arm and hand and as this occurs *going into an even deeper level of hypnosis.* [If the arm remains lifted, instruct the participant to lower the arm to the chair.]

Imagery Involvement/Dissociation

And now something *very interesting* is going to happen...it is possible to *hear my voice with one part of your mind*...and with another part of your mind...to find that *you will feel as if you are in a different place*...soon you will find that you can feel as if you are *no longer in this room* and *instead* you will *be in a beautiful flower garden*...and when this occurs, you will be able to see everything there...You will experience every sight,...sound, smell,...and feeling in this garden...when this occurs, you will find that...you feel as if you are no longer in [state present place] and instead you will, in a sense, be in a flower garden experiencing everything *there.*

Now, as you hear my voice, at the same time seeing before you a gate that leads into the flower garden...seeing the gate now...and as I *count from one to four* you will find that you are walking through that gate and into the flower garden...more than just imagining it... soon *you will be in a flower garden*...walking through the garden.

One...going through the gate now.

Two...as you go into the garden, you can see the flowers that are there.

Three...able to continue to hear my voice as you are there...experiencing every sight, sound, smell, and feeling in this *flower garden.*

Four...*now* you are there...you are *in a flower garden.*

[Pause for 5 seconds and then proceed]

Good. It is a warm day...and yet you can feel a gentle cool breeze in the air...it is very pleasant...feeling safe, secure, and relaxed...before you is a path. As you walk down this path, notice that there are flowers all along the path. The grass is very green and there are many beautiful flowers. Now, notice the colors of the flowers...whether you see red, yellow, or any other colors.

There...There is a very beautiful red *rose...*you can see this rose... now, stopping there for a moment...go close enough to *smell the wonderful sweet aroma* of this beautiful rose...the aroma of the rose becomes stronger now...it is a pleasant smell...now take a breath and...*just smell the rose...*and notice how *strong* the smell is.

[Pause for 5 seconds]

Now...as you are *there...*you can describe what you are experiencing without interrupting your experience of hypnosis. Please describe what you are experiencing.

Where are you?	
What do you see around you?	
Do you see the rose?	
Do you smell the rose?	
Other comments:	

[If the subject does not respond to the first question, prompt with "You can answer verbally..." Record responses to each question.]

*Very good...*now, soon returning to this room at [state present place] and the present time...as you remain *deeply hypnotized...*now walking back through that gate and returning to the present time and back to [state present place]...you are now here deeply hypnotized and comfortably experiencing hypnosis.

Alerting

[Note: Alerting or proceeding to clinical suggestions can occur at this time. If alerting is intended, then the following alerting suggestions should be given.]

All right, in a few moments you can return to conscious alertness. As I count the numbers from 1 to 10 returning to conscious alertness now. [Note: Increase the volume of your voice when counting.]

1, 2, 3...beginning to return to conscious alertness.

4, 5...more alert and eyes beginning to open.

6, 7...eyelids opening and returning to alertness.

8, 9...alert and refreshed.

And 10...fully alert.

Do you feel alert?...good. [Note: Assure that the subject reports alertness before proceeding with the Posthypnotic Scoring Inquiry.]

EHS CLINICAL FORM SCORING SUMMARY

EXAMINER: ________________ DATE: ____________________

TIME TO COMPLETE EHS:_______________

Item	Criteria	Score
Arm Heaviness/ Immobilization	No heaviness.	0
	Subjective report of heaviness.	1
	Heaviness. Immobilization occurred.	2
Arm Levitation	No weightlessness.	0
	Subjective report of lightness.	1
	Subjective report of lightness and effortless arm levitation.	2
	Effortless elbow lift.	3
Imagery Involvement/ Dissociation	No experience—just listening.	0
	Experienced clear imagery, but no dissociation.	1
	Experienced clear imagery, and dissociation.	2
Rose Olfactory Hallucination	No experience.	0
	Reports faint smell.	1
	Reports distinct smell.	2
Total		9

0–3	Low
4–7	Middle
8–9	High

Posthypnotic Scoring Inquiry

ARM HEAVINESS/IMMOBILIZATION SCORING INQUIRY

Earlier I suggested to you that your right arm and hand would feel heavy and then I suggested that they would be too heavy to lift. I want to find out what your experience was.

Item	Detail
When I suggested that your right arm and hand would feel heavy, did you feel a sense of heaviness in your right arm and hand? Did they feel heavier? (Determine if the subject experienced *any* feeling of heaviness.)	☐ Yes ☐ No
(If the hand/arm did *not* lift, ask:) *Did you try to lift your hand and arm?* Determine if there was an effort to lift the hand and arm. *Were they too heavy to lift? Did they feel stuck to the chair?*	☐ Yes ☐ No
Did the subject's hand and arm remain immobile and "stuck" to the chair? Review previous observations to determine if the subject's hand and arm remained on the chair with just minimal, temporary movements. Inquire as needed to determine if arm immobilization occurred. *(Note: Small finger movements or* temporary *slight movements often occur with* successful *arm immobilization. Arm immobilization refers to an inability to lift the hand and arm.)*	☐ Yes ☐ No

Arm Heaviness Item Scoring	
0	If no heaviness.
1	If the subject reports feeling a subjective sense of heaviness.
2	Beyond slight movements, the hand and arm did not lift. Arm immobilization occurred.

ARM LEVITATION SCORING INQUIRY

Earlier, I asked you to experience a very light and weightless feeling in your left arm and that the arm would lift all by itself.

Inquiry	
Did your arm feel lighter? Even if your arm did not lift, did it feel lighter?	
(If the arm lifted, ask:) *Did it float up* all by itself *without any willful effort on your part?* (Inquire as needed to clarify the subject's experience. Determine if the subject experienced a sense of involuntary lifting.) *Could you feel it floating up all by itself or did you feel like you were lifting it? Did it feel like the balloons were pulling it up?*	
Arm Lightness Item Scoring	
0	Score 0 if the answer to the first question is no, whether or not the arm lifted. Score 0 if there is no subjective description of lightness.
1	Score 1 if the answer to the first question is yes, but the arm *did not lift out of its resting position.* (Score 1 if a *subjective sense of lightness is reported* and the hand did not lift.)
2	Score 2 if the answer to the second question is yes, and the arm did lift out of its resting position. (Score 2 if a subjective experience of lightness is described and there is some movement of the hand from the chair *with* a subjective description of an involuntary movement.)
3	Score 3 if the answer to the second question is yes and the elbow lifted. (Score 3 if a subjective experience of lightness is described and there is a movement of the hand of 1 inch or more with a subjective description of an involuntary movement and the elbow lifts.)

IMAGERY INVOLVEMENT/DISSOCIATION SCORING INQUIRY

Also, earlier, I asked you to experience going for a walk in a flower garden.

Inquiry
1. *Were you able to experience what I suggested or were you just listening to my voice*? (If no imagery or only vague imagery is reported, state, "*Some people do not experience clear imagery.*")
2. *Did you* imagine being in the flower garden? *Was the image clear? Could you really imagine being in a flower garden?* (Determine if the subject was able to imagine being in a garden. Determine if the image was clear or only vague [i.e., colors but no specific imagery of the flower garden].)
Review the previous observations and the subject's verbal responses to the questions presented during the item. Determine if the subject's response to the questions "Where are you? What do you see around you?" indicate that the subject may have experienced dissociation (i.e., felt that the subject was actually in the garden). 3. If the subject's responses suggested possible dissociation, ask: *Did you feel that, in a sense, you were no longer in this room and instead you were actually in a flower garden, experiencing everything there?* (Determine if the subject experienced an alteration in perception in which the subject *felt* that he or she was no longer in the room and instead experienced being in a flower garden. Continue inquiry as necessary to distinguish between questions 2 and 3: "Did it feel like you were actually experiencing *(insert subject's report of sensations)* while you were *in the garden* or that you were here and imagining it?"

Mental Imagery/Dissociation Scoring Inquiry	
0	If the answer to the first question is no (no imagery or only vague imagery).
1	If the answer to the second question is yes (clear imagery but no dissociation).
2	If the answer to the third question is yes (clear imagery and dissociation).

ROSE OLFACTORY HALLUCINATION SCORING INQUIRY

Now, I also suggested to you that you could smell a rose.

Inquiry		
Did you smell the aroma of a rose? Did you actually smell it?		
0	If the answer is no. *Did not actually smell the rose (even if it was imagined).*	
1	If the answer is yes. *Smell was faint.*	
2	If the answer is yes. *Smell was distinct.*	
Establish the subjective rating of the intensity of the aroma. Check the subject's rating of the aroma: *How strong was the aroma? Please rate it as none, faint, or distinct.*		
☐ None	☐ Faint	☐ Distinct

APPENDIX B

MINDFUL SELF-HYPNOSIS DAILY PRACTICE LOG

Date Completed (MM/DD/YYYY): ___________							
Week #: 1☐	2☐	3☐	4☐	5☐	6☐	7☐	8☐

Did you practice mindful self-hypnosis using a prerecorded hypnotic induction?

Yes ☐ No ☐

Did you practice mindful self-hypnosis on your own, without an audio recording?

Yes ☐ No ☐

RATING OF RELAXATION BEFORE MINDFUL SELF-HYPNOSIS

Please mark the line at the point that best represents your feelings of relaxation and mindfulness before mindful self-hypnosis practice.

Not Relaxed at All **Very Relaxed**

RATING OF RELAXATION AFTER MINDFUL SELF-HYPNOSIS

Please mark the line at the point that best represents your feelings of relaxation and mindfulness after mindful self-hypnosis practice.

Not Relaxed at All **Very Relaxed**

Comments and reflections regarding feelings of mindfulness (non-judgmental awareness of breathing, sensation, thoughts, feelings, self, compassion):

APPENDIX C

RESOURCES

Books

Brahm, A. (2005). *Who ordered this truckload of dung? Inspiring stories for welcoming life's difficulties.* Somerville, MA: Wisdom Publications.

Elkins, G. R. (2014). *Hypnotic relaxation therapy: Principles and applications.* New York, NY: Springer Publishing.

Elkins, G. R. (2017). *Handbook of medical and psychological hypnosis: Foundations, applications, and professional issues.* New York, NY: Springer Publishing.

Germer, C., Siegel, R., & Siegel, R. D. (2013). *Mindfulness and psychotherapy* (2nd ed.). New York, NY: Guilford.

Goldstein, J., & Kornfield, J. (2001). *Seeking the heart of wisdom: The path of insight meditation.* Boston, MA: Shambhala.

Gunaratana, H. (2002). *Mindfulness in plain English* (2nd ed.). Boston, MA: Wisdom.

Hammond, D. C., & Elkins, G. R. (1994). *Standards of training in clinical hypnosis.* Chicago, IL: ASCH Press.

Hayes, S., Follette, V., & Linehan, M. (Eds.). (2004). *Mindfulness and acceptance: Expanding the cognitive-behavioral tradition.* New York, NY: Guilford.

Kabat-Zinn, J. (1990). *Full catastrophe living: Using the wisdom of your body and mind to face stress, pain, and illness.* New York, NY: Delacorte Press.

Kabat-Zinn, J. (2005). *Wherever you go, there you are: Mindfulness meditation in everyday life* (10th ed.). New York, NY: Hyperion.

Kornfield, J. (2008). *The wise heart: A guide to the universal teachings of Buddhist psychology.* New York, NY: Bantam Books.

Olendzki, A. (2010). *Unlimiting mind: The radically experiential psychology of Buddhism.* Somerville, MA: Wisdom Publications.

Olendzki, A. (2016). *Untangling self: A Buddhist investigation of who we really are.* Somerville, MA: Wisdom Publications.

Pollak, S., Pedulla, T., & Siegel, R. D. (2014). *Sitting together: Essential skills for mindfulness-based psychotherapy.* New York, NY: Guilford.

Raz, A., & Lifshitz, M. (2016). *Hypnosis and meditation: Towards an integrative science of conscious planes.* Oxford, UK: Oxford University Press.

Salzberg, S., & Kabat-Zinn, J. (2008). *Lovingkindness: The revolutionary art of happiness*. Boston, MA: Shambhala.

Thera, N. (1973). *The heart of Buddhist meditation: Satipatthna: A handbook of mental training based on the Buddha's way of mindfulness*. New York, NY: Weiser Books.

Yapko, M.D. (2011). *Mindfulness and hypnosis: The power of suggestion to transform experience*. New York, NY: W. W. Norton.

Websites

Acceptance and Commitment Therapy: http://www.acceptanceandcommitmenttherapy.com

American Mindfulness Research Association: https://goamra.org

Dialectical Behavior Therapy: http://www.behavioraltech.com

Guided Mindfulness Meditation Practices with Jon Kabat-Zinn: http://www.mindfulnesscds.com/pages/videos-of-jon-teaching

Guided Meditations from the University of California's Mindfulness Awareness Research Center: http://marc.ucla.edu/mindful-meditations

Guided Meditations from the Center for Mindful Self-Compassion: http://centerformsc.org/practice-msc/guided-meditations-and-exercises

Journal for Mindfulness Practitioners: http://www.inquiringmind.com

Recordings from Dharma Talks given at Various "Western Buddhist" Retreat Centers: http://dharmaseed.org

Journals

International Journal of Clinical and Experimental Hypnosis: http://www.tandfonline.com/loi/nhyp20

American Journal of Clinical Hypnosis: http://www.tandfonline.com/loi/ujhy20

Psychology of Consciousness: http://www.apa.org/pubs/journals/cns

BMC Complementary and Alternative Medicine: https://bmccomplementalternmed.biomedcentral.com

Organizations

AMERICAN SOCIETY OF CLINICAL HYPNOSIS

140 North Bloomingdale Road
Bloomingdale, IL 60108-1017
Phone: (630) 980-4740
Email: info@asch.net

Website: www.asch.net

CENTER FOR MINDFUL SELF-COMPASSION

https://centerformsc.org

CENTER FOR MINDFULNESS IN MEDICINE, HEALTH CARE, AND SOCIETY

University of Massachusetts Medical School
55 Lake Avenue North
Worcester, MA 01655
Phone: 508-856-2656
Website: https://www.umassmed.edu/cfm

INSTITUTE FOR MEDITATION AND PSYCHOTHERAPY

http://www.meditationandpsychotherapy.org

INTERNATIONAL SOCIETY OF HYPNOSIS

PO Box 602
Berwyn, PA 19312
Phone: (800) 550-4741
Fax: (800) 541-4558
Email: contact@ishhypnosis.org
Website: www.ishhypnosis.org

MILTON H. ERICKSON FOUNDATION

3606 North 24th Street
Phoenix, AZ 85016
Phone: (602) 956-6196
Website: www.erickson-foundation.org

SOCIETY FOR CLINICAL AND EXPERIMENTAL HYPNOSIS

305 Commandants Way, Commoncove Suite 100
Chelsea, AM 02150-4057
Phone: (617) 744-9857
Email: info@sceh.us
Website: www.sceh.us

BIBLIOGRAPHY

Alladin, A., & Alibhai, A. (2007). Cognitive hypnotherapy for depression: An empirical investigation. *International Journal of Clinical and Experimental Hypnosis, 55*, 147–166. doi:10.1080/00207140601177897

Alman, B. (1983). *Self-hypnosis.* San Diego, CA: International Health Publications.

Astin, J. A., Berman, B. M., Bausell, B., Lee, W. L., Hochberg, M., & Forys, K. L. (2003). The efficacy of mindfulness meditation plus Qigong movement therapy in the treatment of fibromyalgia: A randomized controlled trial. *Journal of Rheumatology, 30*(10), 2257–2262.

Aucoin, M., Lalonde-Parsi, M. J., & Cooley, K. (2014). Mindfulness-based therapies in the treatment of functional gastrointestinal disorders: A meta-analysis. *Evidence-Based Complementary and Alternative Medicine, 2014*, 140724. doi:10.1155/2014/140724

Banyai, E. I., & Hilgard, E. R. (1976). A comparison of active-alert hypnotic induction with traditional relaxation induction. *Journal of Abnormal Psychology, 85*(2), 218–224. doi:10.1037//0021-843x.85.2.218

Bates, B. (1993). Individual differences in response to hypnosis. In J. W. Rhue, S. J. Lynn, & I. Kirsch (Eds.), *Handbook of clinical hypnosis* (pp. 23–54). Washington, DC: American Psychological Association.

Beck, A., Rush, A., Shaw, B., & Emery, G. (1979). *Cognitive therapy of depression*. New York, NY: Guilford.

Benson, J. K. (1975). *The relaxation response*. New York, NY: William Morrow.

Bernheim, H. (1886). *Hypnosis and suggestion in psychotherapy*. New Hyde Park, NY: University Books. (Reprinted 1964)

Bodhi, B. (2000). *The connected discourses of the Buddha: A translation of the Samyutta Nikaya.* Sommerville, MA: Wisdom Publications.

Bongartz, W. (1985). German norms for the harvard group scale of hypnotic susceptibility, form A. *International Journal of Clinical and Experimental Hypnosis, 33*(2), 131–139. doi:10.1080/00207148508406643

Bowen, S., Witkiewitz, K., Dillworth, T. M., Chawla, N., Simpson, T. L., Ostafin, B. D., … Marlatt, G. A. (2006). Mindfulness meditation and substance use in an incarcerated population. *Psychology of Addictive Behaviors, 20*(3), 343–347. doi:10.1037/0893-164X.20.3.343

Brahm, A. (2005). *Who ordered this truckload of dung?: Inspiring stories for welcoming life's difficulties*. Sommerville, MA: Wisdom Publications.

Brown, D. C., & Hammond, C. D. (2007). Evidence-based clinical hypnosis in obstetrics, labor, and delivery and preterm labor. *International Journal of Clinical and Experimental Hypnosis, 55*(3), 355–371. doi:10.1080/00207140701338654

Brown, D. P., & Fromm, E. (1986). *Hypnotherapy and hypnoanalysis*. Hillsdale, NJ: Lawrence Erlbaum Associates.

Bryant, R. A., Creamer, M., O'Donnell, M., Silove, D., & McFarlane, A. C., (2008). A multisite study of initial respiration rate and heart rate as predictors of post-traumatic stress disorder. *Journal of Clinical Psychiatry, 69*(11), 1694–1701. doi:10.4088/jcp.v69n1104

Bryant, R. A., Moulds, M. L., Guthrie, R. M., & Nixon, R. D. (2005). The additive benefit of hypnosis and cognitive-behavioral therapy in treating acute stress disorder. *Journal of Consulting and Clinical Psychology, 73*, 334–340. doi:10.1037/0022-006X.73.2.334

Carson, J. W., Keefe, F. J., Lynch, T. R., Carson, K. M., Goli, V., Fras, A. M., & Thorp, S. R. (2005). Loving-kindness meditation for chronic low back pain: Results from a pilot trial. *Journal of Holistic Nursing, 23*(3), 287–304. doi:10.1177/0898010105277651

Castel, A., Pérez, M., Sala, J., Padrol, A., & Rull, M. (2007). Effect of hypnotic suggestion on fibromyalgic pain: Comparison between hypnosis and relaxation. *European Journal of Pain, 11*(4), 463–468. doi:10.1016/j.ejpain.2006.06.006

Casula, C. (2017). Laws and principles of hypnotic inductions. In G. Elkins (Ed.), *Handbook of medical and psychological hypnosis: Foundations, applications, and professional issues* (pp. 43–55). New York, NY: Springer Publishing.

Cordi, M. J., Hirsiger, S., Mérillat, S., & Rasch, B. (2015). Improving sleep and cognition by hypnotic suggestion in the elderly. *Neuropsychologia, 69*, 176–182. doi:10.1016/j.neuropsychologia.2015.02.001

Daubenmier, J., Kristeller, J., Hecht, F. M., Maninger, N., Kuwata, M., Jhaveri, K., … Epel, E. (2011). Mindfulness intervention for stress eating to reduce cortisol and abdominal fat among overweight and obese women: An exploratory randomized controlled study. *Journal of Obesity, 2011*, 651936, 13. doi:10.1155/2011/651936

De Pascalis, V., Bellusci, A. N. N. A., & Russo, P. M. (2000). Italian norms for the Stanford hypnotic susceptibility scale, Form C. *International Journal of Clinical and Experimental Hypnosis, 48*(3), 315–323. doi:10.1080/00207140008415249

De Pascalis, V., Russo, P., & Marucci, F. S. (2000). Italian norms for the harvard group scale of hypnotic susceptibility, form A. *International Journal of Clinical and Experimental Hypnosis, 48*(1), 44–55. doi:10.1080/00207140008410360

Elkins, G. R., Cheung, A., Marcus, J., Palamara, L., & Rajab, H. (2004). Hypnosis to reduce pain in cancer survivors with advanced disease: A prospective study. *Journal of Cancer Integrative Medicine, 2*(4), 167–172.

Elkins, G. R., Fisher, W. I., Johnson, A. K., Carpenter, J. S., & Keith, T. Z. (2013). Clinical hypnosis in the treatment of post-menopausal hot flashes: A randomized controlled trial. *Menopause, 20*, 291–298. doi:10.1097/GME.0b013e31826ce3ed

Elkins, G. R., Jensen, M. P., & Patterson, D. R. (2007). Hypnotherapy for the management of chronic pain. *International Journal of Clinical and Experimental Hypnosis, 55*(3), 275–287. doi:10.1080/00207140701338621

Elkins, G., Johnson, A., & Fisher, W. (2012). Cognitive hypnotherapy for pain management. *American Journal of Clinical Hypnosis, 54*(4), 294–310. doi:10.1080/00029157.2011.654284

Elkins, G., Marcus, J., Stearns, V., Perfect, M., Rajab, M. H., Ruud, C., ... Keith, T. (2008). Randomized trial of a hypnosis intervention for treatment of hot flashes among breast cancer survivors. *Journal of Clinical Oncology, 26*(31), 5022–5026. doi:10.1200/JCO.2008.16.6389

Elkins, G., White, J., Patel, P., Marcus, J., Perfect, M. M., & Montgomery, G. H. (2006). Hypnosis to manage anxiety and pain associated with colonoscopy for colorectal cancer screening: Case studies and possible benefits. *International Journal of Clinical and Experimental Hypnosis, 54*(4), 416–431. doi:10.1080/00207140600856780

Enqvist, B., Björklund, C., Engman, M., & Jakobsson, J. (1997). Preoperative hypnosis reduces postoperative vomiting after surgery of the breasts: A prospective, randomized, and blinded study. *Acta Anaesthesiologica Scandinavica, 41*(8), 1028–1032. doi:10.1111/j.1399-6576.1997.tb04831.x

Epstein, S. (1994). Integration of the cognitive and the psychodynamic unconscious. *American Psychologist, 49*(8), 709–724. doi:10.1037//0003-066x.49.8.709

Ewin, D. M. (2009). *101 Things I wish I'd known when I started using hypnosis*. Williston, VT: Crown House Publishing.

Flammer, E. (2006). Die wirksamkeit von hypnotherapie bei angstörungen. *Hypnose-ZHH*, 1(2), 173–198.

Fogarty, F. A., Booth, R. J., Gamble, G. D., Dalbeth, N., & Consedine, N. S. (2015). The effect of mindfulness-based stress reduction on disease activity in people with rheumatoid arthritis: A randomised controlled trial. *Annals of the Rheumatic Diseases, 74*(2), 472–474. doi:10.1136/annrheumdis-2014-205946

Forman, E. M., Herbert, J. D., Moitra, E., Yeomans, P. D., & Geller, P. A. (2007). A randomized controlled effectiveness trial of acceptance and commitment therapy and cognitive therapy for anxiety and depression. *Behavior Modification, 31*, 772–799. doi:10.1177/0145445507302202

Frankel, F. H., Apfel, R. J., Kelly, S. F., Benson, H., Quinn, T., Newmark, J., & Malmaud, R. (1979). The use of hypnotizability scales in the clinic: A review after 6 years. *International Journal of Clinical and Experimental Hypnosis, 27*, 63–73. doi:10.1080/00207147908407547

Friedlander, J. W., & Sarbin, T. R. (1938). The depth of hypnosis. *Journal of Abnormal and Social Psychology, 33*(4), 453–475. doi:10.1037/h0056229

Fromm, E., & Nash, M. R. (1992). *Contemporary hypnosis research*. New York, NY: Guilford.

Galovski, T. E., & Blanchard, E. B. (1998). Treatment of irritable bowel syndrome with hypnotherapy. *Applied Psychophysiological Biofeedback, 23*(4), 219–232. doi:10.1023/A:1022209631047

Gay, M. C., Philippot, P., & Luminet, O. (2002). Differential effectiveness of psychological interventions for reducing osteoarthritis pain: A comparison of Erickson [correction of Erickson] hypnosis and Jacobson relaxation. *European Journal of Pain, 6*(1), 1–16. doi:10.1053/eujp.2001.0263

Gaylord, S. A., Palsson, O. S., Garland, E. L., Faurot, K. R., Coble, R. S., Mann, J. D., … Whitehead, W. E. (2011). Mindfulness training reduces the severity of irritable bowel syndrome in women: Results of a randomized controlled trial. *American Journal of Gastroenterology, 106*(9), 1678–1688. doi:10.1038/ajg.2011.184

Gilligan, S. (1987). *Therapeutic trances: The cooperative principle in Ericksonian hypnotherapy*. New York, NY: Brunner/Mazel.

Golden, W. L. (2012). Cognitive hypnotherapy for anxiety disorders. *American Journal of Clinical Hypnosis, 54*, 263–274. doi:10.1080/00029157.2011.650333

Goleman, D. (1980). A map for inner space. In R. N. Walsh & F. Vaughn (Eds.), *Beyond ego* (pp. 141–150). Los Angeles, CA: Tarcher.

Gordon, R. (1978). Look! He has come through! *Journal of Analytical Psychology, 23*(3), 258–274. doi:10.1111/j.1465-5922.1978.00258.x

Gruzelier, J. H. (2006). Frontal functions, connectivity and neural efficiency underpinning hypnosis and hypnotic susceptibility. *Contemporary Hypnosis, 23*(1), 15–32. doi:10.1002/ch.35

Haanen, H. C., Hoenderdos, H. T., van Romunde, L. K., Hop, W. C., Mallee, C., Terwiel, J. P., & Hekster, G. B. (1991). Controlled trial of hypnotherapy in the treatment of refractory fibromyalgia. *Journal of Rheumatology, 18*(1), 72–75.

Hammond, D. C. (1990). *Handbook of hypnotic suggestions and metaphors*. New York, NY: W. W. Norton.

Hanh, T. N. (1999). *The heart of Buddha's teachings: Transforming suffering into peace, joy, and liberation.* New York, NY: Broadway Books.

Hawkins, R. M. F. (2001). A systematic meta-review of hypnosis as an empirically supported treatment for pain. *Pain Reviews, 8*(2), 47–73. doi:10.1191/0968130201pr175ra

Heap, M., Brown, R. J., & Oakley, D. A. (2004). *The highly hypnotizable person: Theoretical, experimental, and clinical issues.* London, UK: Routledge.

Hilgard, E. R. (1965). *Hypnotic susceptibility.* New York, NY: Harcourt, Brace & Jovanovich.

Hilgard, E. R., Crawford, H. J., & Wert, A. (1979). The Stanford Hypnotic Arm Levitation Induction and Test (SHALIT): A six-minute hypnotic induction and measurement scale. *International Journal of Clinical and Experimental Hypnosis, 27*(2), 111–124. doi:10.1080/00207147908407551

James, W. (1890 by Henry Holt & Company; 1950 reprint). *The principles of psychology.* New York, NY: Dover Publications

Jensen, M. P. (2011). *Hypnosis for chronic pain management: Therapist guide.* Oxford, UK: Oxford University Press.

Jensen, M. P., Abresch, R. T., Carter, G. T., & McDonald, C. M. (2005). Chronic pain in persons with neuromuscular disease. *Archives of Physical Medicine and Rehabilitation, 86*(6), 1155–1163. doi:10.1016/j.apmr.2004.11.028

Jensen, M. P., Barber, J., Romano, J. M., Hanley, M. A., Raichle, K. A., Molton, I. R., … Patterson, D. R. (2009). Effects of self-hypnosis training and EMG biofeedback relaxation training on chronic pain in persons with spinal-cord injury. *International Journal of Clinical and Experimental Hypnosis, 57*(3), 239–268. doi:10.1080/00207140902881007

Jensen, M. P., Barber, J., Romano, J. M., Molton, I. R., Raichle, K. A., Osborne, T. L., … Patterson, D. R. (2009). A comparison of self-hypnosis versus progressive muscle relaxation in patients with multiple sclerosis and chronic pain. *International Journal of Clinical and Experimental Hypnosis, 57*(2), 198–221. doi:10.1080/00207140802665476

Jensen, M. P., Ehde, D. M., Gertz, K. J., Stoelb, B. L., Dillworth, T. M., Hirsh, A. T., … Kraft, G. H. (2011). Effects of self-hypnosis training and cognitive restructuring on daily pain intensity and catastrophizing in individuals with multiple sclerosis and chronic pain. *International Journal of Clinical and Experimental Hypnosis, 59*(1), 45–63. doi:10.1080/00207144.2011.522892

Jensen, M. P., Jamieson, G. A., Lutz, A., Mazzoni, G., McGeown, W. J., Santarcangelo, E. L., … Terhune, D. B. (2017). New directions in hypnosis research: Strategies for advancing the cognitive and clinical neuroscience of hypnosis. *Neuroscience of Consciousness, 3*(1). pii: nix004. doi:10.1093/nc/nix004

Jensen, M. P., Moore, M. R., Bockow, T. B., Ehde, D. M., & Engel, J. M. (2011). Psychosocial factors and adjustment to chronic pain in persons with physical disabilities: A systematic review. *Archives of Physical Medicine and Rehabilitation, 92*(1), 146–160. doi:10.1016/j.apmr.2010.09.021

Juster, R. P., McEwen, B. S., & Lupien, S. J. (2010). Allostatic load biomarkers of chronic stress and impact on health and cognition. *Neuroscience and Biobehavioral Reviews, 35*, 2–16. doi:10.1016/j.neubiorev.2009.10.002

Kabat-Zinn, J., Lipworth, L., & Burney, R. (1985). The clinical use of mindfulness meditation for the self-regulation of chronic pain. *Journal of Behavioral Medicine, 8*(2), 163–190. doi:10.1007/bf00845519

Kabat-Zinn, J., Lipworth, L., Burney, R., & Sellers, W. (1986). Four-year follow-up of a meditation-based program for the self-regulation of chronic pain: Treatment outcomes and compliance. *Clinical Journal of Pain, 2*(3), 159–774. doi:10.1097/00002508-198602030-00004

Kallio, S. I., & Ihamuotila, M. J. (1999). Finnish norms of the harvard group scale of hypnotic susceptibility, form A. *International Journal of Clinical and Experimental Hypnosis, 47*, 227–235. doi:10.1080/00207149908410034

Kane, S., & Olness, K. (2004). *The art of therapeutic communications: The collected works of Kay F. Thompson*. Williston, VT: Crown House Publishing.

Kaplan, K. H., Goldenberg, D. L., & Galvin-Nadeau, M. (1993). The impact of a meditation-based stress reduction program on fibromyalgia. *General Hospital Psychiatry, 15*(5), 284–289. doi:10.1016/0163-8343(93)90020-O

Kearney, D. J., McDermott, K., Malte, C., Martinez, M., & Simpson, T. L. (2013). Effects of participation in a mindfulness program for veterans with posttraumatic stress disorder: A randomized controlled pilot study. *Journal of Clinical Psychology, 69*(1), 14–27. doi:10.1002/jclp.21911

Kekecs, Z., Bowers, J., Johnson, A., Kendrick, C., & Elkins, G. (2016). The Elkins Hypnotizability Scale: Assessment of reliability and validity. *International Journal of Clinical and Experimental Hypnosis, 64*(3), 285–304. doi:10.1080/00207144.2016.1171089

Kenny, M. A., & Williams, J. M. G. (2007). Treatment-resistant depressed patients show a good response to Mindfulness-based Cognitive Therapy. *Behaviour Research and Therapy, 45*(3), 617–625. doi:10.1016/j.brat.2006.04.008

Khoury, B., Lecomte, T., Fortin, G., Masse, M., Therien, P., Bouchard, V., … Hofmann, S. G. (2013). Mindfulness-based therapy: A comprehensive meta-analysis. *Clinical Psychology Review, 33*, 763–771. doi:10.1016/j.cpr.2013.05.005

Kiecolt-Glaser, J. K., Marucha, P. T., Atkinson, C., & Glaser, R. (2001). Hypnosis as a modulator of cellular immune dysregulation during acute stress. *Journal of Consulting and Clinical Psychology, 69*(4), 674–682. doi:10.1037//0022-006x.69.4.674

Kirsch, I., Montgomery, G., & Sapirstein, G. (1995). Hypnosis as an adjunct to cognitive-behavioral psychotherapy: A meta-analysis. *Journal of Consulting and Clinical Psychology, 63*, 214–220. doi:10.1037//0022-006x.63.2.214

Koszycki, D., Benger, M., Shlik, J., & Bradwejn, J. (2007). Randomized trial of a meditation-based stress reduction program and cognitive behavior therapy in generalized social anxiety disorder. *Behaviour Research and Therapy, 45*, 2518–2526. doi:10.1016/j.brat.2007.04.011

Kristeller, J., Wolever, R. Q., & Sheets, V. (2014). Mindfulness-based eating awareness training (MB-EAT) for binge eating: A randomized clinical trial. *Mindfulness, 5*(3), 282–297. doi:10.1007/s12671-012-0179-1

Kroger, W. S. (2008). *Clinical and experimental hypnosis in medicine, dentistry, and psychology*. Philadelphia, PA: Lippincott Williams & Wilkins.

Lamas, J. R., Valle-Inclan, F. D., Blanco, M. J., & Diaz, A. A. (1989). Spanish norms for the harvard group scale of hypnotic susceptibility, form A. *International Journal of Clinical and Experimental Hypnosis, 37*(3), 264–273. doi:10.1080/00207148908414477

Lang, E. V., Benotsch, E. G., Fick, L. J., Lutgendorf, S., Berbaum, M. L., Berbaum, K. S., … Spiegel, D. (2000). Adjunctive non-pharmacological analgesia for invasive medical procedures: A randomised trial. *Lancet, 355*(9214), 1486–1490. doi:10.1016/S0140-6736(00)02162-0

Lankton, S. R., & Lankton, C. H. (1983). *The answer within: A clinical framework of Ericksonian hypnotherapy*. Psychology Press.

Laurence, J., & Perry, C. (1982). Montreal norms for the harvard group scale of hypnotic susceptibility, form A. *International Journal of Clinical and Experimental Hypnosis, 30*(2), 167–176. doi:10.1080/00207148208407381

Liebeault, A. A. (1889). *Le Sommeil Provoqué et les États Analogues* [Induced sleep and analogous states]. Paris, France: Doin.

Ludwig, A. M. (1966). The formal characteristics of therapeutic insight. *American Journal of Psychotherapy, 20*, 305–318.

Manicavasgar, V., Parker, G., & Perich, T. (2011). Mindfulness-based cognitive therapy vs. cognitive behaviour therapy as a treatment for non-melancholic depression. *Journal of Affective Disorders, 130*, 138–144. doi:10.1016/j.jad.2010.09.027

Matthews, W. J., & Isenberg, G. L. (1995). Hypnosis with signing deaf and hearing subjects. *American Journal of Clinical Hypnosis, 38*(1), 27–38. doi:10.1080/00029157.1995.10403175

McCauley, J. D., Thelen, M. H., Frank, R. G., Willard, R. R., & Callen, K. E. (1983). Hypnosis compared to relaxation in the outpatient management of chronic low back pain. *Archives of Physical Medicine and Rehabilitation, 64*(11), 548–552. doi:10.1080/00029157.1995.10403175

McConkey, K. M., Barnier, A. J., Maccallum, F. L., & Bishop, K. (1996). A normative and structural analysis of the HGSHS: A with a large Australian sample. *Australian Journal of Clinical and Experimental Hypnosis, 24*, 1–11.

Montgomery, G. H., David, D., Winkel, G., Silverstein, J. H., & Bovbierg, D. H. (2002). The effectiveness of adjunctive hypnosis with surgical patients: A meta-analysis. *Anesthesia and Analgesia, 94*(6), 1639–1645. doi:10.1213/00000539-200206000-00052

Montgomery, G. H., DuHamel, K. N., & Redd, W. H. (2000). A meta-analysis of hypnotically induced analgesia: How effective is hypnosis? *International Journal of Clinical Hypnosis, 48*(2), 138–153. doi:10.1080/00207140008410045

Morgan, A. H., & Hilgard, J. R. (1978 Oct–1979 Jan). The Stanford Hypnotic Clinical Scale for Children (SHCS:Child). *American Journal of Clinical Hypnosis, 21*(2–3), 148–169. doi:10.1080/00029157.1978.10403969

Muses, C., & Young, A. M. (1972). Trance-induction techniques in ancient Egypt. In C. Muses, & A. M. Young (Eds), *Consciousness and reality* (pp. 9–17). New York, NY: Outerbridge and Lazard.

Neron, S., & Stephenson, R. (2007). Effectiveness of hypnotherapy with cancer patients' trajectory: Emesis, acute pain, and analgesia and anxiolysis in procedures. *International Journal of Clinical and Experimental Hypnosis, 55*(3), 336–354. doi:10.1080/00207140701338647

Olness, K., MacDonald, J. T., & Uden, D. L. (1987). Comparison of self-hypnosis and propranolol in the treatment of juvenile classic migraine. *Pediatrics, 79*(4), 593–597.

Omidi, A., Mohammadi, A., Zargar, F., & Akbari, H. (2013). Efficacy of mindfulness-based stress reduction on mood states of veterans with post-traumatic stress disorder. *Archives of Trauma Research, 1*(4), 151–154. doi:10.5812/atr.8226

Öst, L.-G. (2008). Efficacy of the third wave of behavioral therapies: A systematic review and meta-analysis. *Behaviour Research and Therapy, 46*, 296–321. doi:10.1016/j.brat.2007.12.005

Palsson, O. S., Turner, M. J., & Whitehead, W. E. (2006). Hypnosis home treatment for irritable bowel syndrome: A pilot study. *International Journal of Clinical and Experimental Hypnosis, 54*(1), 85–99. doi:10.1080/00207140500328666

Patterson, D. R., & Jenson, M. P. (2003). Hypnosis and clinical pain. *Psychological Bulletin, 129*(4), 495–521. doi:10.1037/0033-2909.129.4.495

Patterson, D. R., & Ptacek, J. T. (1997). Baseline pain as a moderator of hypnotic analgesia for burn injury treatment. *Journal of Consulting and Clinical Psychology, 65*, 60–67. doi:10.1037//0022-006X.65.1.60

Peale, N. V. (2003). *The power of positive thinking* (1st Fireside ed.). New York, NY: Fireside/Simon & Schuster.

Piccione, C., Hilgard, E. R., & Zimbardo, P. G. (1989). On the degree of stability of measured hypnotizability over a 25-year period. *Journal of Personality and Social Psychology, 56*(2), 289–295. doi:10.1037/0022-3514.56.2.289

Piet, J., Würtzen, H., & Zachariae, R. (2012). The effect of mindfulness-based therapy on symptoms of anxiety and depression in adult cancer patients and survivors: A systematic review and meta-analysis. *Journal of Consulting and Clinical Psychology, 80*, 1007–1020. doi:10.1037/a0028329

Prior, A., Colgan, S. M., & Whorwell, P. J. (1990). Changes in rectal sensitivity after hypnotherapy in patients with irritable bowel syndromes. *GUT: An International Journal of Gastroenterology and Hepatology, 31*(8), 896–898. doi:10.1136/gut.31.8.896

Repka, R. J., & Nash, M. R. (1995). Hypnotic responsivity of the deaf: The development of the University of Tennessee Hypnotic Susceptibility Scale for the Deaf. *International Journal of Clinical and Experimental Hypnosis, 43*(3), 316–331. doi:10.1080/00207149508409973

Sapp, M., & Hitchcock, K. (2001). Harvard group scale with African American college students. *Sleep and Hypnosis, 3*(3), 111–117.

Sephton, S. E., Salmon, P., Weissbecker, I., Ulmer, C., Floyd, A., Hoover, K., & Studts, J. L. (2007). Mindfulness meditation alleviates depressive symptoms in women with fibromyalgia: Results of a randomized clinical trial. *Arthritis Care and Research, 57*(1), 77–85. doi:10.1002/art.22478

Schoenberger, N. E., Kirsch, I., Gearan, P., Montgomery, G., & Pastyrnak, S. L. (1997). Hypnotic enhancement of a cognitive behavioral treatment for public speaking anxiety. *Behavior Therapy, 28*, 127–140. doi:10.1016/S0005-7894(97)80038-X

Spanos, N. P., Radtke, H. L., Hodgins, D. C., Bertrand, L. D., Stam, H. J., & Dubreuil, D. L. (1983). The Carleton University responsiveness to suggestion scale: Stability, reliability, and relationships with expectancy and hypnotic experiences. *Psychological Reports, 53*, 555–563. doi:10.2466/pr0.1983.53.2.555

Spanos, N. P., Stenstrom, R. J., & Johnson, J. C. (1998). Hypnosis, placebo, and suggestion in the treatment of warts. *Psychosomatic Medicine, 45*, 333–339.

Spanos, N. P., Williams, V., & Gwynne, M. L. (1990). Effects of hypnotic, placebo, and salicylic acid treatments on wart regression. *Psychosomatic Medicine, 52*(1), 109–114. doi:10.1097/00006842-199001000-00009

Spiegel D., & Bloom J. R. (1983). Group therapy and hypnosis reduce metastatic breast carcinoma pain. *Psychosomatic Medicine, 45*, 333–339. doi:10.1097/00006842-198308000-00007

Spiegel, D., Hunt, T., & Dondershine, H. E. (1988). Dissociation and hypnotizability in posttraumatic stress disorder. *American Journal of Psychiatry, 145*(3), 301–305. doi:10.1176/ajp.145.3.301

Spiegel, H., & Spiegel, D. (2004). *Trance and treatment: Clinical uses of hypnosis*. Washington, DC: American Psychiatric Publishing.

Spinhoven, P., & Linssen, A. C. (1989). Group therapy and hypnosis reduce metastatic breast carcinoma pain. *Psychosomatic Medicine, 45*, 333–339. doi:10.1097/00006842-198308000-00007

Strauss, C., Cavanagh, K., Oliver, A., & Pettman, D. (2014). Mindfulness-based interventions for people diagnosed with a current episode of an anxiety or depressive disorder: A meta-analysis of randomised controlled trials. *PLoS One, 9*(4), e96110. doi:10.1371/journal.pone.0096110

Tart, C. T., Puthoff, H. E., & Targ, R. (Eds). (1979). *Mind at large: Institute of Electrical and Electronics Engineers symposia on the nature of extrasensory perception*. New York, NY: Praeger.

Tellegen, A., & Atkinson, G. (1974). Openness to absorbing and self-altering experiences ("absorption"), a trait related to hypnotic susceptibility. *Journal of Abnormal Psychology, 83*(3), 268–277. doi:10.1037/h0036681

Vidrine, J. I., Businelle, M. S., Cinciripini, P., Li, Y., Marcus, M. T., Waters, A. J., … Wetter, D. W. (2009). Associations of mindfulness with nicotine dependence, withdrawal, and agency. *Substance Abuse, 30*(4), 318–327. doi:10.1080/08897070903252973

Weitzenhoffer, A. M., & Hilgard, E. R. (1959). *Stanford hypnotic susceptibility scale: Forms A and B*. Palo Alto, CA: Consulting Psychologists Press.

Weitzenhoffer, A. M., & Hilgard, E. R. (1962). *Stanford hypnotic susceptibility scale: Form C*. Palo Alto, CA: Consulting Psychologists Press.

Wong, S. Y. S., Chan, F. W. K., Wong, R. L. P., Chu, M. C., Kitty Lam, Y. Y., Mercer, S. W., & Ma, S. H. (2011). Comparing the effectiveness of mindfulness-based stress reduction and multidisciplinary intervention programs for chronic pain: A randomized comparative trial. *Clinical Journal of Pain, 27*(8), 724–734. doi:10.1097/AJP.0b013e3182183c6e

Woody, E. Z., & Barnier, A. J. (2008). Hypnosis scales for the twenty-first century: What do we need and how should we use them? In M. R. Nash & A. J. Barnier (Eds), *The Oxford handbook of hypnosis: Theory, research and practice* (pp. 255–281). Oxford, UK: Oxford University Press.

Woody, E., & Sadler, P. (2016). What can a hypnotic induction do? *American Journal of Clinical Hypnosis, 59*(2), 138–154. doi:10.1080/00029157.2016.1185004

Zachariae, R., Sommerlund, B., & Molay, F. (1996). Danish norms for the harvard group scale of hypnotic susceptibility, form A. *International Journal of Clinical and Experimental Hypnosis,44*(2), 140–152. doi:10.1080/00207149608416076

Zautra, A. J., Davis, M. C., Reich, J. W., Nicassario, P., Tennen, H., Finan, P., … Irwin, M. R. (2008). Comparison of cognitive behavioral and mindfulness meditation interventions on adaptation to rheumatoid arthritis for patients with and without history of recurrent depression. *Journal of Consulting and Clinical Psychology*, *76*(3), 408–421. doi:10.1037/0022-006X.76.3.408

Zeig, J. K. (2006). *Confluence: The selected papers of Jeffrey K. Zeig*. Phoenix, AZ: Zeig, Tucker & Theisen.

Zeig, J. K. (1980). *Teaching seminar with Milton H. Erickson*. New York, NY: Brunner/Mazel.

Zernicke, K. A., Campbell, T. S., Blustein, P. K., Fung, T. S., Johnson, J. A., Bacon, S. L., & Carlson, L. E. (2013). Mindfulness-based stress reduction for the treatment of irritable bowel syndrome symptoms: A randomized wait-list controlled trial. *International Journal of Behavioral Medicine*, *20*(3), 385–396. doi:10.1007/s12529-012-9241-6

INDEX

www.ingramcontent.com/pod-product-compliance
Ingram Content Group UK Ltd.
Pitfield, Milton Keynes, MK11 3LW, UK
UKHW021845100926
8556IPUK00019B/1060